The Art and Science of Happiness
in Body, Mind and Soul

The Art and Science of Happiness in Body, Mind and Soul

—▬—

Exploring Happiness - A Physician's Perspective

Om P Sharma MD

ISBN: 153006256X
ISBN 13: 9781530062560
Library of Congress Control Number: 2016902821
CreateSpace Independent Publishing Platform
North Charleston, South Carolina

Printed in the United States of America

First Printing 2016

US Copyright © TXu 1-947-211

kindlehappiness@gmail.com
theartandscienceofhappiness@gmail.com
www.theartandscienceofhappiness.com

To my wife, Rajni
for guiding me to
experience spirituality in a different light

Table of Contents

Preface

THE LONG JOURNEY of human existence has posed different challenges in different eras of civilization. In the beginning the progress had been slow but steady with imperceptible advances measured by scientific designs not in years or decades but hundreds and thousands of years. However, there has been a flood of rapid advances in all scientific fields with unimaginable innovations in the last century. Technologic discoveries in the last few decades have transformed our lives comfortable full of amenities. Newer concepts have taken our lives into uncharted and unimaginable territories.

The quest for happiness has been engraved in the human mind since the beginning of time. Affection for happiness and aversion for pain and suffering have always occupied our minds and is engrained in the very human conscious. The Eastern and later on Greek and other ancient philosophies tried to demystify and explore this issue. Hindu philosophy brilliantly illustrated and discussed this in Vedas and Upanishads as far back as 5000 BC to 3500 BC. They expounded on interrelationship of body, mind and soul to each other and to the inner-self for everlasting happiness. They believe in ever exiting omnipresent Creator God. Various religions have tried to do metaphysical analysis to define their own beliefs in this reality. Buddhism found that sufferings are integral part of life. Most sufferings are of our own making and are due to greed and cravings of our mind.

Greek philosophers like Aristotle, Socrates and Plato dealt with subject of soul and happiness. In sixteenth century French philosopher Rene Descartes found the mind to be non-physical and different from body. However, this concept already existed in Vedic and Buddhist literature thousands of years earlier.

Spiritual writings placed non-physical mind in the realms of the heart as the seat of desires. Vedas placed it in the bosom, in the lotus of the heart. Mind and the heart are two distinct entities. The propelling function of the heart as a pump to revitalize the body with circulation of blood throughout the body was first discovered by William Harvey in 1628. Taking this vital aspect aside, there is a complex link between the mind, the heart, the soul and the happiness.

Recent understanding of bio-physiology and other aspects in neurosciences, as well as psychology, philosophy, psychiatry and genetics have shed new light on mind, emotions and behavior, on thoughts and intellect and on memory and reward mechanisms. Pet-scans (Positron emission tomography), SPECT (Single-photon emission computed tomography), TMS (Transcranial magnetic stimulation) and fMRI (functional Magnetic Resonance Imaging) have defined areas of brain involved in some of these mechanisms. Our mind resides in the realms of the brain. Many behavior disorders like depression, addiction and bipolar disorders have major genetic predisposition. Newer therapies are evolving with better understanding of etiologies of mental disorders. We have better tools to bring some happiness in the lives of these people. Even a 'pill for happiness' at least theoretically is not too far away.

Individual happiness can never be enjoyed and retained if our neighbor is unhappy. Macrocosmic happiness or happiness of society at large is the accumulation of microcosmic satisfaction at individual level. Gross Happiness Index (GHI) is more pertinent for overall well-being of a society or a country than GDP (Gross Domestic Product). Social well-being depends not only on happiness alone but also on being able to meet the necessities of life.

Recently discovered technological gadgets have made our lives more interesting and comfortable and luxurious but at the same time challenging with both up and downsides. Materialism is increasing at the cost of spirituality. Ideology, ethics and morality need preservation amidst tide of easily available gratifications. World leaders like Dalai Lama and Pope Francis plead for equality and ethics and morality and compassion to bring happiness at everybody's doorstep.

This book is written to elaborate on some of the important aspects of happiness in day-to-day life that include the body, mind and the soul. It also deals with emotional and behavioral aspects of man with some insight into the impact of modern scientific, philosophical and materialistic attitudes and last but not the least the spiritual aspect of life. Our diverse pluralistic world needs compassionate ideology, inclusive ethics, considerate resolve, tolerant principals and selfless altruistic minds to bring forth happiness.

This book explores the Hindu religion and some aspects Buddhist philosophies and tries to blend it with concepts of non-believers and modern day interpretations in face of newer understandings in the art and the science of happiness. Its sixty-two chapters not only deal with our basic as well as scientific and technological aspects of happiness but also physical, behavioral, spiritual and ideological aspects in pursuit of happiness.

Current printing of this upgraded edited book contains a new chapter 'Live a Purposeful Life' added to the part six, The Ultimate Goal. The chapter 'Ignorance, Misconceptions and Illusions' is deleted. Newer medical concepts and advancement and other relevant data have been incorporated in the text.

Part One

The Essentials of Life and Happiness

CHAPTER 1

The Meaning of Life

'Life is not finding about yourself. Life is about creating yourself.'

~ MARY MCCARTHY

LIFE IN ITSELF is a unique gift to every living creature. Happiness is the aspiration and the ultimate goal of every human being. The pursuit of happiness is the inalienable right of each and every one of us living on this planet earth. Joyous smiles and laughing expressions can kindle and spread the spirit of happiness all around us. Above all making others happy preserves personal happiness.

To ask the philosophical question as to what is the meaning of life is to try to explore the very basics of our existence. This question has intrigued the minds of philosophers, theologians, psychiatrists, psychologists and scientists in various fields since the beginning of time. Interpretations also vary in accordance with ones own cultural and religious beliefs. It is widespread and multidimensional exploration of various aspects of life from different angles. It explores the relationship of life to right and wrong and good and evil as well as its relationship to ethics and morality and ideology. It explores the very concept of The Creator as well as the human mind, the body and the soul and its relationship to happiness, pain and pleasure.

Unlike many other living creatures, humans are blessed with an intelligent mind with discriminating power and hence can learn and express and expand one's horizon. It can experiment and progress beyond any imaginable aspect of our existence. It can question itself as to 'Who am I?' and 'What is true meaning of my existence?' 'How and why was my life created and who is the Creator?' We humans have a unique capacity to question everything. Is the sole purpose of life merely to enjoy all the pleasures and comforts of our family life and to play our role in the world stage and one day take the last breath and leave this world? It is hard to think that the life is just an illusion as believed by some.

Our existence is not measured by number of years we have lived or the extent of luxuries we have enjoyed. 'We came empty-handed in this world and are going to leave the same way, empty-handed.'[110] Are we going to leave any mark in the world? Are we leaving any legacy behind? Have we tried to understand the mysteries about God? Is there a God to whom we pray and worship by different names? Have we made any spiritual connections? Was the universe created in 6 days? Is the creation of this world a scientific experiment or is it the result of evolution that took millions of years of transformation or is it just the result of an 'A Big Bang' as believed by some scientist?

Is happiness the ultimate goal in life? Satisfaction in personal and social life is the essential ingredient to lead a balanced happy life. Personal achievements are necessary for progression. One needs to advance in all spheres of life that includes educational aspects, professional satisfaction, wealth and a happy family life. Social interaction connects individual harmoniously to the community to make life more meaningful and complete. Each individual is like a flower in the landscape of a community, a metaphor to a well-planned beautiful garden of different species and colors.

Life span of human beings is divided into four stages of life (*Ashramas*) in Vedic philosophy.[19-21, 24, 71, 113] These are '*Brahamacharya*' (first phase for education and self-control), '*Grihastha*' (householder), '*Vanaprastha*' (partially ascetic with partial detachment in life) and '*Sanyasa* '(full detachment and renunciation). These slightly modified stages fit in present-day framework of culture as:

1. First Stage for *physical and mental growth*, self-control, general and professional education and knowledge to excel.

2. Second Stage: as a married '*householder*' with accumulation of wealth and other material objects and to rear children in a happy comfortable environment.

3. Third Stage: *Retirement* with partially relinquishing responsibilities and attachments of the householder, with enough time for reading, volunteering, other hobbies and altruistic goals.

4. Fourth Stage: *Spiritual Growth*- true '*Sannyasa*' with self-introspection in modern day is to take the free time for the spiritual journey, focusing on self-advancement, to renounce all egocentric activities, to understand God and his mysteries and serve and help the needy with compassion. Pragmatically we gradually learn the path of spirituality since childhood.

The world is dynamic and is constantly changing and the mind has to constantly adapt to so many evolving concepts. Nothing stays forever. There is impermanence (*Anyata, Anicca*) in every dimension of life including our surroundings.[21] The changes including shedding of old cells and regeneration of new cells in our body are very subtle and imperceptible, and all these changes have constancy and occur in an orderly transition. There are ups and downs in life with both good and bad moments, moments of happiness where one wants to stay forever and the moments of sad and painful sufferings that one wishes never to face again. At times life can be like a dark forest with dense trees where even the rays of light can not permeate; it is pitch dark with scary fierce winds and frightening noises of intimidating ferocious animals. It is where the traveler is lost completely and is too frightened to find his way out. There can be trails and paths going in different directions that may end up in a lion's den, or in a beautiful mesmerizing lake and a stunning waterfall or in a the lost dwelling·[105] It is those scary moments that bring faith and hope to the mind. These moments make us look around to understand complexities in life and teach us how to avoid dangerous pitfalls and ultimately help us reach our goals in life. Life is a movement of conflicts, problems and challenges.

Human life has momentary existence in the universe just like scripted life of an actor on the stage. We are condemned to die the day we are born.

Nobody knows when? The life is dynamic and ever changing. It is far more unpredictable than even the weather, where the rains and the dust storms, dark clouds over the sunshine, hurricanes and tornados and tsunamis can come from nowhere and change life forever.

Mind is always interacting with the world in quantum leaps and is constantly transforming, as it understands and unties complexities of the cosmos. Our energy and spirit are minute expressions of cosmic energy. Our body mind and intellect are constantly reacting to and expressing variedly to the daily dynamic challenges of the world. Shutting our mind to the outside world is like uprooting our very existence.

To truly understand the meaning of life one ought to look deep inside by self-reflection and contemplation. We are not Buddha, but at least we can try to take baby-steps towards truth and righteousness. We have abandoned the values of life due to greed and ignorance for transient pleasures. We don't spare time to sit and relax. A focused concentration, contemplation and meditation needs years of practice to achieve tranquility of mind. Instead, we have lost our patience, and want all the answers right now in seconds and want to Google all the questions for immediate answer. Can our life long quest be answered by few clicks of a mouse?

Man has ability to work, to strive and to achieve by his sincere efforts.[19] The purpose of a meaningful life for the struggling poor and the helpless, who lack even the basic necessities of life like food and shelter, is to *somehow survive*. A true meaning of life is to understand everyone around us and to know of their needs and shortcomings and to share the burdens of the society. Everyone should learn to share the space and his possessions with others to make a little difference in this macrocosm.

> *'You make a living by what you get, but you make a life by what you give.'*
>
> ~ LEIGH HUGHES

CHAPTER 2

The Quest for Happiness

'Happiness is as a butterfly, which when pursued, is always beyond our grasp, but which, if you sit down quietly, may alight upon you.'

~ NATHANIEL HAWTHORNE

LIFE'S IS A long challenging pilgrimage; there is movement of life from the first to the last breath. Man is constantly motivated and propelled towards two inevitable emotions during his lifetime that originate in the mind: these emotions are love (affection, attraction) and hatred (aversion, repulsion). There is an inborn desire to seek happiness and avoid unhappiness resulting in an endless chase for happiness.

Fundamental question is 'What is happiness?' Is it outside expression of pleasant experiences of life? 'Happiness is defined as mental or emotional state of well-being characterized by positive or pleasant emotions ranging from contentment to intense joy.' [118] Is peace of mind an essential prerequisite to be happy? Can happiness coexist in an agitated mind? Does happiness go beyond material world? After all what is true happiness?

Plato (428-348 BC) defined it as, 'A man is happy when all three parts of soul: the reason, the will and the desire, are in balance.' According to Aristotle (384-322 BC): 'Happy is he who develops his virtues and abilities.' 'The inner happiness comes from inner peace.' (Epicurus- 341-270 BC)

Sonja Lyubomirsky reported in her book 'The How of Happiness' [70] that human happiness is genetically determined in 50% of people, it is affected by external living conditions in 10% and in the remaining 40% happiness can be influenced by the mind of a person.

Material possessions including wealth do not necessarily bring more happiness. Some of the million dollar lotto winners have become penniless destitute as they end up spending it all without any planning. Suddenly, they end up having too many propped up desires with too little know-how and hardly enough experience to handle that kind of money. 'Easy comes easy goes.' Many rich people seem to be enjoying life on the surface but are unhappy internally. All the wealth of the world can't make one happy or healthy. Happiness can be achieved only by contentment and control of the mind and by living a healthy balanced life.

Happiness is a state of mind that brings satisfaction with pleasant experiences. It is a joyous satisfaction of mind on materializing our dreams, desires and goals. Unlike sorrow, happiness is always a welcome sign. Our desires have an inherent tendency to grow limitless and become inexhaustible. In our present day- to-day life we have unending craving for more and more materialistic possessions: flat or curved LED TVs, luxurious cars, inflated bank accounts, bigger houses and ever growing affluence. This temporary happiness of acquiring material things and fulfillment of desires consumes our inner joy.

The art and the science of happiness have remained the subjects of our exploration since dawn of civilization. We are constantly seeking better ways to secure and sustain happiness and overall wellbeing. This quest entails spiritual, philosophic, theological and scientific research in many fields like psychiatry, psychology and neurophysiology. It has volumes of literature with many controversial conclusions and innumerable unanswered questions. Unlike science the art is a study of the intangibles. This aspect of the quest of happiness is strikingly fascinating as well as spiritually challenging. Somehow it remains elusive. Despite abundance of literature it is rather confusing. It raises more questions than giving satisfactory answers.

Religious background and culture plays a dynamic role in making us happy and content. Our undue expectations are major source of unhappiness. Fulfillment of desires makes us 'happy' for a little while, but we're miserable again, because of our ever-increasing expectations. Poor man at the bottom of the ladder dreams of owning a small house. He plans to get married and have a happy family life with his wife and wants to have healthy beautiful children. He wants to put them in good schools, give them the best education and opportunities to enjoy all the amenities of life in a bigger and better home. This is a common sought after dream of everyone's life. But soon our desires multiply with no end in sight that makes us agitated, dissatisfied and unhappy.

We are always chasing happiness and running away from pain and sorrow. 'We are usually unhappy for not being happy.'[110] Happiness grows in direct proportion to acceptance of our fate or fulfillment of our desires, and in inverse proportion to our expectations.[19-21] This equation is not that simple. Happiness also depends on intensity, urgency, quality and probability of achieving those desires. One needs to cut down quantity and increase the quality of desires but at the same time desires should be reasonable and pragmatic.

Peace and tranquility of mind are essential prerequisites for happiness. State of the mind determines feeling of joy or sorrow, as happiness is only a subjective phenomenon. When mind is agitated we experience sorrow but a tranquil mind is filled with joy. We should control our mind and try to remain equanimous in joys and sorrows, which are nothing but only passing phases of life. Worldly possessions only give fleeting experiences of happiness. Undue expectations on our part are the major source of discontentment and unhappiness in this world. We have agitation and restlessness of mind as we 'struggle to gain' more, 'try to guard' what we have and 'get rid of all unpleasant things' that we don't want.

True happiness can be attained when you understand your inner-self and are contented irrespective of success or failure.

You have to keep your mind focused, stable and strong as well as positive and contented to be happy. You can achieve 'inner happiness' by controlling your egoistic desires.

Happiness is when our life is in harmony and the mind is full of love, connectedness and compassion. Happiness is felt both in love and pain. 'No pain and no love' go with no happiness as well. It is said, 'It is better to have loved and lost than never to have loved at all.'[110] Pain of love brings in a new understanding in life. Sometimes most loving moments are painful. Joy of newborn's cry after a painful delivery is overwhelming. The competitive supports cause exhaustion and lots of aches and pains before giving euphoria of happiness on victory. Accidents and near-death experiences and other tragedies are sometimes turning points in our lives to make us a more positive to enjoy the present moments.

Pleasure and pain are like shadows. 'Darkness is followed by light and sorrow by comfort.' Pain and suffering invariably follows pleasure as sooner or later when the pleasure and its euphoria ends, as it always does, it is again followed by depression, discontentment, anger and frustration. A spiritually disciplined contented mind is needed to escape from this universal cycle of pain and pleasure.

True celestial happiness comes with contentment and satisfaction in a spirit of detachment. One needs to remain positive and be patient. Don't remain imprisoned in shackles of fear, anger and frustration as only a positive attitude can set you free. You don't need best of everything to be happy, 'you have to make best of everything that you have.'[110] Aristotle eloquently emphasized, 'Happiness depends on ourselves.'

> 'Desires are insatiable. They keep growing as we try to satisfy
> them just as the fire becomes more inflamed when oil is poured
> into it.'

> ~ MANUSMRITI 2-94[71]

CHAPTER 3

The Philosophy of Mind

'Om Bhur-Bhuvah Svah, Tat Savitur Varenyam
Bhargo Devssya Dhimahi, Dhiyo Yo Na Parchodyat'

~ GYATRI MANTRA *YAJUR VEDA 36-3 RIG VEDA 3-62*

Translated as:
    'Om, The Giver of life, The Dispeller of miseries and the bestower of happiness, we mediate upon that creator… inspire and illuminate thought-flow in our intellect.'

Earliest documentation of happiness and human mind is depicted in 'Vedas' (5000-2500 BC). General assumption is that at the dawn of civilization either Vedas were revealed by God to 'Rishis' (sages), or revealed themselves to the Rishis. The word 'Veda' is derived from Sanskrit root 'Vid' means 'to know', the knowledge imparted by God at the dawn of civilization for the harmonious development and guidance of mankind. Since there was no written language in the beginning, Rishis, the original recipients of Vedic knowledge transmitted Vedas by word of mouth ('shruti') successively through generations. Thousands of years later these were documented in hand-written Sanskrit on 'bhojpatras' (carefully preserved dried leaves).

    'Gyatri Mantra' has been accepted as the one of oldest divine hymns. It is the divine prayer to God to illuminate and guide thought-flow in our mind and intellect in the right direction. This mantra is one of the oldest scholarly connections of our mind to intellect and thoughts.

The philosophy of mind, body and soul has intrigued human race since antiquity. According to Darwin theory of evolution, it took millions of years for our species to evolve into able minded human being. But if we believe in evolution and the God as the Creator, then why it took Him that much time to germinate the powers and ambiguities of the mind in us. It did not take long for Adam and Eve to unlock the mysteries of life.

The world was created in 6 days according to Genesis. It was created in 6 days or periods based on Qur'anic verses. There is another valid theory of evolution as to how the all-knowledgeable omnipotent God created us. He did not wish to create the world in utter chaos without any discipline and direction. At the beginning he created the teachers and prophets along with others. The earliest teachers of the universe were the most learned, and the noble ones, the manifestations of perfectionists full of all knowledge and experiences to lead the mankind. It is no coincidence that revelation of Vedas to the sages and emergence of prophets of all religions descended to earth in the beginning of civilization. [17] Abraham, Moses, Jesus, Mohammad, Krishna and Buddha, all of them showed us the path of divinity, righteousness and ultimate liberation of humans in the practice of spirituality embedded deep in their religious philosophies, teachings and beliefs.

Evolution of philosophy of mind and its relationship to body and soul has been dealt in detail in the ancient times in Eastern religions. Hinduism has been constantly evolving. It is not merely practice of the religion but it is a way of how to lead the life in diverse circumstances. 'Hinduism is not a religion but a way of life.' [115] Vedas and Upanishads brilliantly bring an unparalleled focus on philosophy of mind, body and soul and their relationship to The Creator. Lord Krishna's elaborate preaching of this flawless philosophy to Arjuna in the battlefield of Kurukshetra is depicted so wisely in Bhagwad Geeta.[19]

The Buddhist, the Chinese and the Inca philosophies antedate that of Greek and Romans. The basic quest has been to somehow transform human sufferings to happiness. The downfall of many civilizations of the past resulted from erroneous beliefs of their superiority.

Great philosophers extensively analyzed the ambiguities of mind in the past. To our amazement the mysteries of mind and the concepts and origin of our pains and pleasures are still evolving with newer research.

'I the Lord search the heart and examine the mind, to reward a man according to his conduct, according to what his deeds deserve.' -Jeremiah 17:20. This and other quotes depict ample philosophy about man and the mind in the Holy Bible.

The philosophy of mind deals with the study of mysteries of mind and its relationship to the physical body. It is relation between the non-physical mental faculties of mind and the material objects and the body. It deals with metaphysics, fundamental nature of being and the world as to 'what is there?' and 'what is it like?', ontology and cosmology. [118]

In philosophy of dualism, mind and body are considered two deferent entities with complex inter-relationship dealing with non-physical mind's influence over physical body. Plato, Aristotle and Rene Descartes subsequently emphasized this ancient Vedic philosophy.

Aristotle and Plato believed in multiple souls. According to them there is 'Nutritive soul' that deals with all plants and also animals and human beings. 'Sensitive soul' is present in animals. 'Rational soul' is the perceptive soul of pain, pleasure and desire in human beings.

'It is mark of an educated mind to be able to entertain a thought without accepting it.' (Aristotle)

In fifteenth century French philosopher Rene Descartes[25] considered by many to be 'father of modern philosophy', popularized the idea that humans are two things: mind and body. Mind and body are not identical as mind is non-physical. The input passes by sensory organs to the brain and from there to immaterial spirit. The mind is immortal and survives after death of the body. Descartes described the mind as the seat of conscious awareness and the intelligence dwelling in the brain. Still many believe in Cartesian dualism in the present century.

In monism view of Baruch Spinoza (17th century) and others, mind and body are not ontologically distinct entities. They argue that there is only one 'primal substance' that is neither mental nor physical but it has both attributes. There is a unifying sustenance or essence.

Body, mind and soul are the three different facets of human life with complex, intricate interrelationships. Buddha preached no soul doctrine of '*Anatta*'.[15]

We must try to keep our mind open and under control. All the wrongdoings arise because of misdirected mind. 'If mind is transformed, can wrongdoing remain?'[15] We must try to assess any problem or confrontation with a cool mind and take time to give a suitable response. The intelligent in-depth determination results from weighing the past experiences, knowledge and understanding.

Mind need to be evolved into the next stage for humanity, the so-called 'supermind' according to Shri Aurbindo.[113] At this stage mind is equipoised, out of dualities of concepts like darkness and light and the pain and the pleasure. It is the joyous transcendence of humanity beyond death to blissful eternal happiness.

'Small are the numbers of people who see with their eyes and think with their minds.' Said Albert Einstein. Many conflicts in the world can be averted by proper use of an unbiased mind.

> '*Our species needs, and deserves, a citizenry with minds wide awake and a basic understanding of how the world work.*'
>
> ~ CARL SAGAN

CHAPTER 4

What is mind?

'Most people believe the mind to be a mirror, more or less accurately reflecting the world outside them, not realizing on the contrary that the mind is itself the principal element of creation.'

~ RABINDRANATH TAGORE

MIND IS THE key to mysteries of our existence as it unfolds the real mentality. Life is manifestation of *'manas'* (mind). It is the seat of our thoughts, desires, and wills, attention, interests and imaginations that are essential for functioning of life. Life without a mind is metaphorically a candle without light. Body without a mind is dead and inert like a light bulb without electricity. Hinduism has dealt extensively with the exploration of philosophy of mind. Swami Chinmayananda teachings give practical application of the oldest Eastern religious philosophy of mind to the modern day-to-day life.[19-21]

Mind reflects on the individual and it is a mirror of his demeanor. 'Mind is a complex cognitive faculty that enables consciousness, reasoning, thinking, perception and judgment that are characteristic features of human beings and some other life forms.'[118] According to American Heritage Dictionary: 'Mind is the collective conscious and unconscious processes in a sentient organism that directs and influence his mental and physical behavior.' Complexity of mind makes its definition difficult. Religion, philosophy, psychology, physiology, neurology, biology, cybernetics and other disciplines of science all come up with different interpretations of mind and consciousness.

Life is governed by the whims of mind. Body and mind are complexly entangled, body feels what the mind knows and the mind knows what the body feels.[15]

Life is compared to flow of water in a river. Like river life is not straight, it bends, changes its course and never flows with a constant speed. Ups and downs of the course control the speed of water. Life is confronted with many challenges at every crossroad: problems at home, at work, with children in their upbringing, and education, their life styles, the list goes on and on. Mind acts as banks of a river and it controls the flow within its embankments, making sure it doesn't spill over. Determination of mind and character of man are the most powerful tools that keep the fast flowing water under control within its confines. If the banks of the river are solid and re-enforced passionately by a determined mind, there is no danger of water overflow and thereby preventing floods. Weak mind and flawed character can't hold turbulent waters within its confines. When an agitated and confused mind full of desires gets out of control; the water overflows the weak fragile banks causing havoc with catastrophic floods. Weak mind with lack of determination and integrity leads to agitation, chaos, confusion, unhappiness and depression.[21]

Neurophysiology of Mind: Nervous system is diverse traffic system composed of connections, signals, and intertwined fibers with brain that is acting as the 'control tower'. Afferent nerves bring sensations from periphery and extremities to the spinal cord. These fibers ascend to medulla oblongata at base of the brain, decussate and cross to opposite side to reach various centers in the brain. Brain has faculties of sensory, motor, vision, speech, and coordination and balance etcetera. Motor impulses travel downwards through efferent fibers in spinal cord to peripheral nerves that innervate various muscles for actions and responses. Most of the actions are controlled by higher centers in the brain while some rudimentary reflex responses occur at spinal cord level. Seat of intelligence resides in the prefrontal gyrus of the brain. Memory is spread over many brain areas. Memory loss in Alzheimer is associated with various changes in the brain: its shrinkage, reduced utilization of sugar (glucose) in brain areas associated with memory, amyloid deposits and other emerging explanations. There is evidence of biologic inheritance of memory and intelligence. The mysteries of DNA revolution have just begun. Intelligence in the brain may not be localized but may result from effectiveness of information travelling through the brain. It may be clustered in the frontal and parietal lobes of brain. Intelligence may be determined by effectiveness and communication between parietal and frontal lobes, so called Parieto-Frontal Integration Theory (P-FIT).[16] Presently understanding of complex brain functions is enhanced by use of PET (Positron Emission Tomography) scans and fMRI (functional Magnetic Resonance Imaging) and other newer technological advances. The imaging techniques assess the changes in brain functioning like blood flow and other activities when exposed to a neurologic challenge or an event.

Mind is a powerhouse of thoughts and emotions that can electrify our body to chase sensuous objects of desire. Sensory perceptions lead to 'thought' of desires for indulging, avoiding or suppressing that impulse leading to conflicts. 'To do or not to do' (Sunkalpa or Vikalpa) conflicting resolutions lead to confusion and turbulence of mind. It is the gateway through which all ideas and impulses have to pass.[123] Determinative power of discernment of right from wrong (viveka) and contemplation (vichara) comes from wisdom after transformation of mind through faculty of intellect (mind-intellect complex) directing our thoughts, actions, and speech.

According to Buddhism there are three poisonous afflictions of mind: ignorance, attachment and hatred.[62] We have to learn to educate and restrain our mind to cure these afflictions to discard our sufferings and to gain peace and happiness. It needs physical, mental and intellectual discipline.

Mind directed 'outward' to sensory world bring all kind of desires with anxiety and agitation, whereas, when directed 'inwards' towards the inner-voice it becomes tranquil and happy.

Mind and thoughts can't be collected in a test tube to be analyzed, weighed or measured. Mind equipped with its thoughts and emotions colors the landscape of perceived reality with diverse spectrum of human personality by its own interpretations that are varied and dynamic. Happiness resides within positive contented mind.

'Greater part of our happiness or misery depends on our dispositions and not on our circumstances.'

~ MARTHA WASHINGTON

CHAPTER 5

Objective and subjective Mind for Happiness

'Objective Reality and Truth requires neither ones consent nor dissent'

~ R ALAN WOODS

MIND IS A product of impressions and experiences. It is constantly bombarded with external stimuli. Objective and subjective are two concepts of categories of reality. Objective is the reality outside your mind while inner reality of mind is a subjective phenomenon, subject to your experience and interpretations and this subjective interpretation can be biased.

You can't be selected as a jury if you know any one of parties involved in litigation, plaintiff or defendant, as you can't be objective in your judgment.

You see something hanging from a tree in the dark; you think it is a snake. As you go closer to it with a flashlight it turns out to be a rope. In this case snake and the rope are subjective and objective assessments respectively in your mind. [19-21] Similarly realities in life can be hidden under cover of ignorant beliefs that you hold dear to your heart.

Some writings, rituals or views can easily become subjective realities in our mind. We become oblivious to reasoning and tend to defend our subjective convictions. There are holy wars and conflicts because of these religious convictions. We should try to remove doubts and superstitions by objectifying our biased subjective beliefs.

'Scientific definitions' of objective and subjective: As described above subjective opinion is *subject to your experience* and is determined and accepted by the mind. On the other hand, objective opinion is outside and independent of our mind. It is a sound fact based on scientific conclusions that are verifiable. The subjective determination is based on conclusions of a person or a group of persons or on anecdotal experiments. This is a raw scientific determination and scientifically it is considered the lowest grade of evidence. On the contrary, objective findings are scientific conclusions based on facts rather than individual observations. Here strict guidelines are used to select, implement and interpret data that is verifiable, reproducible and statistically significant.

Objective mind based on facts and conclusions is *conscious* mind, whereas, subjective mind is *unconscious* (or subconscious) as it acts at that level. All our memories, habits, beliefs, likes, dislikes and preferences are encoded subconsciously in our subjective mind.

Is our subjective mind living divinity? Is it the site of our soul or closely connected to it? This mind is ever awake, always actively listening to suggestions, conflicts, issues and sermons and suggestive advertisement at subconscious level without our awareness or our permission.

In short, to put in simple words: objectivity means facts of the universe, the way things are. Some of our present day thinking and the facts may change in future, depending on newer concepts and research and development. Most of the facts are, however, true forever. Earth will always be 'round' and all planets will always 'revolve around the sun'.

Conscious mind is the reasoning faculty that protects the unconscious mind from incorrect programming. Subjective mind is inner-self; it is a personal belief (as to what objective is). We can make our objective and subjective minds messed up and their distinctions blurred or overlapped. When improperly used mind can lead to all miseries and conflicts.

Vedantic Interpretation of Mind: is described in the vast literature that includes 'Brihad-Aranyaka Upanishad' [90,105] and The Holy Geeta[19] and other books.[20,95] The mind facing various objects is the outer-objective mind and is called 'manas' (mind) in Sanskrit. It faces the world of external stimuli from various sources (five sensory organs). The inner-mind is subjective mind called 'Budhi' (intellect or determinative faculty) in Sanskrit. It is facing-within and reacts to stimuli received. Mind should be under influence of intellect for peace and harmony. Wisdom based on our intellect tries to put brakes on egoism, confusion, agitation and turmoil in our lives. Objective mind is like the receiving station that takes call from external stimuli. If it reacts reflexly or emotionally or impulsively without guidance from intellect (Budhi), it will lead to confusion and chaos, discontentment and dissatisfaction. Instead impulses are taken over by Budhi, in-charge of our intellect that assesses a suitable response.

This is done at subconscious level without our knowledge from information brought by past experiences. Although the objective mind seems to be the controller, the subjective mind stores all the information intelligently and thus is equipped with ready to use material discriminately. It is very powerful, as it provides instantaneous input in the mind like data in the hard disc in a computer. When awake and active external stimuli are constantly keeping our conscious mind engaged in making judgments, while subjective mind sits back and absorbs all the processed information. While in deep sleep (and during hypnosis) our mind shuts down our sensitivity to the outside world and our unconscious mind comes to the forefront. The processes of unconscious mind occur automatically and are not available for introspection. It includes thought processes, memory, affect and motivation.[116]

An individual is healthy and in peace when outer and inner mind work in harmony. Intellect is the discriminating faculty with disciplining influence on the mind. A discord in their relationship leads to agitation and confusion. Between these two faculties is the layer of egoistic desires. Greater the distance between these two aspects of mind, greater is the inner confusion and agitation in a person.[19] All the experiences and stimuli lead to ever-increasing irrepressible desires; an overindulgence of these is like putting layers of dirt on subjective mind, making it dull, unreflective and inefficient in controlling objective mind.

Wisdom is noble and pious character of the person based on his thoughts and deeds nurtured by the sound knowledge and judgment of mind-intellect complex. Intellect is under influence of outer world through experiences of mind but it transcends under subconscious influences from within.

Some responses are natural and normal, some of these reflexes may be defensive and do not need much cognitive function. You reflexly withdraw your hand when you touch any hot object. Even an infant does the same. Many reflex actions are automatic and without our control. Even animals share the same of the same responses.

Many species have cognitive awareness. Living corals recoil to touch. We are well aware about the intelligence of many living species, i.e. sharks, elephants, domestic animals just to name a few. Tales of elephants having a 'long memory' are well known. Salmon hatch in stream and rivers and swim to ocean to eat and grow. Towards the end of their life span (3 to 8 years) they swim back to their place of birth, up the rivers and streams for spawning. Salmon are attuned to planet's magnetic field and use their sixth sense to navigate hundreds of miles (up to 3000 miles) in open water of lakes and rivers to find their way home. Setting of its internal guidance system to local earth's magnetic field shapes their route of migration. The direction of approach is very sensitive to earth's magnetic field.

Mind and intellect refine and mature with knowledge and self-realization with spiritual guidance. One should keep ones' mind restrained, avoid overindulgence in desires and keep intellect firm and determined to maintain peace and harmony in life to enjoy everlasting happiness.

'The secret of success behind all 'men of achievement' lies in the faculty of applying their intellect in all their activities without being misled by any surging emotions or feelings.'

~ CHINMAYANANDA [20]

CHAPTER 6

Wandering and Drifting Mind

'The mind can go in a thousand directions, but on this beauti-
ful path, I walk in peace. With each step, the wind blows. With
each step, a flower blooms.'

~ THICK NHAT HAHN[41]

OUR MIND NEVER stays still; it is wandering (chunchal) all the time. It anchors on all kinds of flights of imagination and ideas as well as prone to blind faith and belief in all kinds of miracles without any regard to wisdom and common sense.[2] It is speedier than wind and faster than the sound and the lightening. Its imaginative powers can take us to any place or time in a millisecond Imaginative mind can make us travel in an instant from bottom of the sea to the top of highest mountains or travel as far away as to the surface of the moon and other galaxies.

Mind is like a boat roaming freely in the 'ocean of life'. It can touch any shores or flow aimlessly round and round in a whirlwind. Maybe human life itself is a boat, 'a boat of life' navigated with mind as its pedals. This boat is constantly jolted in the high and low tides. Tides and the high winds can easily capsize this boat. These tides of turmoils are easily generated by over-indulgence in our emotions or by ego and jealousy and by incessant pursuit of material objects. Our mind needs to be focused to navigate us free from all these hurdles. We need its intellectual sense of determination and its dis-criminatory powers to take us to the chosen shores and thus achieve peace and tranquility. Our character, nobility and spiritual beliefs can help to lead us to the right path of peace and harmony. It is correctly said, 'Mind can move mountains.'[110]

Recently it has been shown scientifically how a quadriplegic can move some muscles directed by focusing the thoughts in his brain (mind?)? Stephen Hawking, a theoretical physicist, one of the great geniuses of our times contracted Amyotrophic Lateral Sclerosis (ALS, also called 'Lou Gehrig's Disease) in 1963 and was given only 2 years to live at that time. Despite this crippling progressive neurological disorder, his best works are yet to come.[45] His body is twisted and wasted but his mind (brain) is intact. With miracles of modern technology, by focusing his thoughts in the brain, he is able to express his thoughts and actually speak through a computer-generated voice. You can watch his videos on Internet sites and 'you-tube'. His latest book 'Grand Design' was published in 2010.

According to Buddhism, life is like a log of wood caught in current of a rapidly flowing river. It can jostle around aimlessly by the flow of thoughts generated by the currents of our cravings. It is like the burning flame of a candle caught in intense winds or like a restless forever jumping ape.[15] It can easily be swayed by sudden impulsive mind to unknown territories. One can be sitting in a holy place of worship absentminded to the sermons but engaged in mindful of thoughts totally opposing spiritual advice.

Mind can charismatically touch ones' innovative self to set goals for ones achievements and attain success after success, or it can be destructive enough to ruin one's concentration and focus to achieve nothing but failures. The human mind is dynamic, constantly changing reacting to ever shifting causes and conditions amidst panorama of the world. Mind full of greed is clouded with ignorance. It is fertilized with rain of craving desires and is irrigated by willfulness of egos that results in wrong actions. Man chases these impure, often unobtainable desires that cause restlessness of mind and pain and sufferings.[15]

Good mind is the free mind, free from the desires and divisive conflicts and free from selfish egocentric attitudes.[55] Only mind that is free from outer-sensory world can look inwards to enjoy real happiness in tranquility.

Mind is the unique power but one who has control over his mind is the most powerful person. Chattering mind is perpetually occupied and never still or silent to be able to concentrate and enjoy in solitude of tranquility. We need to rechannel our mind and bring it under physical, mental and intellectual control. Uncontrolled wandering mind leads to a whirlwind of unending desires but a control over it brings contentment, peace and happiness. Mind can transform and transcend with single pointed focus to blend with infinite blissful truth. 'Still mind is like an open window' through which you can see reflections of reality.[19]

'What is that world, by which the wandering mind can be restrained? What are those teachings by which you can endure pain and pleasure?'

~ SRI GURU GRANTH SAHIB

CHAPTER 7

Where is Mind Located?

'Consciousness and cognition are essential elements without which the other qualities of mind do not seem to register...conclusion that the brain is the organ of the mind and the quality of the mind depends on the quality of the brain.'

~ PHIROZE HANSOTIA, MD

MIND IS INTEGRAL part of our body. Full cognitive awareness of human mind is essential to enjoy happiness. It is one of the most powerful and unique tools. Mind is an unending source of all emotions, thoughts and deeds. Mind can bring us closer to divinity in realization of God or away to question His existence. Just like soul, mind is not a physical entity that can be discovered on anatomical dissection or scanned by investigatory procedures or slain by any means. Mind resides within us. The exact location of mind has been debated and questioned since thousands of years. Mind is elusive. It is formless without any shape, size or location. It can neither be seen nor photographed. It has intangible abstract conceptual existence. When we look for it in the body it is nowhere and yet everywhere.

Mind is the energy, the consciousness that fuels the feeling of pain and pleasure, and stimulates and maintains human spirit. Does it exist in our bosom, as it is intimately associated with echoes from our heart? Is it near lotus of the heart where the soul pervades according to Hindu philosophy? Is it located in the heart as according to the Bible this organ has direct relation to the God? Vital air, food and water nurtures and sustains life ('*prana*'), whereas, mind sustains human spirit.

Since mind and intellect go hand in hand, where thoughts germinate and blossom, does it reside in our brain like intellect? The modern research with all its newly innovative tools like fMRI (functional Magnetic Resonance Imaging) has placed it in the realms of the brain. Vast neurologic network and neurochemicals and neuropeptides play an integral part in its actions. Dr. Cadence Pert concluded that human brain is the primary analyzer, whereas; mind is information processing-field spread across the body in every cell of the body as integrated body-mind complex.

The mystery of consciousness has always remained a challenge since beginning of time. Philosophers, theologians, psychologists, historians and scientists have tried to unveil its secrets. We are trying to understand the complex functioning of billions of neurons (cells of nervous system) and their inter-relationships to awareness, memory, knowledge and intelligence. Scientific research on consciousness is exhilarating and mysterious. Major religions locate consciousness of mind in the soul. The soul resides in the inner-self; it is believed to reside in the lotus of the heart.[19] It leaves the body after death to merge with cosmic mind and go through cycle of rebirths.

According to Penrose and Hameroff[42] consciousness reside in cytoskeletal microtubules and other structures within each of brain neurons. It provides evidence of pre-conscious to conscious transition. In future human intelligence will radically evolve beyond biology and has to compete 'the artificial intelligence.'

In the 'Pattern-recognition theory of mind,' brains are general purpose learning machines.[57] Neocortex that constitutes 80% of our brains is largely a grid structure of about 300 million pattern-recognition modules. Each set of modules runs the same basic algorithm that is a set of rules of identifying patterns (e.g. face recognition, grammar etcetera.).

Self-awareness is a complex cognitive function of brain integrated through insular cortex, anterior cingulate cortex and medial prefrontal cortex.

The ambiguities of mind have continued to elude us forever. Our understanding of it is merely the tip of the iceberg. Human mind germinates thoughts and emotions and is a powerful manipulator of human spirit on the world stage and makes us feel success and failure, pain and pleasure, happiness and sorrow.

'Mind lies where heart throbs'.

~ UNKNOWN

CHAPTER 8

Knowledge Illuminates Path of Happiness

*'An ignorant man has eye to see but sees nothing, has ears to
hear but hears nothing, has tongue to speak but speaks nothing.
The ignorant can never understand the mysteries of knowledge.'*

~ *RIG VEDA, X, 17, 4* [24]

GROWTH IS FUNDAMENTAL to all living beings. Growth of body, mind and
intellect are essential elements of life. Physical growth of the body is universal,
equally applicable to plants, animals and human beings. Growth of the mind
is attained by two basic prerequisites: knowledge and intellect. Knowledge is
the key to bring happiness.

Knowledge ('Gyana', 'Jnana', 'Vidya') is the light that eliminates darkness of ignorance. It illuminates the path for success in life. It is education
and in-depth study acquired from parents, teachers, educational institutes,
from study of books, and from other ever-increasing sources of knowledge for
education. Basic 'worldly education' is the foundation, on which we expand
our horizon in any sphere or profession: whether it is technical, mechanical,
medical and any other specialties. Education is the key to success in life. We
cannot make progress without it. Acquiring knowledge leads to perfection,
wisdom, character and integrity. In children knowledge is essential to develop
both their bodies and mind to fullest extent, so that they can mold their
future life in nobler thoughts and deeds.

'Intellectual knowledge' (Baudhik-gyan) is obtained from personal experiences in life. It can be gained from basic interactions and teachings from parents

and teachers and from basic to philosophical and spiritual books and discourses. Essentially intellectual knowledge can be obtained from anybody who is learned and wise. Anybody or any event that rubs you right or wrong way leaves an imprint on your mind. This acquired knowledge alone is the cause of individual progress. Instinctive knowledge is natural and limited. It is neither sufficient nor progressive in nature. Children learn the wisdom of right and wrong and virtue and vice from parents and teachers in their formative years.[24]

Intellectual knowledge ((Baudhik-gyan) in Hindu philosophy is defined in 'Yoga Shastra'[24] consisting of moral discipline (Yamas) and physical discipline (Niyamas) for practicing in everyday life.

A), Rules of Behavior: Five principals of 'moral discipline' (Yamas) are: harmlessness (Non-Violence, Ahimsa), strict discipline to veracity (Truthfulness, Satya), non-stealing (Asteya), self-control —never be lustful and non- covetousness (Aparigraha) with abstinence from pursuit of worldly desires and freedom from vanity.

B), Rules of Self-Discipline: Five principals of 'physical discipline' (Niyamas) are: cleanliness (purity -physical and mental), contentment (Santosha), equanimity of mind (Tapasa) and devotion to duty regardless of consequences, acquisition and dissemination of true knowledge and devotion to God.

In Judaism, sages say, 'da'at kanita ma chasarta, da'at chasarta ma kanita'. It means, 'if you have gained knowledge (da'at) you lack nothing, if you lack knowledge (da'at) what have you gained?'[112] In Kabbalah there are the pathways of Wisdom ('chochmah'), the gateways of Understanding ('binah') and the bridges of Knowledge (da'at).[49]

Knowledge is limitless and ever growing. 'Greatest enemy of knowledge is not ignorance; it is illusion of knowledge,' says Stephen Hawking.[45] The more you read, the more you realize as to how ignorant you are. Many self-proclaimed knowledgeable persons ('Gyanis') who blow their own trumpet are basically ignorant illiterates ('Agyanis'). They are intoxicated by their ego and have undue exuberance about their abilities. Basic worldly knowledge (Gyan) gives only a little more than a tunnel vision. Only way to increase your horizon is with the intellectual growth (Baudhik-gyan). Both these facets have unending limits; there is always room for improvement. Ignorance is darkness of mind while knowledge is the incandescent candle that illuminates our mind. Ignorance can also result from wrong education with incorrect knowledge. Information is power and knowledge is the key.

Human knowledge is growing fast but it has its own limits. Man's physical resources are also limited and finite. We can only see so much with our eyes and hear so much with our ears. There are newer ways to augment and enhance our limitations. Reading glasses improve vision when vision is impaired; telescope and microscope are extensions of our visual perception. Random sound waves in the atmosphere can be recorded. There are newer explanations and avenues for knowledge. Seekers of knowledge don't accept anything blindly but with a discerning thoughtful analysis. Knowledge reflects with intense luminosity that lightens up all the dark corners of ignorance and shows the right path.

Knowledge of self (Atam-gyana) is the path of spiritual knowledge to ask inquisitively as to 'who am I?' It is a spiritual insight that brings tranquility of mind. The knowledge of the human spirit is the spiritual knowledge as opposed to knowledge of material world (material or worldly knowledge).

The material knowledge is 'Apara Vidya' -lower knowledge.

Material knowledge pertains to five basic material elements- space, air, fire, water and earth. Entire material universe and our bodies are composed of these five material elements in varied proportions.[28,123]

Spiritual knowledge encompasses the knowledge of the Divine Principal, the eternal Creator. It is –higher knowledge 'Para Vidya' (Mundaka Upanishad).[28] The spiritual knowledge is the path to self-realization. The Self-Realized (Tattwa-Darshi)[123] person is free from all bondages and enjoys eternal bliss.

Emotional growth gives stability and control over mind to understand others and be compassionate and to develop inter-relationships and self-restrains. Spiritual growth results from our quest to understand purpose of life, the creator and the creation.

Despite advancement in scientific knowledge, which brings all the comforts and amenities in life at our doorsteps, there is unhappiness in this world that is full of jealousy, envy, apathy and selfishness. Spiritual knowledge is needed to direct us to the right path of happiness that is full of peace, love, compassion and humility.

Human mind seek answers to the mysteries of the world. All aspects of growths are essential to overall development as all these factors are intertwined. Man has capacity to guide his actions by checks and balances, using his power of discrimination. His sound judgment and intellect to discern right from wrong can sway him away from momentary impulses and feelings. Religion guides our intellect by giving sound choices at every moment of our life. Rightful choices in the walk of life depend on mind-and-intellect. Intellectual development brings harmony and peace of mind. In order to attain happiness and peace, mind needs to be well versed in human relationships and be able to pick the right choice of words and deeds. Absent-minded professor or a certified PhD in sciences could have a tunnel vision and be totally naive in human relationships.

Just as watering and fertilization of the soil is essential for the seed to germinate and bloom, in a similar manner, knowledge is essential to germinate the mind with the intellect (that acts as a fertilizer) to bloom into the light of wisdom. Unlike wealth, knowledge is an inexhaustible treasure; the more you spend it, the more it grows. Knowledge guides not only in complexities of situations, but also helps us in day-to-day life. How to speak the right words? How and when to display our charm? When to keep quiet and let the event pass without confrontation? Knowledge and intellect act synergistically to keep mind under control and to keep it happy in peace and harmony.

'Knowledge, the object of knowledge and the power are the three factors, which motivate action: the senses, the work and the doer comprise the three-fold basis of action' Bhagavad Gita.[19]

*'Education and teaching are the most powerful weapons which
you can chose to change the world. If people can learn to hate,
they can be taught to love.'*

~ Nelson Mandela

CHAPTER 9

Mind and Religion

*'The highest art is always the most religious, and the greatest
artist is always a devout person.'*

~ ABRAHAM LINCOLN

MIND AND INTELLECT are guided in the right direction of peace and tranquility by spiritual connection. According to Vedas[19-21,24,113-115] there are 11 'Indriyas': 5 sense organs ('Punch Jnanendriyas': ears, eyes, nose, tongue and skin), 5 organs of action ('Punch Karamendriyas': hands, feet, mouth, rectum and genital organs) and Mind ('Manas'). The words 'Punch Jnanendriyas' and 'Karamendriyas' are derived from the Sanskrit roots: 'Punch' (5, five), 'Jana' (wisdom), 'Indra' (God of sensory haven), 'Indriyas' (organs) and 'Karma' (act).

There are many religions preaching different messages and modes, but basically all point to the same goal, which is: to overcome our deficiencies, to do the virtuous deeds and to become good human beings to bring peace and contentment to everyone in the universe and bring us closer to The Divine Creator. There is no correct English synonym for 'Dharma'. The word religion comes closer but its true message can be lost in translation. The word 'righteousness' is more akin to 'Dharma'- always leading to the right path, performing your duty towards everybody in the world: your duty to your wife, husband, parents, children, fellow human beings, your community, your country and the whole universe.

To do your duty is real or true 'Dharma'. Performance of duty is seldom sweet unless performed by passion and when your determination and love greases the wheels to make it run smoothly without any friction.[114,115] (Vivekanand-91) Patience, forgiveness, control of mind, external and internal purity, control of indriyas, truthfulness and a resolve to not to steal or have any anger or hatred and in addition spiritual growth with knowledge of 'atman' (soul) are essentials of 'Dharma' -Manusmriti VI-92.[71]

Universal Dharma is to be kind, considerate, humble and compassionate person who doesn't insult, cheat or hurt any other person. It is a predictable right response to any situation.

Character, personality and integrity of a person is molded by experiences of life by the mind and the intellect, whereas, religion brings harmony by stabilizing the mind and educating the intellect bringing perfection. Peace and tranquility of mind can be attained by renunciation of all desires at best, or at least avoiding over indulgence in seeking materialistic objects and pleasures. Yoga through practice of concentration and meditation, restrains the mind from agitation.

Religion and 'Dharma' is like a stop sign that reminds us to be righteous, truthful, compassionate and considerate to everyone, it reminds us to stop whenever we are tempted to do a wrong or non-virtuous act. 'Dharma' is virtuous moral behavior that sustains life on earth by maintaining social order. Religion is a link between man and God. It is a way to God.

Discernment ('Viveka') is the process of making detailed judgment and the value and quality of a certain subject or event.[118] It is a process of evaluation by exhibiting keen insight, perception and good judgment. In Christianity, it is the process of determining God's desire in one's life or in a situation. It describes an interior search for an answer. In the Hindu philosophy of 'Dharma', one needs the power of 'viveka' to discern right from wrong and to be able to follow the noble path.

Discernment is well illustrated in Code of Canon Law, Rule of Faith and other theology literature.

According to Buddhism,[15] the world is full of sufferings. The desires to acquire wealth, honor, comforts and pleasures are its source of sufferings and are due to greed and ignorance of mind. According to Buddhist philosophy everything in the world is impermanent; it is a delusion of mind. Still it is same mind that gets illuminated in the Enlightenment. 'To conquer oneself is a greater victory than to conquer thousands in a battle.'[15]

Spiritual discipline and morality are engraved in the teachings of any religion. Our beliefs are the anchors of our hopes and dreams that fuel the fire within us to never lose the resolve of our mind. Despite success and failure, we must learn how to keep our mind tranquil and at peace, contented and happy.

*'I reject any religious doctrine that does not appeal to reason
and is in conflict with morality.'*

~ *MAHATMA GANDHI*

CHAPTER 10

Who are we? Where from and Why do we exist?

'Not until we are lost do we begin to understand ourselves.'

~ HENRY DAVID THOREAU

'THE MEANING OF life' cannot be fully grasped unless we try to understand ourselves as to 'Who are we? Who am I?' 'What is our origin? And why do we exist?' Without knowing our own-self we cannot solve the mystery of others surrounding us. Understanding is the key to true happiness.

We have to ask ourselves: 'Are we just physical bodies playing our roles in life on the world stage or are we eternal souls temporarily housed in physical bodies that will eventually wither away? [2] We have to define our purpose and goals in life. We are all mortals and have momentary existence like a tiny dot in the world clock of timelessness.

We have complex cognitive consciousness that sometimes reacts unpredictably in this constantly changing environment of dynamic world. We are so much involved in the fast day-to-day life that we have hardly any time to ourselves. The day passes so quickly from the time we wake up, we get ready and commute to work and there try to solve the stresses of workplace, and get something accomplished and finally at the end of the day rush home to juggle in the work at home. Involvement gets more time consuming with demands from all directions. In a growing family with children one gets engrossed in their care, their education, schooling, school reports, their soccer matches and so on. This is the story of a busy middle class family. If you are relatively poor, your day and night is consumed by worrying as to how to make enough to provide for their basic needs and to feed and educate the children and to have

36

a roof over their head and to secure their future? Complexities of life unfold every day to face new challenges.

You are consumed by so much distractions that there is hardly any time to sit and relax and think and introspect. There is no contentment as to what we have and what gifts God has bestowed on us. We are consumed by worries and are unhappy and overwhelmed by negative feelings. We don't have time to look in the window of our mind with a positive attitude to discover happiness as it lies within us.

Positive psychology is conducive to happiness. Persons who try to explore the answers to the puzzle, to understand as to 'who am I' and 'what we are here for' are the ones who realize the foundation of happiness. The very idea that we are looking for these answers means the start of an idealistic and spiritual quest in the journey of life to explore the meaning of our existence on earth. A person who fails to grasp and recognize his own self can't understand others. Know thyself first before you can know someone else.

The personality and mannerism of a person depends on his background, his composure and behavior and his character and his general outlook in life. The gestures, the way of talking and walking, the eye contact and the body language tell a lot about one's self-esteem and attitude in life. The problem is that we lie about ourselves all the time. We want to project a positive happy and contented image to others and portray ourselves as someone else. We transmit this fake imagery everywhere including on social media like Facebook and Twitter. We are impersonators as we have fake masks on our faces, wrong clothes on our body and phony smiles and empty laughter. We have to stop lying about ourselves and to be honest and straightforward about our true feelings, our desires and likes and dislikes. As Socrates said, 'Know thyself'. Khalil Gibran also echoed the same feeling in the last century, 'Knowledge of the self is the mother of all knowledge.' Understand yourself before you can understand others, love yourself before you can truly love others, have faith in yourself before you can inculcate faith in anyone else and strive to be happy yourself before you can make anyone else happy.

Once you look inside by introspection to understand yourself and start realizing that 'no one is perfect'. Instead of being judgmental and critical of others you start admiring their abilities and try to be considerate and compassionate. Encouraging words and a helping hand means a lot when one is in distress as these words bring a ray of the new hope and alter one's negative behavior. Yours and my happiness are interlinked in universal idealistic approach to life. One can never be really happy if the person next to him is miserable and in pain. Macrocosmic happiness or happiness of society at large is the accumulation of microcosmic satisfaction at individual level.

"Life's most persistent and urgent question is, what are we doing for others?" eloquently said Dr. Martin Luther King Jr.

Egoistic self-centered activities to seek materialistic gains merely gives transient happiness, whereas, by leading a life of giving you seek real happiness. 'Happiness is upbeat moods and experiences on receiving while meaningfulness is beyond self and is about giving with deeper sense of satisfaction.'[97,110]

You will open new vistas in life once you transform your attitude to be more giving, more tolerant, better and kinder, compassionate and loving person. You easily grasp the feelings and needs of all those that are around you. You are no longer confined in the walls of seclusion created around you. You increase your horizon as you evaluate the world with a new insight. You muster enough strength to do angelic deeds, like the legions of God's angels you guide the people and bring the message of love, peace, compassion and benevolence. The real angels may be mythical but in modern age these are ordinary people without any wings who try to help others and give them hope and a shoulder to cry in their distress. They try to allay their fears and with their compassionate deeds, bring a smile amidst their tears and a ray of hope of happiness amidst their sorrows. These are the true angels who understand the true meaning of life and are blessed by the Gods.

'What counts in life is not the mere fact that we have lived. It is what differences we have made to the lives of others that will determine the significance of the life we lead.'

~ NELSON MANDELA

Part Two

The Material Life

CHAPTER 11

The Pursuit of Happiness

'Success is what you want, happiness is wanting what you get.'

~ W.P. KINSELLA

BODY MIND AND soul are three facets of human existence. True happiness entails all of these three aspects of life, which is happiness of body, mind and the soul. Happiness of body is easily attainable. It is lowest form of happiness. How happy an animal looks when eating his favorite food? Human beings are meant to enjoy a higher plane of happiness that resides in their thoughts and in their minds. Many human beings persistently overindulge and chase to satisfy their bodily happiness. We passionately pursue the superficial life by falling prey to desires for worldly objects, but the highest pinnacle of happiness lies within us in the inner-self. This brings state of true happiness and bliss from within.

What makes us happy? Is it a happy family life, lots of money, love, success, luxuries and worldly possessions and other gratifications in life? The neurotransmitter dopamine stimulates the 'pleasure center' of the brain to elicit pleasurable sensations. These are perceived by various means like consuming delicious food or a drink or other stimulants. One is happy on getting a promotion, or on winning a sporting event or achieving other successes and accomplishments. All the mechanisms that trigger happiness in the human mind are probably not mediated by a single brain chemical. The complex neuro-chemical changes underlying human happiness are a puzzle that is gradually being explained by newer scientific discoveries. Recently in 2013 scientists at UCLA (University of Southern California Los Angeles) led by Jerome Siegel reported that hypocretin, a neurotransmitter peptide, is markedly increased when subjects are awake, happy and while having social interactions. It is decreased when one is asleep, is sad or in pain.[10,100] Another peptide MCH (Melanin-Concentrating Hormone) increases when asleep and is lowest when interacting socially or in pain. These associations will shed new light on our understanding and treatment of addiction, depression and sleep disorders. This opens a new avenue to the path of happiness in future. There may even be a pill for happiness in future.

'Happiness is when, what you think, what you say and what you do are in harmony.' said Mahatma Gandhi. Happiness lies in coordinated harmonious response of mind transpiring in positive thoughts, in words and in deeds. Firm determination of the mind and contentment bring positive attitude in life. 'Think not what you don't have in your life; instead be grateful for what you have.' [110] Don't look into other people's possessions with greed and envy, instead look at your own achievements with contentment and you will have a lot to be thankful for.

The world is full of people less fortunate than you. Share some of your possessions with them to allay their hunger. The greatest gift you can give to anyone is the gift of knowledge to educate them so they can free themselves from clutches of ignorance and poverty and become productive members of the community. Progress starts with grass-root efforts. By giving part of what little or a part of big you possess can usher happiness. Noble acts of sharing, sacrifice, forbearance, empathy and compassion always enrich ones' mind, body and soul with tranquility and lasting happiness.

The newly invented technologic gadgets loaded with luxury, expensive watches, 3D LED televisions, newer generations of iPhones and other smart phones, iPads and tablets and myriad of other innovations have lead our mind astray and confused. We have a keen desire to possess all these luxuries initiating a cycle of agitation, greed and unhappiness in our inability to possess. There is decline of optimism due to lack of affordability. Middle class is shrinking and the poor are getting even poorer, whereas, the rich are getting richer. The world is getting smaller due to info-technology, 24-hour news coverage and easier transportation across the borders. Geographical or political borders do not confine luxuries of life. Desires to have the luxurious goods have multiplied to a dangerous degree. Vanity is on the rise. Narcissism is the motto of the day, 'I want it all and I want it now, I can't wait for it, tomorrow is too late. I should have had it yesterday.'

A wealthy man can have a valuable art and is very happy that he owns this priceless piece. But only a true art lover with knowledge of the art can really appreciate and fully enjoy it.

Happiness is a state of mind that changes with the changing environments. Some people are always looking for pretexts for being unhappy and consequently have a negative attitude in life. There are also 'myths about happiness'. In this world one is bombarded with false notions and hopes every day that 'I will be happy if....' Examples of this 'if' are countless. 'I will be happy if I get a promotion, or if I have a pay raise or if my boss get fired or if I get a divorce or if I marry that girl. I will be happy if I have a bigger house and a bigger television or if I could go on a cruise or win a lottery. The list goes on and on. Even on getting all the wishes fulfilled somehow we find that happiness is deceptive and short-lived and there are more and more desires propping up that make us unhappy. 'Happiness is like chasing the butterfly that is elusive and always a step away.'[110]

Be happy in adversity with your positive willpower and spirit of forgiveness, and smile peacefully in stoic silence. Keep your cool in unfriendly environment by eliminating any destructive negative emotions that originate in your mind.

Happiness is within us, discover and enjoy it in the moments here and now. Existing opportunities of happiness should never be postponed for the future. There was a story I read recently in Time Magazine that touched the core of my heart. There was an Indian who immigrated to Nairobi from Ahmedabad, India in 1920s. He and wife lived a simple thrifty life. They used to save a lot to plan a comfortable life in future in India. They bought a house there and filled the rooms with all the luxury goods and furnishings, which they planned to enjoy and to live a comfortable happy life after retirement. One day the wife suddenly died from heart attack in her 50s. The husband left Nairobi to come back to Ahmedabad. He felt lonely and depressed, as he could not live in his dream house. Within a month he sold his house and all the things they had accumulated so fondly and he left for London. This entire episode had a powerful influence on his son who started living every day of his life in pursuit of happiness. He enjoyed life, enjoyed his entire possessions, played guitar at home and in clubs, played cricket for his college and took vacations. Unfortunately, he died at age 34 from congenital heart disease. Despite being devastated his father was very proud of his son because his life was not spent deferring-happiness. He enjoyed every day to the fullest and did not defer happiness for tomorrow. Nobody has ever seen tomorrow.

You should learn to live your life happily with a positive attitude. Happiness lowers blood pressure and boosts immune health. Avoid anxiety by not being overly sentimental and emotional; let your inner-self guide your actions.

We have to train our mind to higher intellectual goals, restrain our desires and restrict our greed. We can have happiness through control, contentment and compassion of mind. An uncontrolled mind addicted to pleasures is never satisfied as it clouds our vision, eclipses our intellect, pollutes our wisdom, magnifies our ego and taints our soul. Mental equilibrium with evenness of mind and desireless actions are conducive to lasting happiness.

'Let us be grateful to the people who make us happy; they are the charming gardeners who make our souls blossom.'

~ MARCEL PROUST

CHAPTER 12

Shades of Happiness

'Pain and pleasure, like light and darkness, succeed each other.'

~ LAURENCE STERNE

PAIN AND SUFFERING, happiness, pleasure and joy are the emotional states that are part of life's journey like night and day, darkness and sunshine. Everyone wishes to be happy and avoid pain and suffering altogether if possible. Only a person who has suffered at the hands of pain and misery can appreciate real happiness. It is like finding a long lost love suddenly or like a full and dramatic recovery from a chronic debilitating disease or a serious near-death illness.

There are many shades of happiness

1. *'Hedonism'* is a school of thought that argues that pleasure is the only intrinsic good emotion. It is a focused pursuit of happiness, pleasure and gratification without any hint of pain. Hedonists try to maximize net pleasure, which is pleasure minus any pain.[118] Aristippus, a student of Socrates started ethical hedonism. German philosopher Friedrich Nietzsche was one of the many critics of Hedonism. He believed in morality and 'Will of Power'. He perceived suffering as a necessary device for cultivating human excellence.[118] Michael Onfray, a dedicated French contemporary philosopher defined hedonism 'as an introspective attitude to life based on taking pleasure and pleasuring others, without harming yourself or anyone else.'[5]

There is a famous Paradox about happiness: 'By pursuing happiness itself it moves farther away, but by pursuing something else happiness comes closer.'[110]

'Pleasure' is different from happiness and joy and it is considered a trap.[58] Sensory gratification or satisfaction is a feeling that comes after having delicious food or a drink or sexual enjoyment. Satisfaction can be a feeling after finding a lost piece of a valuable jewelry, or even after relaxing in your own home after a long and exhaustive journey. Pleasure is an emotional state that results after getting something –in material (buying a new car), in experience (like praise, spending time with family), in thoughts or accomplishment (passing an examination, getting acclamation in sports).[58] In this sense life will be barren without these pleasant experiences.

Pleasure always results from some sort of gratification. It is brief as it is associated with something that comes and goes. After brief period of pleasure boredom ensues. There is emotional cycle of desire and frustration, pleasure and boredom. Pleasure being a feeling of enjoyment, delight and satisfaction and can be addictive. You like a glass of wine once in a while socially. You start taking it once a week, and without realizing soon you are taking it more than once a day. It gives you pleasure and a sense of euphoria after you take a few drinks. It becomes part of your habit and before you know you get addicted to it. You feel restless and agitated unless you have a drink. Drinking gives you a momentary pleasure. This becomes a vicious cycle of gratification with pleasure and boredom with restlessness.

2. *'Happiness'* on the other hand is an experience of feeling good. It comes from within and is an emotional state of wellbeing and contentment. Happy people have a positive attitude and willpower. They have a high self-esteem and are contented with their life. They see the glass as half full and not half empty. They dwell in happiness and are by nature forgiving, compassionate and altruistic. It is impossible to quantify happiness. Happiness is an outward expression of the inner feeling and is displayed through a smile or happy facial expressions or

even exuberance. Often unexpected good news makes one jump with happiness. No one can hide happiness.

3. *'Joy'* is another aspect of happiness. 'Joy and happiness' are more or less similar and are associated with positive and desirable experiences. Many a times there is no clear-cut boundary between happiness and joy. You are happy and everyone knows it, you can't hide it. Joy relates to a more meaningful experience in life. It is the intense inner feeling of well-being which exists in spite of whatever is going on around us. It is like a child beaming with simple innocent expression of joy on getting his favorite toy. It is intense feeling that you get on watching your child take the first baby step. So in essence pleasure is a sensory gratification and joy is more a state of an inner awareness that makes you happy. For moral and spiritual fulfillment one should follow the path of joy rather than the path of pleasure.[58]

These terms have no defined boundaries and are often used as synonyms. Many consider joy to be an extreme happiness. Joy can be found on the face of an innocent child on seeing his mother. A person living a simple life can be full of joy under difficult circumstances. Any big or small achievement can initiate this spark of satisfaction. This inside expression does not depend on any specific events in life as it occurs in a person with well-functioning, clean and open psyche. Joy has an inner spiritual connection. It is described in Upanishads as the path of introspection and self-realization. The reward is a tradeoff of short-lived pleasures of life by long-lasting joyous self.

4. *'Bliss'* is the stage of intense joy, ultimate 'ananda', a state of bound-less happiness stemming from inner-self. A blissful mind is full of universal love, peace, compassion, and serenity and unending inner bountiful joy on merging with super-consciousness.

Positive psychology enhances well-being to bring happiness. Seligman and Royzman reported in 2003,[97] that authentic happiness is rooted in three ratio-nal theories: Hedonism theory (the pleasant life), desire theory (the engaged life) and objective theory (the meaningful life). Father of present day 'Positive

Psychology' Martin Seligman describes: 'Life-changing lesson of *Authentic Happiness* (in his book with the same name, published in 2002) is that by identifying the very best in ourselves, we can improve the world around us and achieve new and sustainable levels of authentic contentment, gratification and meaning.'

Everyone has an inherent wish list for *maximizing pleasure and minimizing pain.* Gratification of various objects and instruments of pleasure only brings happiness in a limited way and is transitory. Overindulgence in pleasures is not true happiness and it should not dominate one's life. However, some pleasures in life are essential ingredient of a good life.

You experience a high level of satisfaction engaging in activities where your personal preferences, your strengths and likings are shaped into your work. You are completely wrapped up in your surroundings[89] and working passionately and completely engrossed enjoying your work.[19,21,24]

People with extraordinary achievement bring a purpose to life by higher ideals.[21] It is achieved by knowing and using your highest strengths and talents in service of something bigger than you.[97] This unique way of meaningful life can be accomplished by positive contributions to society like educating, teaching sports, helping children of single moms and helping elderly in various ways and by volunteering.

It has been known that helping others augments immune system; triggers brain reward circuitry and bring true happiness.

The global way to understand one's life is the belief that 'the life itself is meant for a greater purpose.'[110]

We have been seeking a script for happiness forever. The solution for happiness has consumed philosophers, religious scholars, psychiatrists, psychologists and researchers. You can never buy happiness. You need a positive attitude in life and a need to discover it within yourself.

'I ask you to ensure that humanity is served by wealth and not ruled by it.'

~ POPE FRANCIS

CHAPTER 13

Fulfillments of Goals with Positive Willpower

'True victory is the victory of the mind; True defeat is defeat of the heart.'

~ *UNKNOWN*

GOALS IN LIFE are your dreams, aspiration and priorities. Progress in life is sustained by ongoing incessant efforts to improve one's life. It is not only by accumulation of material possessions but also acquiring worldly as well as spiritual knowledge. The passionate drive to achieve something higher than what one presently possesses is the aim of everyone. The common goals in life are proper education, gainful employment, raising a family, accumulation of wealth to live a comfortable life and to have some affluence in society etcetera. The personal goals are dynamic and change and evolve with time depending on one's needs and circumstances. These are part of a broader vision. A child dreams of becoming a firefighter or a policeman or to become an astronaut and to be on the surface of moon but his goals change as he grows and strives to become a doctor, a scientist or an artist or worker in a lab or in a factory.

Once you mature with age and become a responsible adult, you define your goals with your sound judgment and pursue them diligently. Haphazardly changing your course in the middle causes confusion and restlessness and is unhealthy and can be counterproductive.

Every person in this world is born with certain inborn nature, 'the gunas' (attributes, temperaments) described in Bhagavad-Gita.[19] This inborn nature

49

is characterized by three qualities of goodness, energy and dullness defined as 'Satvic', 'Rajsic' and 'Tamasic'[19,51]

'Satvic' willpower is sublime, selfless, compassionate, and always ready to help others. It originates from inner-self resulting in peace and relaxation of mind.

'Rajsic' will originate in egoistic and selfish mind. Always full of activity in seeking success that will make 'me happier, wealthier and more prosperous.'

'Tamasic' will belongs to a lethargic and lazy person who is utterly self-centered, jealous, revengeful, angry and has erroneous impression that everyone is conspiring to derail his project and are hindrance to his success. He is agitated, anxious, confused and fearful. He can't sleep, as he is full of negative energy and thoughts. Every negative thought bounces back at that person with more intensity, weakening his mind, worsening his disposition, making him more fearful, depressed and lonely.

Everyone has a mix of these three traits in their lives, but one of these attributes is usually predominant in an individual and that determines his personality and character at large. Those with overwhelming 'rajsic' tendencies like scientists, discoverers and entrepreneurs passionately pursue their goals to achieve success. Those with predominant 'satvic' traits like Mahatma Gandhi or Mother Teresa are wise noble and the learned role models that help uplift society.

Remain positive and dream big. Dreams originate in the subconscious mind in our sleep. 'Dreams are expression of unconscious desires', said Sigmund Freud. People with negative thoughts are miserable, depressed, fearful, agitated and down in the dumps, Negativity transpire into negative or bad dreams. You are afraid to sleep, as it will bring premonitions or bad omens. Positive thoughts, on the other hand, bring happiness with bright ideas and enthusiasm. When one is objectively engrossed in positive outlook in one's conscious mind, even one's dreams are good and positive. Your goals are your dreams, an inspiration of your heartfelt imaginations and should never be imposed by others.

Define your goals. The moment to start defining one's objective goal is now. Postponing it may alleviate one's desire for a long time if not forever.

The spark of adventure may lie dormant for a long time in the depth of one's heart. One should cultivate hope, passion, patience and perseverance in one's endeavors. It is prudent to attain one's goals first in one's mind, consciously plan, and then emphasize enough for it to penetrate in one's subconscious mind to mark it as the factor of determination in one's psyche. One can draw spurts of unending enthusiasm and energy from positive willpower generated from one's inner cosmic mind like rays of the sunlight. One must let the mind take guidance from inner-voice. Marinate the idea in your subconscious.

Positive psychology germinates and sustain a positive will power and 'incorruptible hope' to achieve one's target. Remaining positive in one's determination even in adversities that act as hurdles, to create an environment conducive for positive thinking. 'Every action one aspires and performs in the battle of life with hope and the faith of a positive willpower will reinvigorate one's determination and infuse it with renewed energy and courage.'[52]

Positive mind and thoughts are essential to achieve a positive willpower. Don't breed negativity in the mind. 'A negative mind will never bring positivity in life.' One needs to define ones' goals by careful thinking and research as to what is suitable and appropriate to pursue. Don't fall prey to an emotionally hurried decision. One must reach at the decision or the idea by careful analysis and deep thoughts and by igniting the creative spark of light in the darkness of one's mind. That spark does not originate on demand, but it depends on one's intelligence, inspiration, ambition, and imaginativeness of mind that ignites with persistent determination and perseverance. It needs lots of time thinking and planning to seed creative ideas in your brain. These can also crop suddenly in one's brain like a bolt from the blue. These creative desires originate in the occipital lobe of the brain or in insula where we feel emotions or in our areas of intelligence in the brain aided by the mind. These biologic mysteries are open for exploration in the future.

Challenging hurdles in the path of success need to be tackled. Success usually starts in microscopic increments like baby steps.

Neither run away and nor magnify the problem. At times it is advisable to distance oneself from the problem for a while. Changing one's perspective and assessing the problem with an open mind from another angle can be productive. 'Like a golfer you may hit perfectly with precision using an iron with a different angle.'[124]

Once in a while there is emergence of a single individual who undeniably changes the course of history. These great men can change the tide of human events. In the modern times entrepreneurs like Steve Jobs, Bill Gate and Warren Buffet, thinkers like Stephen Hawking and Albert Einstein or researchers like Marie Curie and Nobel laureates who discovered Human Genome are to be revered and emulated.

Opportunity is waiting at your doors. Both external and internal resources need to be tapped to attain success. One should passionately pursue ones' goals with zeal, the confidence, the patience and the perseverance. Don't ignore or postpone it, instead passionately pursue it. 'There are a thousand failures for every success.'[110] The path to success is full of distractions, impediments and hurdles. Don't be afraid of past failures, as those are your illuminating guides.

You can strive to achieve your pursuits, don't get dismayed but march ahead and turn your failures into inspiring fuel for achieving your goals. Your success depends on you. It has everything to do with your heart and mind, passion, character, ability, determination and dedication to your goal to make a difference in everyone's life.

'I sometimes think in life you have got to dream big by setting yourself seemingly impossible challenges...catch up with them. You can make what people believe is impossible possible if you set a big enough target. If you don't dream nothing happens. And we like to dream big.'

~ RICHARD BRANSON

CHAPTER 14

Let Your Failures Define Your Goals

'Take risks in your life, if you win you can lead. If you lose, you can guide.'

~ SWAMI VIVEKANANDA

YOUR GOALS DEFINE you. Goal originates in your mind and intellect to achieve something that is presently beyond your hold. It can be something ordinary or may be something even beyond your imagination. Imagination is the seed of innovations and it is the fuel that ignites our aspirations. Discoveries result from the combined result of aspirations and imaginations.

One can waste one's time, energy and other resources aimlessly unless one has at least some plans or some set of goals in life. Planning goals in life is essential rather than trying to accomplish something haphazardly. The results of your efforts are not always rewarding and can vary from partial success to utter failure. Complete success at first attempt is 'as rare as overnight success.'[110] Failures teach us to be persistent and humble at the same time. Goals are transforming milestones. No goal is too small to seek or too big to pursue. 'Planning is bringing the future into the present so you can do something about it now.' (Alan Lakein). Once you define a goal, go for it with all your passion. 'Think big, start small, move fast.' (Mayo Clinic, Post-It note).

Goals can be many types:[110]

1. *Basic and personal goals*: Everyone has some personal strategy in life. You chose the field of education with a goal of gaining some rewarding

53

profession or start a business venture. Owning a house, raising a family, educating your children, enjoying with the family, saving money for old age, these and many others are all basic personal aspirations in life and need careful planning as well as timely implementation. Preparation for these basic needs is essential to avoid failure and disappointments in life.

2. *High stake goals*: are chosen by high achievers and visionaries. All major discoveries and inventions took place as those pioneers always looked beyond the present. Not satisfied with current knowledge and inventions, they aimed high beyond the horizon. World would have been incomplete without foresight and persistent efforts of great men like Thomas Edison, Graham Bell, Henry Ford, Wright Brothers, Marie Curie, Bill Gates, Paul Allen and many others.

3. *Altruistic goals* can make you a noble human being. These unselfish acts bring immense satisfaction and peace and happiness in ones' life. All compassionate deeds, big or small, are commendable. These can be as simple as sharing food with poor and needy or giving them time and monetary help, or they can be as monumentus acts like pledge to wipe out polio or malaria in the world or helping AIDS stricken patients or being part of 'Doctors without borders.'

4. *Angelic goals* are followed by selfless teachers, humble divinely servants of humanity and torchbearers of the world. These great people of the rarest breed are born rarely in a generation. Mother Teresa, Mahatma Gandhi, Dalai Lama, Nelson Mandela and Pope Francis are shining examples.

Alternately easy living is within sleepy confines of your day-to-day living. You face challenges and failures when you transgress your boundaries and follow your guts.

Passionate pursuit of noble goals brings at least the satisfaction of mind, if not fame and glory. There is no goal worth pursuing if it is without inherent threat of problems and failures. 'If you look for a problem everything can become a problem.'[110] Instead it is good to seek solutions with an open mind.

The metamorphosis of mind occurs in quantum leaps. Goal is set for the future. It is like planting a tree today and to reap its' fruits in the future; to seek shelter under its shade decades later. Iran had been major exporter of pistachio nuts and other dry fruits in the past. After Iranian uprising and crisis with United States over American hostages in US embassy in Tehran in 1979, Iran was isolated with economic sanctions. Seeing this opportunity, farmers of California planted pistachio trees. Commercial production of pistachio nuts began in the late-1980s. The trees start bearing fruit in 5 to 8 years; full bearing of nuts takes 15-20 years. Meanwhile California has become the major exporter of these nuts. "China going nuts for California pistachios' was posted in a recent blog. We are grateful for the courage and conviction and the foresight of these farmers in achieving their goal.

DNA and human genomes research are one of the major discoveries of last few decades. This is playing a major role in forensic medicine; many innocent death row inmates have been released through 'The Innocence Project'. Our understanding of genetics is increasing every day, gene therapy for treatment of cancer, and many incurable diseases is already being implemented. Further research is going to improve the quality of life and alley the sufferings of many.

Don't lose hope in face of failures. Dream big and dream success to have a positive demeanor. Winning boosts secretion of testosterone and suppresses the release of stress hormone cortisol.

When you think you have lost everything and you think that you are an utter failure in life and you are at a point of no return, at these darkest moments only hope left is to move forward, follow your instincts and find confidence and courage in your beliefs. These moments define your character and integrity. Your karma is to work passionately, without asking for a reward, don't worry about success or failure as you have only a limited control over it. Sometimes there is unexplained downward spiral in your luck, when you think positive outcome is certain and within your grasp, the opposite happens for no obvious reason.

If your achievements are easily accomplished maybe you are too soft on your goals. 'The starting point of all achievement is desire. Weak desires bring weak results,' said Napoleon Hill. Goals beyond reach are worth pursuing.

Maybe a hard laborious road full of disappointments and hurdles is worth pursuing, as it will bring intense sense of achievement at the end. You will be happy if you achieve even a fraction of the unachievable.

It is pragmatic to make peace with bitterness of negative experiences in life with a calm, collective and tranquil mind and come to terms with reality. No life is without mistakes, failures and mishaps. At this juncture it is essential to forget the past, instead redefine yourself and march ahead with a new zeal and hope. "It is during our darkest moments that we must focus to see the light." Said Aristotle Onassis.

One has to passionately pursue one's goals without bragging about one's accomplishments. Persons with low self-esteem sometimes brag in order to feel good and get approval of others. It is always advantageous to carefully listen to critique and suggestions of others.

Simple goals may not seem that simple in the beginning. Plan the goals with a positive attitude and enthusiasm following your mind; it's aptitude and the resources. Vehemently pursue the goals with relentless determination of mind.

Don't get discouraged and disheartened by your failures, as these are the stepping-stones. Never make excuses for your failures. As is wisely said by Sir Alec Guinness, 'Failure has thousand explanations. Success doesn't need one.' The failures should not deter you or curb your enthusiasm. These are the defining moments guiding your destiny. Renew your commitment each morning with a renewed zeal. Begin each day with affirmation of your desire and willingness to stay on course to attain your goal. Simply assert in your mind and even say, "I can do it. I know I can do it." Write your goal and a personal positive massage to yourself on a paper; paste it all around you, on the wall, or on the mirror. It will constantly reinforce positivity in your mind. A positive mind can achieve miracles. It brings ultimate satisfaction and happiness.

'The real loser is never the person who crosses the finishing line last. The real loser is the person who sits on the side. The person who does not even try to compete.'

~ Sheila Pistorius

CHAPTER 15

Giving – a path to Happiness

'Be charitable. Give-in faith or without faith. For fame or through shame. Give-Whether through fear of public opinion or simply for keeping your word. Always give.'

~ *TAITTRIYA UPANISHAD*

SUCCESS IN THE journey of human life is not reflected in accumulation of wealth, enjoyment of materialistic possessions and comforts and fulfillment of our desires but is exhibited in pursuing altruistic deeds of compassion. One of cherished goals for many of us is to have a prosperous family living leisurely in a comfortable lifestyle in nice exclusive neighborhood. Our inability to fulfill limitless desires leads to anguish, restlessness and agitation of mind. An ultimate success in life lies in attaining peace and happiness of mind body and soul by liberation from undue desires.

All of us want bigger, better and more material possessions to satisfy our self-centered ego. Poor homeless man dreams of a small hut to live in. On the contrary a rich person is not satisfied even with a million-dollar mansion. Accumulation of wealth and other materialistic pleasures of the world do not necessarily bring contentment of mind but instead usually lead to disappointments due to unfulfillment of ever-increasing desires. One has to learn to control one's greed and cravings and to be considerate, compassionate and charitable.

Mahatma Gandhi often said, "We have enough to satisfy man's needs but not enough to satisfy his greed. It is sinful to multiply one's wants unnecessarily."

Sri Aurbindo said. "All wealth belongs to God and those to hold it are only trustees." French Nobel laureate Romain Rolland bluntly said over a century ago. "...man who has more than necessary for his livelihood is a thief." Albert Einstein put it more mildly, "It is everyman's obligation to put back in the world at least the equivalent of what he takes out of it."

Money beyond basic needs does not necessarily bring more happiness. Some of the craziest despicable men have been very rich. It is said that Nizam of Hyderabad, one of richest man of his times was also a famous miser, who had a pay phone in his mansion for his guests.

Money cannot buy happiness or health despite ability to afford topnotch health care. "Idolatry of money," warned Pope Francis, "would lead to a new tyranny."

Every individual has to give something back to the society. Spending lots of money on yourself, your family or on your possessions is a display of material wealth. In fact, it is the richness of heart that counts. Rich are those persons who gladly part with their possessions to help the needy. Rich is that person who splits his only loaf of bread with a hungry man. Only on true introspection we realize that most of us are blessed with plentiful. Many of us shrink from our responsibility of sharing our possessions with the less fortunate.

Everyone needs to give one's fair share back to the society. According to Vedic philosophy: 'The rich who does not utilize his wealth for noble deeds or offer to the needy and the poor fellow-beings, but only looks after his own needs, is selfish and has earned the wages of sin.' One of the wealthiest billionaires Warren Buffet quotes, "You're the luckiest 1% of humanity; you owe it to the rest of humanity to think about the other 99%." "Is the rich world aware of how four billion of the six billion live? If we were aware, we would want to help out; we'd want to get involved." Says Bill Gates.

Give and help with humility. Let there be circulation of material possessions. Give with love and passion, be compassionate and empathize with the needy. Be generous in giving with your heart and mind. Most human beings are generous in nature. Generosity is not hallmarks of the rich as rich people are a minority in the world. 'The value of a man resides in what he gives and not what he is capable of receiving,' said Albert Einstein.

The acts of kindness and giving lights up the reward circuitry of the brain granting happiness to the giver. Steven Cole, Professor of Medicine at UCLA, found that 'Individuals whose happiness comes primarily from *doing good to others* show much better gene profile than hedonistic individuals who are always busy in self- centered feel good pursuit. Altruistic people have less inflammation and better antibody and antiviral activity.'[117] Altruistic acts bring out the best within us, taking us to an extraordinary height of eloquence and human dignity.

'Life is a gift, and it offers us the privilege, opportunity, and responsibility to give something back.' (Anthony Robbins). 'To give away money is not an easy matter and is in man's power. But to decide whom to give and how large and when, and for what purpose and how, is neither in every man's power nor an easy matter.' (Aristotle). 'The highest use of capital is not to make more money but to make money to do more for the betterment of life.' (Henry Ford). Be compassionate and help the needy. 'If you can't feed a hundred people, then just feed one.' Said Mother Teresa. 'Better off you are, the more responsibility you have for helping others. I believe it is my duty to make money and still more money and to use the money I make for good of my fellow man according to the dictates of my conscience.' Said John D Rockefeller. 'If service is the rent you pay for your existence on this earth, are you behind in your rent? I resolved to stop accumulating and begin the infinitely more serious and difficult task of wise distribution.' Said Andrew Carnegie. Benevolence by acts of sharing increases happiness without depleting the giver's possessions. American poet Anne Sexton apparently influenced by the spirit of 'Isha Upanishad' eloquently wrote:

'Then the well spoke to me.
It said: Abundance is scooped from abundance
Yet abundance remains.'

Ancient philosophy of giving is well documented in Chandogya Upanishad: '...have neither prides nor vanity for charities ...Give but not with pride. Give generously but not with egotism. Give freely but not with an eye for fame. Give but not as something that is yours, but as something given to you by the spirit for giving to others.'

'Blessed are those who give without remembering and take without forgetting.'[110]

All religions believe in charity, in helping others and in treating everyone with respect. Charity is not just recommended by Islam, 'Zakat' is mandatory for every financially stable Muslim. It is one of the Five Pillars of Islamic practice. 'Zakat' means 'purification'.

In the end, It does not have to be money that we give. One of the most charitable gifts is the gift of education that can be in any sphere of knowledge. There is inexhaustible treasure of knowledge: more you give the more it grows.

'You give but little when you give of your possessions
It is when you give of yourself that you truly give
There are those little of much which they have-and they give it
for recognition
And their hidden desire make their gift unwholesome
And there are those who have little and give it all
They are the believers in life and the bounty of life
And their coffer is never empty
There are those who give with joy and joy is their reward,
And there are those who give and know not pain in giving,
Nor do they seek joy, nor give with mindfulness of virtue
Through the hands of such as these God speaks,
And from behind their eyes, He smiles upon the earth'

~ KAHLIL GIBRAN[37]

CHAPTER 16

Poverty and Hunger – an
Ever-growing World Dilemma

'Poverty is worst form of violence'

~ Mahatma Gandhi

Poverty and hunger rob humans of their happiness and dignity. Imagine a world devoid of all these afflictions and that will be an unimaginable state of heaven on earth. But such an outcome exists only in our dreams or in fairy tales. There are different concepts of poverty, which is a state of a person with insufficient monetary and material possessions to maintain basic needs for living for himself and his family. *Destitute* is absolute poverty with complete deprivation of basic necessities of life including food, water and sanitation. *Relative poverty* is the economic inequality that exists in every society. A person in relative poverty in a rich country may be well to do in relation to the norms of a poor country. Fundamental dilemma is how can anyone remain happy while surrounded by rampant poverty and hunger.

There will always be people in poverty so long as there is life on this planet earth, with many people living miserably with desperate needs. About 80% of humans live with less than $10 a day. Many people do not even make $10 a month. Over 75% of the wealth in the world is with the 5% of the people. I am appalled to read a recent report in 2016 by Oxfam that 62 mega rich persons have as much money as half (3.5 billion) of the world's population. 'The wealth of 8 richest people in the world equals that of poorest 3.6 billion' (Oxfam 2017).

Poverty in children produces a whole host of different problems. According to UNICEF about 28% of children in the world are stunted or are

61

underweight. About 22,000 children die every day due to poverty. Extreme poverty is abundant in Southeast Asia and Sub-Saharan Africa. Many countries like Rwanda are constantly in clutches of poverty and famine. There are pockets of poverty even in wealthy countries. Social programs with public assistance for food, education, health and other necessities are provided in many Western countries. However, the situation is awful in many developing countries. Poor people are often illiterate and are unemployed or end up in low-wage entry-level jobs. Their diet is usually cheap with high carb and lacks sufficient proteins and milk. It affects their growth and development and they remain undernourished, weak and stunted. They have low life expectancy and die early, many in their childhood. Surviving adults are weak uneducated and unemployable. Poor families cannot get out of this spiral and so successive generations of people end up in a cobweb of poverty.

There are many UNO sponsored programs like UNICEF, food for work and food for education programs.[120] Many programs for food such as soup kitchens for the homeless and other poor people are sponsored by various charitable organizations and foundations and religious groups like churches. These monumental efforts hardly scratch the surface of the problem. Perhaps genetically modified foods in future will bring global sustainability and alleviation of poverty.

Approximately quarter of a billion children age 14 and under work instead of going to school. They often work in hazardous or unhealthy conditions.[120]

Poverty is the biggest curse to mankind. Is the concept 'accidental-birth' true, as someone is born in riches and the others in poverty? Or is it aftermath of Karma? Is it that your fate is determined by past karma, which gives one the reward or punishment to be born with a silver spoon or not even a piece of bread? It is a cruel punishment to be born and then die from disease or starvation during childhood. Those pictures of malnourished children with potbellies, shriveled limbs and flies hovering over deathly eyes without hope are heart rendering. These images put us to shame in this 21st century when so much advancement has been achieved in this global community.

Poverty and inequalities are unfortunately part of every culture. Poverty due to the lack of basic necessities or wealth due to its over-abundance does not define the extent of pain or happiness. Egalitarianism will always be a myth. Persons in extreme poverty are always pursuing for the next piece of bread or a bowl of rice. They are so dejected by lack of response to their prayers that many altogether abandon praying to God. Still millions go to temples, churches, mosques, synagogues and other places of worship and pray for food and pray for absolution of their past sins. Poverty mostly passes from one generation to another. Despite poverty you can see a spark of genuine happiness on their faces when they get a loaf of bread to fill their stomachs. Abundant innocent joy with radiant smile and happiness are evident on their faces when they get something that they never expected. Once basic necessities of life are met these people easily become happy and contented. Even pennies worth of unexpected find can translate into a million dollar smile. Even few moments of happiness are a respite from their sufferings. People are generally overwhelmingly very kind, considerate and charitable irrespective of their financial status.

However, too much wealth does not translate into genuine happiness. Wealth brings more desires with more worries and problems. Some wealthy children lack incentive for progression and achievement and are led astray by addictive pleasures. Poor socioeconomic status in dysfunctional broken families allures some individuals to have easy money by illegal means and invariably ending up being incarcerated. Too much or too little money works as a double-edged sword.

A society where everyone enjoys the comfortable life is undoubtedly a myth. Imagine a world without poverty and hunger and full of hope and happiness where no one would dream of heavens above as they will be living in it.

'Do not waste your time on social questions. What is matter with poor is Poverty; what is matter with rich is Uselessness'

~ GEORGE BERNARD SHAW

CHAPTER 17

Happiness of Community at large

*'Happiness is the meaning and purpose of life, the whole aim
and end of human existence.'*

~ ARISTOTLE

HAPPINESS HAS REMAINED a central point of human endeavor since beginning of times. The philosophy of peace and happiness, both individual and collectively of society has been extensively described in Vedas and Upanishads that can be traced to the beginning of human civilization. Chinese and other beliefs including Buddhism also dealt with this issue. Later Greek philosophers explored the relationship of peace and happiness to the purpose of life.

Aristippus (435-356 BC) who was student of Socrates defined that philosophical goal of life is to seek external pleasure. He is credited as the founder of hedonism. Ethical code of Socrates teaching was advanced by Antisthenes (445-365 BC), who as founder of Cynic Greek philosophy stressed that purpose in life is to live in virtue. He advocated an ascetic life. According to him the life of peace, modesty and virtue dissolves the inner tension leading to inner happiness and enlightenment -inner peace.[49] This philosophy is in conformity with concepts advocated in earlier times in teachings the Vedas, Buddhism and even the Chinese Taoism.

Another student of Socrates, Plato (428-328 BC) stated that human soul has three parts: the reason, the will and the desire. Man is happy when all three parts of soul are in balance. He believed that philosophy of happiness should be central focus of a happy society.

Epicurus (341-270 BC), another Greek philosopher believed that a happy, tranquil life results from peace, freedom from fear, absence of pain and from living a self-sufficient life in company of friends. According to Plato's student Aristotle (384-322), happiness is the ultimate goal of human thoughts and action. Wealth, intelligence and courage are valued in relation to other things while happiness is the unique and incomparable entity.

Enlightenment was a historical cultural movement of 'new age' by intelligentsia in the 17th and 18th centuries for reforming the society by newer progressive ideas. Rather than sticking to old traditions and values this experiment was to advance knowledge with newer concepts of individual rights for the citizens in the face of irrationality, superstition, and autocratic oppressive abuses of power by the church and the state. This adventure of enlightenment started in Europe from England, Germany and France and spread to other parts of Europe and to the American Colonies.

The spirit of Enlightenment also provided a framework for the American and the French Revolutions. The works of philosophers like Bruce Spinoza, Voltaire, Isaac Newton, David Hume and Denis Diderot (who edited great Encyclopedia in 1751-72) had a major impact on the world history. Fredrick the Great of Prussia enforced the laws for equality of men and for religious tolerance. Catherine the Great of Russia tried in vain to bring this age of change to Russia. Many of the political ideals of Enlightenment influenced American forefathers like Thomas Jefferson, John Adams, Benjamin Franklin, James Madison and many others who played a major role in the American Revolution. They incorporated progressive principals in drafting Declaration of Independence of America and the United States Bill of Rights. George Washington emphasized 'immense value of national union for collective and individual happiness.'

Philosophically individual happiness is no good without happiness of the society as a whole. The teachings of Vedas and Upanishads, Buddhism and ancient Greek philosophy believe in virtuous conduct and in living a moral modest life to achieve inner happiness. Public well-being is elementary to happiness of everybody. "The happiness of society is the first law of government." Said James Wilson. The state is created for happiness of society. "Happiness of society is the end of government," said John Adams. Thomas Jefferson was given the task to author the document for Declaration of Independence. There were so many drafts and edits of The Declaration of Independence. 'The pursuit of happiness' clause remained a fixture in each version. Jefferson's pursuit of happiness had nothing vague, private or personal in mind. 'It meant public happiness which is measureable; which is indeed, the test of justification of any government' wrote Garry Wills. Declaration of Independence was passed on June 28th 1776 and adopted a week later on July 4th. All the forefathers firmly believed in general wellbeing in this pursuit of happiness.

Ashoka The Great (304-232 BC), Indian emperor of Maurya Dynasty was a great conqueror that converted to Buddhism after witnessing the horrific killings in Kalinga war. Later he become embodiment of non-violence and ruled the nation with primary purpose of public wellbeing and happiness in mind. He built universities, hospitals, rest areas and wells for his citizens whom he treated as his children. It was the golden age of civilization in India at that time. There have been other equally concerned rulers in the world but none can surpass his eloquence, candor and resolve.

In 1729 Kingdom of Bhutan declared that happiness of people is the central goal of the government. Presently general wellbeing and everyone's welfare is considered obligatory measure of happiness of society.[43] This well-being encompasses many facets of daily life from personal issues to education, public welfare, environment and ecology. 'Happiness indexes' encompassing different aspects of public well-being by various organizations including United Nations are regularly compiled and reported from different parts of world under different names.

The culture of compassion is necessary to transcend selfishness and break down the ideological boundaries of divisive confrontations and dogmatic convictions. Collective happiness represents aggregate of individual happiness. The collective happiness at large is a metaphor of an amazing landscape studded with flowers of different species in a rainbow of colors enriching the universe.

'No one should remain content with his or her own well-being but on the contrary should regard his or her well-being in consonance with well-being of others' said Swami Dayanand Saraswati in the ten principals of Arya Samaj.[24]

The Vedas and Upanishads have repeatedly stressed about individual and collective happiness at large.

Ethical behavior and moralistic attitude dwelling in a positive mind full of compassion and humility are essential ingredients of happiness of any society at large. Ridicule and anger kindle a sense of hatred and revenge, whereas, spirit of forgiveness and inclusiveness exuberates with love and happiness.

The healthy human body depends on harmonious and proper functioning of all the body organs. 'Just as organs are to the body so are the members to the family, to a community or to a society or to the nation.'[113] True universal peace and happiness can only be attained by a resolute determination of each and every member in a united effort. All personal, religious and political biases need be sacrificed to attain universal objectiveness of a broader vision. Everyone is looking to the future when this universe will transcend as one large happy family.

'No one can be perfectly free till all are free;
No one can be perfectly moral till all are moral;
No one can be perfectly happy till all are happy.'

~ HERBERT SPENCER

CHAPTER 18

The Quantification of Overall Happiness

'I am very happy
Because I have conquered myself
And not the world.
I am very happy
Because I have loved the world
And not myself.'

~ SRI CHINMOY

HAPPINESS IS AN emotional state (positive mood and emotion) that can be identified with pleasure and satisfaction. Happiness is opposite to pain, sorrow, sadness and sufferings. Material prosperity has surprisingly modest impact on happiness. In the aftermath of World War 2 Japanese economy went through one of the greatest boom in the world. Though economic output per person grew 7-fold from 1950 to 1970, making war-torn Japan one of the richest countries on earth, yet their lives were not happier in life's satisfaction survey.[69]

According to theory of Easterlin Paradox[32] put forth in 1974 'once basic necessities are met economic growth has virtually no impact on happiness.' People in poor countries did become happier when they could afford basic necessities of life, and after this achievement wealth had little or no impact. Despite massive increase in wealth and income in The United States in the last 60 years, the measured happiness has not increased. According to Gallup poll our happiness index has remained unchanged since 1972 (53% to 57% very happy) despite rise in per capita income. In other polls in United States median income for happiness is around $75,000 to 100,000. A higher income does not necessarily bring more happiness. It has been reported that a 10% increase in income results in temporary non-lasting boost in happiness

Anyone who says wealth brings happiness is living in an illusion. A poor man is happy to earn a decent meal for his family while a millionaire is not contented with his lot and dreams to be on the billionaires' list. Many wealthiest men crave for still more wealth and some of them indulge in questionable and even illegal means to acquire it.

Our perception of happiness is based on cultural, religious, geographical, environmental, political and economic conditions. According to a Global Happiness Index (GHI) released by North Korea[12] their country and its allies are most happy and cheerful countries in the world: happiness index is 100% for China, 97% for North Korea and mere 3% (lowest of any country) for United States. This is simply a useless political statement of no value.

According to Stanford encyclopedia of philosophy, there are two types of happiness: 1), Happiness is a state of mind, and 2), A life that goes well (for the person leading it).

Gross National Happiness (GNH) and other current parameters in the world try to quantify overall happiness in state of mind and overall well-being in all spheres of life including economic, health, education and environment.

In 1729, Hindu kingdom of Bhutan declared a legal code that "if the government cannot create happiness (dekid) for its people, there is no purpose for the government to exist." That was corresponding to the era Enlightenment in Europe. The progressive ideology spread to other parts of the world even influencing the American Revolution. Thomas Jefferson's concept of 'pursuit of happiness' in Declaration of Independence entailed both personal and public happiness and their well–being. John Adam statement 'the happiness of society is the end of the government' was taken in the same context.

In 1972, 4th king of Bhutan, Jigme Singye Wangchuck declared that GNH is more important than Gross National Product (GNP).[43,47] This Happiness Index (GNHI) became a part of constitution of Bhutan in 2008 (article 9). It was enacted to promote conditions that will enable pursuit of happiness.

GNHI is a multidimensional measure for subjective well-being to assess collective as well as personal happiness.

There is wide diversity in mind, thought and perception as different people can be happy and contented or sad and anguished in the same set of circumstances. Policies and programs are geared towards happiness, primarily by improving the conditions of not-yet-happy people.

Bhutan's GNH[43] is a single number index developed from 33 indicators categorized in nine domains: Psychological well-being (overall happiness, emotional, spiritual), Health issues (Overall health, food, health care), Time use (fun, work, exercise, time of poverty), Education, Cultural diversity and resilience, Good governess, Community, Vitality, Ecology and Living standard. Bhutan's first baseline index in 2010 was 0.743 on a scale 1.

Recently Dasho Karma Ura, as president of Bhutan studies and GNH describes four pillars happiness: Good Governess, Sustainable Socio-economic development, preservation and promotion of culture, and environmental conservation. Perhaps fifth pillar is six-hours of deep sleep at night and an hour-long walk in the afternoon. Their happiness index was 91.2 in 2015. Bhutan is relatively a poor country but people are happy and contented due to its social structure and overall sense of well-being. As a result, Bhutan became known as 'the land of the thunder and dragons - the happiest place on earth.'

In 2011, United Nations general assembly passed a resolution to measure happiness in its member nations. Prime Minister of Bhutan chaired their first meeting for this purpose. World Happiness Report[120] (WHR) is derived from 1) 'Cantril Ladder' of variables of happiness in different nations and regions, 2) 'Life-satisfaction' emotions felt a day earlier, assessing prevalence of both 'Positive emotions' (smile and laughter, enjoyment and happiness) and 'Negative emotions' (worry, sadness and anger), and 3) Happiness with life as a whole. Detailed assessment includes Linear Income, Gross National Product (GDP), Life expectancy at birth, Perception of corruption, Donation, Freedom to make choices, Social report and Positive and negative effects. World Health Report 2016 lists Denmark, Switzerland, Iceland, Norway and Finland at the top of the list, Canada 6th, United States 13th, Mexico 21st, United Kingdom 23nd, Russia 56th, China 83rd, Pakistan 92nd, India 118th and Burundi 157th -the least happy.

American economist Richard Easterlin[32] established a long held belief that 'beyond a certain threshold, rising income does not bring more happiness.' All of us have seen that the money temporarily boosts happiness as our buying power increases. But when desires outpace affordability unhappy feelings return. So even rising income can easily result in falling sense of well-being. Happiness never rises as quickly and to the same degree as the income. It is absurd to think that doubling ones' salary can make one twice as happy. There is no linear relationship between income and happiness. Once one's basic necessities are met the positive impact of money on overall happiness is not that steep. The Easterlin paradox is evident in Bhutan, Japan and China.

Overall well-being with different yard-sticks for happiness are being researched, compiled and assessed under different names and categories as: Your Better Life Index, Happy Planet Index (HPI), Canadian Index of Well-being, and different assessment tools of well-being in Great Britain. Recent Gallup poll conducted in 2014 as to how often persons experienced 'positive emotions' like laughter and feeling well-rested, Paraguay topped the list with Denmark 6th, United States 19th and Russia 103rd.

Pursuit of happiness and general well-being is inalienable right of every human being. On a broader vision overall happiness is a part of an individual as well as collective happiness. Your happiness to a large extent depends on happiness of all around you.

This quantification of happiness gives everyone a boost for self-esteem and gives the courage and opportunity to find ways to amplify happiness all over the globe.

> *'Happiness is when you think, what you think and what you say is in harmony.'*
>
> ~ MAHATMA GANDHI

Part Three

The Physical Life

CHAPTER 19

Children bring Happiness- Reality or a Myth?

'One child, one teacher, one book, one pen can change the world.'

~ MALALA YOUSAFZAI

ONE OF THE fundamental polarizing questions raised in last few decades in the Western literature is whether 'Children bring happiness or misery?' Is it a myth that childre bring happiness? Till recently I would have never thought about this controversial subject even in my imagination. Being born and raised in Indian culture I have always thought that the bond of everlasting love between mother and the child is forever entrenched in bountiful of joy and happiness. To think otherwise would have been outrageously absurd. Enough research has been published recently to start the controversy but has not completely tilted the pendulum in the other direction.

One of most intense unparalleled relationship is between a child and his parents. A mother's love for her child is so unique. Words cannot describe its intensity. She nurtures the child in her womb; breast feeds him and keeps him safe close to her bosom. She enjoys his every milestone from baby talk to baby steps. These are the joyous memories forever. She teaches him the first lessons of life in his formative years. She lays the foundations of child's morality, character and integrity, and kindles his spirit and also builds his aspirations and ambitions. She always wishes the best for her child. This bond of everlasting love is eternal and incomparable. On the contrary, the love between husband and wife may erode with time due to myriad of reasons as infidelity and divorces are of everyday occurrence in these modern times. Regardless, any subject about children and grandchildren brings forth radiant happiness in everyone's face.

The child grows into adulthood, becomes a man or a woman, learns the ropes of life and its' intricacies to become a productive part of the society, marries, has children and repeats the 'cycle of life'. He becomes a grown man for the world but still remains a small child in the eyes of his parents. Parents always see their child the same way as they had seen him the day he was born. After all, 'child is the legacy of mortal man.'[110]

A baby is innocent like a flower that blossoms to bring joy and happiness to everyone's eyes during his growing years. A mother gives unconditional love, she wants nothing in return, and she will always love him or her even if her child resents her. Her child's arms around her neck are the most precious gift. No scale can measure or quantify the intensity of love joy and happiness that motherhood brings. Parents are very happy at the birth of their first child.

However, according to modern research happiness gradually decreases at birth of second and third child. On broader scale the world being one large family we as adults should try to inculcate universal love for any and every child, protect their innocence and teach them the right path. We should teach them by our example. They follow what they see and witness.

Parenting is not easy. Raising a child from infancy to adolescence and through teenage years can easily take a toll on anyone. Nurturing and educating their mind and intellect in right direction and building and molding their character and integrity is a slow tedious process. Children with low-empathy develop aggressive behavior, flawed understandings and conflicts in relationships. Peer pressure, easy availability of drugs and other addictive activities or substances and lack of opportunities can all lead to flaws in the growth of a child. In the absence of tender loving care by parents and teachers many end up as problem children at odds with the parents, school authorities and the law. This brings lots of lingering unhappy moments. Some children in extreme cases cross the line of decency and are abusive to parents both verbally and physically.

There is a widespread belief in the world across all cultures that 'children bring happiness'. Is this myth similar to that 'wealth brings happiness'? In a sense parents are both rewarded with happiness and unhappiness in this very life. You are lucky if your children end up being successful and you forget and forgive all the difficulties you encountered during their growing years.

New generation brings new challenges. About 1/3rd of baby boomer's adult children continue to live at home bringing whole set of newer problems to their elderly parents. Under these circumstances relative unhappiness of parents extends far beyond the years that children are financially and physically dependent on them.

The 'me me generation of Millennial kids' are described as high-headed, overconfident, lazy, self-centered, entitled and narcissistic, believing in individualism over community. (Time Magazine, 2013) These twentysomething are unapologetic. However, on a positive note they are independent and motivated and are even responsible for many start-ups in the Silicon Valley. About 30% of young adult millennial kids are not affiliated with any religious belief.

Childcare is progressively becoming more challenging and less satisfying? This challenge is more when you are a single parent especially who is financially insecure, drug addict or socially compromised. Worries about children's education and future prospects can easily make any one insomniac especially if he or she has a problem child.

Recent published reports from United States and Europe in last decade or so have concluded that 'parents have lower level of happiness, life-satisfaction, marital satisfaction and mental well-being compared to non-parents'. This was according to Sonja Lyubomirsky article 'Do children bring happiness- or misery?' in Times Magazine (August 1, 2013). In other studies, parents with kids reported more meaning and satisfaction in their lives compared to their childless counterparts. Working fathers and financially stable mothers are always happier.

Some young parents (ages 17-25 years) and parents who have young children are relatively unhappy. But relatively older married financially stable parents are happier with higher life-satisfaction.

New research by Sarah Damaske from Penn State University in 2014 revealed a lower level of stress hormone cortisol when at work compared to when at home. This finding was consistent irrespective of type of work, being single or married and whether you like the job or not. The difference was more in individuals with children. The cortisol level was same (at home and at work) for those earning more than $75,000 annually. Women were found to be happier at work than men. Decreased stress at work may be related to many factors: like getting paid and appreciated at work, becoming more proficient and because you may start to excel at work with time. There are better work etiquettes and fewer distractions than at home.

Children bring a purpose in life and make it more complete and meaningful. Mothers of young children may be more stressed and sleep-deprived but they are mostly happier.

Our happiness in our old age depends a lot on our children. Our present day children will be adults of tomorrow. If they become responsible adults, positive minded and happy, they are more likely to bring peace and harmony in our old age.

'Children are one of the greatest lessons in happiness, constantly challenging us to enjoy the moment, as next one will not be the same.'

– UNKNOWN

CHAPTER 20

Transition to a Happy Householder

'The householder is the center of life and society'

~ VIVEKANANDA

TRANSITION TO THE next phase in life is most challenging when after finishing the education a person is trying to be gainfully employed and to set and pursue his or her goals and dreams. A happy householder means a happy world all around. It is a major transformation full of rajsic activities to face all and any encounter in any arena of life. In the beginning it is metaphorical to being pushed in the ocean of life without the lifejacket and without full knowhow as to how to face all the ups and downs of life. A person has to steer his boat to shores of safety amidst a myriad of tides from all directions with all ensuing demands. Carefree yesteryears of childhood never come back. Younger age leaves an unforgettable memory and those moments are cherished forever. Old age is too far away and it is too early to worry about. Responsibilities of a householder are the most tedious of all when you are pulled from all directions and the when the hours are few with so many tasks to accomplish.

In Hinduism according to Manusmriti (Laws of Manu)[24,71,113] there are four stages in life: 'Brahamacharya' (celibacy, self-restrain and education), followed by 'Grihastha' (householder) from 25 to 50 years of age and in older age 'Vanaprastha' and 'Sannyasa'.

Proper education is essential to acquire the skills of the trade and to start earning and get settled into this new phase of life. There are unavoidable pressures at the job or at your business with deadlines to finish, jobs to accomplish and hierarchy to please and satisfy. You may need accommodation near place of work and to have suitable transportation. After you marry and get settled there is a lifelong unending list of 'duties and responsibilities' (dharma): for your life partner, to get a house and to furnish it with all affordable comforts and to have children and to rear them with utmost parenting. Every day you learn from challenges and try to lead the life of a responsible husband, a wife, a son or a father and at the same time be a good neighbor and a community member.

The life of a householder is very busy and complicated when as a 'karam yogi' you are actively engaged in all sort of activities at the prime of your life. You are exuberant with energy to pursue your goals and dreams with a passion. It is during this phase of life that many of the so-called 'doshas' (disturbances of mind) make a platform to engage in life with full veracity. These disturbances like desires (kama), anger (krodha), greed (lobha), attachment (moha), and most of all pride (ahamkara) have limited but proper place in this period of life. Eventually these need to be avoided and renounced as we mature for spiritual and moral growth.

As a householder you nourish your 'rajsic' self-centered temperament with unending zeal to have what you want to have in life. You have to satisfy your big fat ego and pride. You have immense love and attachment with your children. You get angry if you can't achieve something dear to you or when your pride gets hurt. Most of the personal achievements are motivated by ego when you want to own the world. You vigorously pursue to earn and to have name, fame and all materialistic possessions including wealth. At the same time, you try to fit in the society as a proud influential man who is caring and considerate. You want to be the happiest family. You may not be able to get everything. You may be poor and struggling to get even the basic necessities for you and your family but you can always have hopes and dreams of happy days ahead.

The world stage is open to you to diligently play your part and fulfill your natural legit desires. Accumulation of wealth by fair means and to your heart's content is a normal desire. It is a part of life so long as you are considerate and are a part by society and contribute your due share to it. It is your duty to acquire wealth and to have decent living for your family and contribute to the society at the same time. Most of the charitable and religious places will close if people who can afford stop parting their money. A person who struggles to become rich by fair means and for a good purpose and is not self-centered is no less than a 'sunnyasi' who has renounced the world.[115]

Enjoy life as husband and wife without any undue restrictions. Fulfill all your worldly desires, legitimate pleasures and your dreams and aspirations. It is essential to control your mind and enjoy your life without any trace of hatred and ill wills. Enjoyment of sensual bodily and mental pleasures is essential for a happy married life. The desire for sex is natural and normal. 'This 'Kama' (sex drive) is the motive force of the wheel of creation in this world and it inspires the desire for offspring.'[113] 'Kama' is best enjoyed within confines of your marriage or between two consenting adults. But one should lead a disciplined life of self-restraints, contentment and moderation as over-indulgence leads to untoward ramifications.

The key to the happiness of everybody from family life to the happiness at large of the entire community and in essence welfare of the whole world is in the hands of the householder who is actively pursuing 'karmayoga' to keep the wheels of life moving. It is like gluing the little droplets of happiness to the vast ocean, a quantum leap from microcosm to macrocosm.

'An ideal householder is a much more difficult task than to be an ideal sunnyasi; the true life of work is not as hard as, if not harder than, the equally true life of renunciation.'

~ VIVEKANANDA

CHAPTER 21

The Golden Years of Happiness?

"'The truth is I'm getting old", I said.
"We are already old," she said with a sigh,
"What happens is that you don't feel it on the inside, but from
the outside everybody can see it."'

~ GABRIEL GARCIA MARQUEZ

HAPPINESS IS A state of mind. Physical body decays and gradually becomes weak with the advancing age but the human mind remains vibrant as ever unless you are afflicted with neurologic decay of the brain. Life is a long tedious journey from first to the last breath. Warmth, kindness and concern for others always bring peace and happiness. Modern era has conquered many challenges, including focus on health issues prolonging life expectancy. In the Vedic era, many of our Rishis lived past 100-years of age. Stress of everyday life, modernization with comfortable life styles and lack of physical endurance to procure necessities of life, brought down our life expectancy. Life expectancy was 46-years of age in 1900 and 76-years of age a century later in the United States. Even today life expectancy is only 38-years of age in Angola.

Human beings are prolific breeders with exponential growth. The world population is predicted to grow from 6 to 9 billion by 2050. It will be a challenge to keep pace with feeding so many people in the face of dwindling world resources.

A centenarian is a person who lives to or beyond the age of 100 years. Presently United States has highest number of known centenarians (53,364) of any nation according to 2010 census with females making up to 82.8%. According to the United Nations there were 316.600 centenarians (51,376 in Japan) worldwide in 2012. Centenarian's population in the United States has already increased to 72,197 in 2014. Senior citizens make it as the fastest growing population in the world and it poses very serious issues.

Besides the chronic health problems elderly have many issues for their day-to-day needs. They suffer from depression from loneliness and other causes. Elderly neglect and abuse is not going to be solved merely by social welfare agencies, assisted living and nursing homes but by a radical change in our concepts in dealing with the problems of older generation. These challenges are beyond comprehension financially for the rich as well as countries with limited resources.

Gone are the days of the past Hindu philosophy when Vedas advised over 50-years of age-group people to take 'vanprastha' (a retired person living a simple spiritual life like a hermit) and beyond 75-years to take 'sanyasa' (renunciation) by renouncing the world and living a tranquil life of happiness and contentment.[24,113] Modernization and recent scientific advances have confronted us with ever-growing new challenges.

Like birth, decay (old age), disease and death are realistic milestones of our journey in life.

Old age has been designated as the golden-years of life, as we have accomplished most of worldly goals as a householder. We have fewer responsibilities and are free from day-to-day worries. 'The Golden Years of Adulthood' also called, 'The Third Age' is a span of good peaceful time that extends from onset of retirement to the onset of age-imposed limitations viz. physical, emotional or cognitive. It falls between 65 to 80+ years of age. It varies depending on mental, physical, spiritual and financial health.[11] 'Third age' gives an opportunity for travel, golf, and exercise. It also gives opportunity for reading, for entertainment and for further education and spiritual insight.

Aging brings physical and mental decline. Youthful attractive looks full of affirmations are replaced with wrinkled, edentulous, spectacled and often an unattractive face. All the modern plastic surgery techniques can't hide the realities of age. A veneer of sparkling white teeth tells the whole story of decay underneath. Physical disabilities are rampantly evident by unsteady waddling gait and walkers and wheel chairs. One often is found panting for breath, unable to effectively walk or talk. Neurologic disorders like stroke, dementia, and Alzheimer's disease can blemish ones physical and cognitive abilities.

Brain deterioration is not irreversible as previously thought. Brain is an organ that reacts like a muscle that atrophies with disuse and improves with use. Inactivity from lack of social interactions and non-involvement in day-to-day activities results in loneliness and depression leading to brain disuse and atrophy. On the other-hand robust involvement in social activities and a keen interest in life keeps the mind occupied and enhances cognitive functions. Recently research is being done on 'superagers': people older than 85-years of age who have memory like that of 30-years younger. Only 10% of over 85 years old are superagers. According to Emily Rogalski[44] superagers have more active neurons (nerve cells) with thicker cortex (grey matter) on brain scan. This is helpful in thinking, attention and memory. Brains atrophy results in cognitive impairment that leads to the vicious cycle of more brain disuse and atrophy as seen in dementia.

An elderly person with all these ailments and weaknesses of old age has traveled the long and tedious road of life and has confronted all the challenges of life with a firm resolve. Eyes that are weak today were witness to all the ups and downs of life including many spring and fall seasons. The ears that are now hearing impaired have heard the sound of music, giggling and laughter of their children and roars of acclamations on personal achievements as well as endured the silence of personal failures. The brain that has now become diseased, atrophied and dysfunctional in many was once robust and vibrant with ideas and discoveries and had been the experiencer of life well respected has now been jolted by the events of life. The skin that is now wrinkled, leathery and full of ugly hyperkeratosis spots had sensed all the pleasures of life, had caressed the beloved, and had felt like soothing balm for children in pain. Limbs that are weak, deformed, rickety and unsteady now have been pillars of strength in the past and have walked and worked to sustain the life's burdens. All these tools of perception, which have been working tirelessly since birth, and are now weak, tired and diseased, and are near the end of a long journey in sojourn of life, need to be appreciated. Don't consider them as a burden to society in terms of dollars and cents. In many cultures old wise men are considered as treasures and are well respected and cared for.

According to Dilip Jeste, Professor of Psychiatry and Neuroscience at the University of California, San Diego, old age can be a time of growth and a helpful resource for younger generation.[77]

Elderly like to be surrounded by warm and kind people that bring love affection and happiness. This is better than to be surrounded by indifferent and hostile persons in an environment of discord and resentment.[59]

Older people are more organized, consistent and dependable, more polite, trusting and compassionate and maintain relationships, but on the other hand, they are less talkative and assertive, have less neuroticism (worrying, feeling stressed, temperamental) as they learn to regulate negative emotions and tend to avoid unpleasant situations.[8]

Somehow society has to adapt to changing times and learn to tap onto the vast store of wisdom and knowledge of the older generation. Old people are like sages. They should be integrated into the family so they feel useful and not a burden. Younger generation should respect them and instead of neglect and disregard seek guidance from their life long experiences and expertise. This will bring peace and happiness for both the givers and takers.

'We don't stop playing when we grow old: we grow old when we stop playing.'

~ George Bernard Shaw

CHAPTER 22

Impact of Age on Happiness

'Cherish all your happy moments; they make a fine cushion for old age.'

~ BOOTH TARKINGTON

THE PERCEPTION AND pursuit of real happiness in man not only depends on the state of mind and wisdom of his intellect but also on dynamic changes of age and age-related problems with both negative and positive impacts. Seed of character and integrity germinate and takes roots in childhood. It needs proper education and guidance. One usually enjoys childhood and youth, as these are relatively carefree periods of life with plenty of time to enjoy and has minimal responsibilities. It is good so long as basic necessities of life are available and individuals are not suppressed. Gradually worries of life start with more responsibilities at home and at work. Happiness waxes and wanes with challenging tides of circumstances that the life confronts everyday. You gradually mature with age, as you understand the true nature of sufferings and happiness by your experiences, your wisdom, your ideology as well as by material and spiritual knowledge.

There is some relief from responsibilities as you grow older and you have a better grip on life. You try to understand the meaning of life and the purpose of your existence. Some people leave enough time to spend on spirituality and idealism. Many elderly people have onset of newer age-related problems and the golden years turn out to be not so golden or happy. Older people have more physical and cognitive disabilities that impact their satisfaction and happiness in life.

Dilip Jeste, Professor of Psychiatry and Neuroscience at the University of California reported that after 50-years of age, the successful-aging perception went up with each decade of life.[77] Recent research in well-being of the elderly in United Kingdom is heartening. Their conclusions on happiness in different age groups were surprising. Happiness levels were quite high in 20s, and then dropped through 30s; decline continued reaching their lowest point in mid-40s. And then after 50 years of age the happiness starts rising through 60s surpassing even amplitude of young age.[83,106] Another research concluded that fairly healthy 70-years old are on average as happy as 20-years old.[83] Happiness curve relative to age is more or less U-shaped. Elderly people have mostly completed their responsibilities. They have limited family related demands and there are no job-related worries. These individuals have adapted to their strengths and weaknesses and have control over their desires and aspirations.[83] They strive to find joys of life in the present moment, to fondly reminisce the past and appreciate the things they love. They keep moving forward with a positive attitude.

Daniel Gilbert, Professor of Psychology at Harvard, argues in his book 'Stumbling on Happiness'[38] that the' joy of children' bears as much of a misconception of happiness as the 'joy of money'. This is a part of popular 'belief-transmission game'. His interpretation is based on newer research compiled with numerous citations in his book. Parent's perceived images of their offspring not only reflect positive images of their gorgeous children but also stress of rearing them up. Newly wedded couples are very happy in the beginning but gradually they become dissatisfied. They get close to levels of original satisfaction only when their last child leaves home. This 'cycle of satisfaction' is also true for women, the primary caretakers of children. Detailed studies show that women are 'less happy' when taking care of their children compared to other day-to-day activities like watching television, shopping, exercise etcetera. However, caring for children is somewhat more pleasant than housework. 'Empty nest syndrome' after the youngest child leaves the household contrary to popular belief elicits more happiness.[38] These days modern parents are around 45-50 years of age when child leaves home. Surge of increased happiness from 50 years up was also seen in other studies.[83,106]

Degree of happiness in rearing their children has cultural and regional differences in Eastern versus Western philosophies and values. The joy of being with grandchildren in older age is immense but if you have to take care of them you become overtired and exhausted by end of the day and are relieved when they go to sleep. You are happy when they are up and about and happy when they go to sleep. Grandparents have only limited responsibilities in rearing them up. Grandparents and the grandchildren certainly cherish memoirs of 'good time' bonding forever. However, grandparent's role to babysit while parents are working is indeed commendable.

There is increased impact of hormonal changes in women with age, as menopausal symptoms increase their anxiety and depression. This coincides with the time when they are no more needed at home and they feel useless. Additionally, there can be significantly more impact of untoward circumstances in older age. These include problem child, addiction, spousal abuse, divorce, chronic ailments, cancer, dementia, demise of life companion and many other challenges. It can lead to loneliness and depression. Most of the older people are mature enough with good coping mechanisms and have learned to live with patience.

Elderly individuals, 65 to around 80-years of age, in so called 'The Golden Age of Adulthood' or 'Third-Age' have these extra healthy years for reading, recreation and happiness in early retirement years.[11] In addition 10% of elderly over 85-years of age are 'Superagers' with memory of 30-years-younger[44] and continue to have more positive outlook in life. Happiness in any age basically depends on positive attitude in a sound body and mind. It can be discovered in ones' bosom if one cares to look deep inside. 'Happiness depends on ourselves' irrespective of age, one should tap the fountain of joy that will perhaps last forever.

> *'Try to keep your soul young and quivering right up to old age, and to imagine right up to the brink of death that life is only beginning. I think that is the only way to keep adding to one's talent and one's inner happiness.'*

> ~ GEORGE SAND

CHAPTER 23

Mind and Health for Happiness -
Healthy Mind for a Healthy Body

'I will not let anyone walk through my mind with their dirty feet.'

~ MAHATMA GANDHI

HAPPINESS DEPENDS NOT only on mental but also on a sound physical health. There is a deep inter-relationship between mind and the health. An unhealthy mind results in unhealthy body and vice versa. Your whole attitude in life, your mood, feelings and thoughts are part of your psychology. Mental health improves by embracing optimistic positive attitude in life instead of living in negativism. Mind cannot only heal the body but it can also rejuvenate.

Many believed until 1800 that many diseases are caused by emotional imbalance and advised patients to visit spas and seaside resorts. Gradually we understood other causes of illness like infections due to bacteria and toxins. Presently diseases like autism and many mental illnesses are found to have genetic and biological bases in a great percentage of cases. There is increasing acceptance that stress jeopardizes health. There is powerful mind-body health connection through which emotional, mental, social, spiritual and behavioral factors directly influence ones' health.[76]

Despite a clean body, human mind can be polluted with unhealthy desires and addictions or afflicted with mental disorders. Cleanliness of mind is as much desirable and necessary as physical cleanliness of body. The cleanliness of mind comes from purity of thoughts and actions that are good for you and the others. The destructive negative and inconsiderate thoughts belong to an unhealthy impure mind that is rarely happy or at peace.

When confronted with imminent danger there are only two options: either defending yourself with all your might or running away from the danger, known as 'fight or flight' response. In face of imminent danger there is secretion of hormones like epinephrine (adrenaline) from adrenal glands leading to palpitation, sweating, increased heart rate and respiratory rate to pump more oxygen in the body for defense. Adrenal glands also secrete glucocorticoids that increase blood sugar level to augment energy sources. Hormone cortisol is known to suppress cytokines that weakens the immune system helping the spread of cancer and infections.

An unhealthy mind can lead to development and precipitation of many disease processes. A negative mind is the source of negative or destructive thoughts like envy, jealousy, hatred, apathy, competiveness, vengeance and selfishness. These snatch away the peace of mind causing agitation, stress, anxiety, anger, lack of sleep, low self-esteem and depression. It can cause various behavior problems including eating disorders like obesity, anorexia nervosa and bulimia.

Optimism helps: Individuals with optimistic positive attitude have lower risk of heart disease, cancer and mortality than those who are pessimist. Negative self-centered people who are pessimistic about other people and think them to be untrustworthy have higher risk of death than individuals with lower cynicism. Upbeat people with positive attitude have lower level of hormone that raise blood pressure and higher population of disease-fighting white blood cells.

Stressful conditions lead to loneliness, low self-esteem, depression and insomnia (inability to sleep). They can also lead to addiction and anger disorders.

The risk of dying from cardiovascular disease including heart attacks is five to six times greater in patients suffering from depression. Depressed people smoke, they are too lethargic to exercise or to take proper diet and medications. Only a fraction of depressed persons are happy. In addition, there is higher incidence of various digestive disorders, headaches, fertility problems, accelerated aging and premature deaths and suicidal ideation.

Healthy and sound mind improves memory and mental focus, and also perception, mood and behavior.

Stress reduction strategies takes pressure off the mind and are beneficial. Mindfulness and relaxation exercises reduce stress and augment the immune system.[88,99] People who pray regularly live longer. Cancer patients who are optimistic in attitude and take the fight head on also live a little longer than their counterparts. In other people you need hope not fear and to learn to relax and be upbeat and resilient with a positive attitude.

Other techniques to augment healing and reduce stress before surgery are massage, meditation and yoga. In the article written by Dr. Mehmet Oz,[85] 'Say "Om" before surgery', patients before heart surgery were asked to: 1), listen to special audiotapes in which a calm voice speaks over gentle music, 2), and urges patients to close their eyes and remember the place where they were very happy and comfortable. It has been shown to have beneficial effects as it reduces stress and helps recovery.[85]

Rather than criticizing others like a hypocrite, introspection is essential to lookout for personal faults and shortcomings and to correct these inadequacies. It is a tedious process and not easy to accomplish. We need to become humble, polite and non-judgmental and start appreciating goodness in other people and treat them on equal footing.

A healthy balanced life is an ideal one. Healthy nutritious foods and participation in various sports, swimming, running, cycling, yoga and other exercises are tiring but are exhilarating at the same time due to the release of endorphins in one's body.

Positive attitude in life coupled with regular exercise routine, balanced healthy diet and adequate sleep reduces stress, augment immune system and add years to quality of life. People with healthy positive minds are full of energy and live a happier fulfilling life. Healthy body and mind are the key to happiness.

'Health is a state of complete harmony of the body, mind and spirit. When one is free from physical disabilities and mental distractions, the gates of the soul open.'

~ *B.K.S. IYENGAR*

CHAPTER 24

Mind and Health for Happiness – Healthy Body for a Healthy Mind

'The doctor of the future will give no medicines, but will interest his patients in the care of the human frame, in diet, and in the causes and prevention of disease.'

~ THOMAS EDISON

A GOOD LIFESTYLE of wholesome and balanced food consumption is essential to maintain a healthy body. Stress and unhealthy life styles including lack of exercise and fast foods have increased the incidence of being overweight and obese. It is a worldwide problem. It is no more a problem of rich and prosperous countries as it is presently rampant in all corners of the world. Over half a billion people in the world are obese and many-times more of that are overweight. It is just a global issue but also a global epidemic. In recent statistics World Health Organization report in 2015, 1.9 billion (39%) adults over age of 18 were overweight that includes 600 million (13%) who are obese. There were 49 million obese children below 5 years of age. Obesity is most rampant in Mexico, United States and India. An increased incidence of obesity in children is creating additional problems for the parents and the society.

Obesity is preventable. It is a high risk factor for diabetes, cardiovascular disease, high blood pressure, stroke and cancer. The incidence of diabetes is highest in India and is rising.

Good nutrition is crucial for keeping a healthy body. Healthy food consists of a balanced proportion of proteins, carbohydrates and fats and daily requirements of vitamins and minerals. Fiber intake is essential to regulate our bowel habits and prevent many digestive disorders such as diverticulitis, irritable bowel syndrome and even bowel cancer.

'Cruciferous vegetables' (called 'super-veges') like cabbage, cauliflower, broccoli and turnip greens are rich in antioxidants, vitamins, carotenoids and minerals. According to National Cancer Institute (NCI)[80] these vegetables have protective effects on some type of cancers due to high content of isothio-cyanates, indoles and phytochemicals. These help protect cells from DNA damage and also inactivate carcinogens. There is also inhibition of tumor blood vessel formation (angiogenesis) and tumor cell migration (inhibiting metastasis). Women consuming four servings of these vegetables a day were found to have 18% reduced chance to develop certain type of breast cancer (hormone receptor-negative), 35% reduced risk of cancer recurrence and 62% reduced risk of cancer mortality. Broccoli helps purge the body of carcino-genic air-pollution toxin benzene that causes carcinoma of the lung.

Powerhouse' vegetables and fruits (PVF): CDC (Center of Disease Control and Prevention) has recently defined PVF as health-protective foods that have 30-40 nutrients with bioflavonoids, polyphenols and other antioxidants with vitamins (A, B, C, D, E, K), trace minerals, certain fats and chemicals. PVF reduce chronic diseases like cardiovascular and neurodegenerative dis-eases and certain cancers. PVF list consists of green leafy and cruciferous vegetables, citrus-orange and berries and is topped by watercress followed by Chinese cabbage and chard.

One should eat plenty of 'fruits and vegetables' as it reduces risks for stroke, heart disease, high blood pressure, and painful intestinal ailments like diverticulitis and also reduces risk of cataracts and macular degeneration in the eyes.

Nuts: In a 30-year study on 119000 subjects by Ying Bao,[7] daily con-sumption of handful of nuts like almonds walnuts and pistachios discovered longevity benefits as they had 20% less chance of death during the study period. These people were also less likely to die from heart disease (29%) and cancer (11%). Contrary to our beliefs 'nut-eaters' stayed slimmer in the study.

A balanced protein, carbohydrates and fat intake is paramount. A wholesome diet consists of fruits, vegetables, whole grain and proteins. Things to avoid are red meat, hydrogenated oils and animal fats. Recently in 2015, CDC has eased restrictions on cholesterol and saturated fats. However, it still remains controversial. Added fine sugars are major concern as average American consumes 22 to 30 teaspoons. Sugars should not be more than 10% of daily calories (no more than 12 teaspoons).

Normal intake in an average adult is around 2000 calories per day. Intake of food high in carbs (4 calories/gram) and fats (9 calories/ gram) that are abundant in fast foods, and soft drinks (that include diet sodas) have led to alarming increase of obesity and type 2 diabetes in the world. Calories from proteins should make 10 to 15 percent of daily intake. New recommendation (2016) for protein intake is 0.8 to 0.9 grams per kilogram of body weight per day for a sedentary person.

The 'food pyramid' has been replaced in current recommendations for nutrition. Visit 'ChooseMyPlate.gov' by USDA (United States Department of Agriculture) to pick a balanced healthy food as a crucial campaign against rising concerns against obesity. The plate is unevenly split into four sections, for fruits, vegetables, grains and proteins. A smaller circle sits beside it for dairy products. One should try to eat fish twice a week and avoid high-fat and salty foods like salami and bologna.

'*Weight gain*' is a slow process of 2 to 5 pounds a year, which adds up over a period of time. If calorie intake is higher than calories (energy) spent, it results in net weight gain. Eating a variety of foods is the key and of course portion control is paramount. Alcohol and wine (especially red) is good for the heart and may be cautiously consumed by adults. But remember that alcohol is notorious for addiction and leads to road accidents that can ruin lives with disabilities and premature deaths. Prolonged use of alcohol leads to brain atrophy, 'alcohol-related dementia', and cancer (throat, esophagus, breast, colon).

You must balance the food you eat with good physical activity and exercise to maintain or lose weight. An average sized person needs to run 5 miles in one hour in order to compensate for the extra calories on consuming one large portion of French fries. Avoid refined carbohydrates and transfats that are abundant in processed junk foods like cookies, cakes and chips as these have contributed to global epidemic of obesity. A simple effective way loose weight is to eat less (20 to 25%) than your caloric needs. Have a smaller serving.

Energy bars and sugar containing drinks are calorie bombs. Carbonated sodas are to be avoided. Coffee, tea and many other drinks have a diuretic effect. Diet sodas are implicated in obesity and type-2 diabetes (as their use changes intestinal flora in rats and lead to Insulin resistance). Liquid calories are not as satisfying. Eating 250-calories worth of apple slices is far more fulfilling than 250-calorie apple juice because fiber content in apple satisfies appetite. Two main sugars are glucose (bread, rice and potatoes) and sucrose (soda, candy, cookies, honey). Sugars are converted to fat in the body by Insulin (secreted by beta cells of pancreas). High sugar intake leads to weight gain, obesity, insulin resistance, beta cell (pancreas) dysfunction and type 2 diabetes and also cardiovascular disease. Sucrose is sweeter than glucose. It is rapidly taken up by liver and converted into fat that is deposited in liver (fatty liver). Some of it is also released into blood stream and is deposited as visceral fat in the abdomen. Compared to fructose in soda (liquid calories) fructose in fruit is balanced by fiber and is delivered slowly to the liver.

Elderly people have decreased thirst mechanism and are usually dehydrated. They should remember to drink at least 4-6 glasses of water daily. Of course they should consult their physician, as in some people their water intake may be restricted because of cardio-vascular disease. However, you may need electrolytes or simple salt water when you are sweating a lot as during exercise and in hot weather.

'Mind Diet' consists of 'brain-healthy' foods such as green leafy vegetables, nuts, beans and berries, whole grain and olive oil. This diet decreases cognitive decline reducing the risk of dementia- Alzheimer, stroke and heart disease.

A diet low in fat and cholesterol is helpful in cardio-vascular disease. Colorectal cancer is common in diet consisting of low-fiber, high red meat (beef, pork, lamb) and processed meat (hot dog, bacon and deli meat) commonly consumed in many western countries. A healthy balanced diet is vital. Moderation is the key. Excess of anything is invariably harmful.

Impact of sleep on health

'Sleep is the single most effective thing that you can do to reset your brain and body for health,' says Mathew Walker, professor of neuroscience and psychology at the University of California at Berkley. During sleep 'neurons pulse with electric signals that wash over the brain in a rhythmic flow …to check balance of hormones, enzymes and proteins. The brain cells contract, opening up spaces between them so that toxic buildup of accumulating debris' is washed out like the 'nightly wash cycle.' (Maiken Nedergaard MD)

Seven-hours of sleep is essential. It is little less (about 6 hours) in seniors and a little more (8 hours +) in children. Sleep deprivation kills mice faster than starvation. Lack of adequate sleep leads to faster aging of nerve cells that can contribute to Alzheimer's disease, which is the leading cause of death in seniors these days. Insomnia can be symptom of underlying stress, depression, schizophrenia and bipolar disorders.

During deep sleep brain tries to recoup and reorganize the events of the day and tries to strip away emotional attachments like grief, fear, anger and joy to come to a rational judgment with a cool mind. During sleep brain is fairly active at molecular level.

(Alice Park, Time magazine, March 6, 2017)

'A healthy body is a guest-chamber for the soul; a sick body is a prison.'

~ FRANCIS BACON

CHAPTER 25

Mind and Health for Happiness - Exercise for a Healthy Body and a Healthy Mind

'The journey of a thousand miles begins with a single step.'

~ LAO TZU

EXERCISE IS GOOD for body and the mind as it nourishes both of these to preserve health and happiness. Presently in United States exercise assessment is called a 'vital sign' that needs to be checked like pulse and blood pressure in the physician's office. CDC recommends 150 minutes of moderate exercise (brisk walking, jogging, and bike riding) per week and muscle strengthening exercises (push-ups, sit-ups, weight lifting, yoga) twice a week. Basically you have to sweat and cautiously increase your heart rate. Guidelines for diet and exercise are easily available from dietician, clinician, your physician and sports medicine consultant and also on Internet. 'Recommendation from your physician regarding any restrictions is paramount.'

Thousands of years ago Patanjali,[24,113] the father of yoga and other Rishis stressed the need of a correct posture to keep a relaxed straight sitting position without any stress on the spine. Correct body posture expands chest resulting in the ability to take a deeper breath that brings in more air (oxygen) in the lungs, giving the person more energy and the ability to focus. When sitting in a chair for a longtime like working on computer a 110-130 degrees backward tilt is optimum. On the contrary, stooping forward posture ends up like 'slump to a hump' that closes in the chest with pressure on liver, spleen and other organs. Incorrect posture leads to backache and other problems.

'Sedentary Death Syndrome' is a major public health burden causing multiple chronic diseases and millions of premature deaths annually.[68] Fifty-seven percent of Americans ages 65 to 74 spend more than 7 hours being sedentary as reported in Time Magazine, February 29, 2016. This lifestyle of physical inactivity leads to malnutrition, low back pain and a higher incidence of obesity, high cholesterol and type 2 diabetes.

One should stop being sedentary and start exercise routine at a slow pace at first and gradually increase your stamina. If one constantly pushes oneself to the point of discomfort, one is apt to lose motivation faster. Start swimming from 5 to 10-15 laps in weeks not days. Most of us make promises at the start of the New Year to pursue a healthy lifestyle by regular exercise, eating nutritious food and losing some weight. The enrolment in gyms and workout places sees a big spurt in the beginning of January with all the New Year resolutions. Soon they lose interest and a majority is back to their basic habits within a few months.

When you start exercise, you may get some aches and pains especially if you have arthritis, but your body will loosen up eventually. Typically, patients with degenerative osteoarthritis have body stiffness and aches on getting up in the morning that improves within about half an hour or so. 'Your physician may help you to choose a suitable exercise program if you have any restrictions.' Primary care physician in United States are required to routinely check patients' fitness levels and prescribe suitably tailored workout regimens.

Walking may be very strenuous activity for very sedentary and obese people. Swimming or walking in water is rewarding because of buoyancy. It takes pressure off the joints and above all it maintains the range of movements. One should gradually increase exercise routine.

Group exercises like water aerobics, biking or jogging with a buddy or hiking and dancing can be motivational and socially inspiring. During workout, you will be able to do more exercise if your mind is engaged in some audiovisual activity. Listen to your favorite music, or look at a TV show.

Despite increased awareness of benefits of physical exercise, only 3.5% of Americans age 20 to 59 get the recommended amount of exercise. Statistics elsewhere is not any better. Walking and jogging can be easily undertaken even in impoverished countries. Other type of group sports like football (soccer in US) and basketball are common around the world.

Healthy life style with regular physical exercise, balanced diet, adequate sleep and a positive attitude is essential for longevity. A happy active 70-year old who is relaxed with a positive attitude will probably have more years to live than sedentary cynical 60-year pessimist.

A good exercise routine and eating a balanced food can maintain a healthy life style for the body and the mind.

'Investing in your health now can pay dividends for the rest of your life. What is one easy thing you can do today to live healthier?'

~ MELANIE GREENBERG

Part Four

The Science Behind Impact of Behavior

CHAPTER 26

Biochemical changes and Biogenetics of Happiness

'The laws of genetics apply even if you refuse to learn them.'

~ ALLISON PLOWDEN

THERE ARE COMPLEX mechanisms of physiology for happiness and other behavior regulations in the human body. These result not only from changes in the environment and from the issues at hand or predilection and attributes of a person but also one's underlying personality and to a major extent on one's genetic predisposition.

Everything in this dynamic universe is impermanent and constantly changing and no two moments are the same. The changes that we confront in life can be insidious and slow or sudden and acute in nature. Both lead to modifications of our behavior, former with a slow and at times imperceptible change because of some element of adaptation and the later with a sudden emotional outburst that only a few can hide.

Irrespective of degree and intensity of the pleasant or unpleasant incidents in life, events mostly result in the same often-predictable behavior. Our natural inherent affection for love, happiness and joy, and a natural aversion and repulsion for pain and sufferings is a universal behavior. There is happiness and joy on hearing the first cry of the newborn or getting a million-dollar lottery and there is shock and painful hurt on the death of a near and dear one or news of someone suffering from a terminal cancer or a progressively crippling neurologic disease. These are normal behavioral responses, however, the intensity and duration of these emotional responses are variable depending on many factors including our overall attitude in life that can be positive or negative. Coping mechanism is essentially a slow process that varies in intensity and duration in different individuals.

The neurologic changes that govern our emotions and behaviors are complex and to a great extent unknown. There are some fundamental biochemical responses in brain chemistry that are beyond our control. The concepts of their neurophysiology are constantly evolving with research by the newer technologic aids. Some of these neurophysiologic, neuropathological, neurochemical and biogenetic research conclusions are as follows:

The *autonomic nervous system* (ANS) is composed of two complimentary systems: sympathetic (SNS) and parasympathetic (PNS). ANS is responsible for regulating the body's involuntary (unconscious) functions. SNS controls the body's responses to a perceived threat and is responsible for the "fight or flight" response, whereas, PNS is responsible for homeostasis and the body's "rest-and-digest" or "feed and breed" activities that occur when the body is at rest like digestion, urination, defecation and sexual arousal etc.

Anger and stress leads to tense muscles in the neck, back and chest wall due to sympathetic over activity. This autonomic imbalance can be corrected by various deep-breathing techniques that include pranayama. Deep abdominal (diaphragmatic) breathing helps oxygenation due to better lung expansion. There is also parasympathetic stimulation through vagus nerve leading to slowing of heart rate, lowering of blood pressure, relaxation of muscular tension and stress reduction.

Vagus nerve with its mind-body connection is the calming nervous pathway of parasympathetic system.

Prana means 'life' in Sanskrit. Pranayama means control of breath, 'life-force control' by various breathing techniques. It purifies and energizes mind-body complex and general wellbeing fighting anxiety and depression. Deep breathing is simple way to reduce stress.

The *fight-and-flight response* occurs on confronting a real or perceived threat to make the individual either fight or run away from the threat. It is a physiologic rapidly occurring reaction in the presence of something that is terrifying either physically or mentally. In this acute stress response there is mobilization of bodily defense mechanisms to counter the threat. Threat stimulates the autonomic sympathetic nervous system and the adrenal gland to trigger the release of hormones i.e. catecholamines: adrenalin and nor-adrenaline, leading to increased blood pressure, respiration and heart rate and palpitation. There is perspiration and flushing of the face. These symptoms can appear in innumerable other situations like accidents, when you get unexpected shocking news or when you are very angry with someone or in a heated confrontation.

'*Brain reward system*' regulates, controls and enforces behavior with pleasurable effects. Human brain is always dynamically working in the face of external stimuli; both physical and thought processes in our mind triggering neurochemical responses. It is always on the lookout for fun and pleasure especially from past encounters and experiences. The pleasurable source can be any particular food, alcohol or any other drug. It could be a potential mate or in the form of innumerable desires, which trigger the cerebral cortex to signal the ventral tegmental area of the brain to release the chemical 'dopamine' by complex interactions at amygdala, the prefrontal cortex and the nucleus acumens. These latter regions of the brain make up the 'reward system'. The coordinated response delivers a sense of pleasure and focuses the attention of the person on repeating the same behavior to seek more and more of the same. The pleasure is usually short-lived and the person seeks more and more gratification, thus creating a vicious cycle of 'dependence'. Most of the persons with a strong will and the control of their mind can cope with these urges but many with weaker willpower are easily persuaded especially if they have genetic predisposition, to become an addict.

-Dopamine through brain pleasure-reward system is involved in 'addictive behavior' as described above.

- In 'Philanthropy' as fMRI (functional Magnetic Resonant Imaging) has exhibited arousal of brain's reward center when one performs an act of kindness, like helping someone in need or by donating to a worthy cause. The brain is flooded with dopamine, the happiness-inducing hormone with intense feeling of pleasure. However, surprisingly brain reward center has similar chemical response with dopamine release in a negative situation.

-Dopamine and Serotonin are feel-good neurotransmitters.

In addition, the following facts are known:[53,54,56]

- *'Novelty-seeking genes'* are involved in behavior genetics that transpires the spirit of adventure.

- DRD4 receptors are members of the dopamine receptor (DR) in G-protein-coupled receptor family that includes D1 to D5. The human D4 receptor gene is localized in chromosome 11 (11q15.5). These receptors are located primarily in the frontal cortex, midbrain, amygdala and the cardio-vascular system.

DRD4 is responsible for neuronal signaling of the brain that regulates emotions and complex behavior. It is one of the most polymorphic DR genes with several forms or alleles ranging from 2 to 11 R (repeat units) with 4 and 7R the most common.[18]

There are gene codes responsible for even-temperedness and reflection, exploratory and impulse behavior and risk-taking and novelty tolerance. Population with repeated migration continues to possess genes favoring exploratory behavior. People with this forward-looking behavior with optimism seek fulfillment and happiness. It varies from 2R (East Asia) to 4R (Africa) and 7R is in the New World.[54]

- DRD4-7R: Dopamine system related genes mark a person's susceptibility to the environment. Children that are carriers of DRD4-7R profit most from positive feedback and remain at lower level of literacy skills in absence of it.[53] Bruce Ellis and Thomas Boyce coined the term 'orchid-dandelion' based on the vernacular Swedish term 'dandelion children,' who (like weed- dandelion) seem to grow up okay in almost any environment. To that they added the term 'orchid children', those who thrive under good care but wilt under bad.[31] This DRD4-7R variance is prevalent in 20 to 30% of Caucasian children. Thus less dopamine producing 'Orchids Children' don't learn well in the presence of negative feedback or distracting environment or poor parenting and can end up depressed, drug-addicted, or as a criminal in jail. However, in the presence of the right environment and good parenting, they blossom to be most creative, successful, and happy people of the society.

- 5 HTTLPR is another gene for Serotonin transport that is responsible for stress-related disorders.[75] This genes allele frequency is less common in the United States with culture of individualism compared to Eastern cultures of collectivism. Genetically optimistic temperament is essential in the biology of happiness.

'Peptide of happiness': is a neuropeptide- 'Hypocretin-1'. Recently Dr. Jerome Siegel (2013), Professor of Psychiatry at UCLA[10,100] found a greatly increased level of hypocretin in subjects that are happy, awake and in social interactions and a decreased level in subjects when they were sad, unhappy and in pain or while they were asleep. Another peptide, MCH (Melanin Concentrating Hormone) has lower levels when subject is awake and increased while asleep. Patients with narcolepsy (excessive sleeping disorders) also suffer from depression and are found to have fewer Hypocretin-nerve cells. This research has opened a newer field for possible future treatments of various psychiatric disorders like depression and narcolepsy. Probably a 'pill of happiness' will become available in the near future. Hopefully it will be different from other addictive hedonistic substances.

Neuroscientist Rob Rutledge from UCL (University College London) published results of research using fMRI in subjects in proceedings of National Academy of Science in August 2014: 'Happiness is not about how well you are doing but rather if you are doing better than expected' as short-term happiness conformed to a predictable mathematical equation.

Payback from Altruism: -According to research of Steven Cole at UCLA 'Individuals whose happiness comes primarily from doing-good-to-others show much better gene profile than those feel good hedonistic individuals who are always self- centered. Altruistic people have less inflammation and better antibody and antiviral activity.'[117]

-It is noted that monkeys are less stressed when they give rather than when they receive grooming. Monkeys spend hours picking and grooming each other's fur (removing lice and other parasites). Grooming lowers their heart rates and stress hormone levels and decreases behavior markers of anxiety.[104]

Old dogma that infant is born with all the neurons (nerve cells) that one is ever going to have is no more valid. It has been discovered recently that new neurons are constantly being born in dentate gyrus of hippocampus that is crucial for learning and memory. Many of these newborn neurons fail to survive. Physical exercise and enrichment help to integrate these cells in neural circuitry to learn new facts and events. Foods rich in flavonoids like berries, grapes, chocolate and tea boost memory and brain function, whereas, stress, alcohol and high doses of nicotine are suppressants. Furthermore, it has also been shown that mental exercise like meditation helps in neuroplasticity.

Good genes are not the only factors that influence our intelligence and behavior. Upbringing, environmental factors and the educational opportunities can influence and transform genetic traits positively or negatively. The inherent drawback and limitations can be manipulated to our advantage by tailoring the living environment to counteract the real or the perceived problems in a growing child. Unfortunately the will and the resources are limited. Hopefully research and development to fully understand our genetic coding and its manipulation to our advantage is not in a too distant future.

Good parenting, a positive stimulating environment and education at school and at home by example can overcome some of the genetic challenges. There are examples of occasional poor and underprivileged children who living in slums with limited doors of opportunities in life have become icons in various professional fields and have become national and world leaders by their persistent hard work and positive outlook. Better understanding of genetic coding and of neurophysiology and neurochemistry can open newer avenues of therapy in genetically predisposed individuals for mental illnesses. This can help bring new rays of happiness and hope in their lives.

'The human genome is a life written in a book where every word has been written before. A story endlessly rehearsed.'

~ JOHNNY RICH

CHAPTER 27

The Control of Mind - Key to Happiness

*'To enjoy good health, to bring true happiness to one's family,
to bring peace to all, one must first discipline and control one's
own mind. If a man can control his mind he can find the way
to Enlightenment, and all wisdom and virtue will naturally
come to him.'*

~BUDDHA

HUMAN MIND AND intellect determines the character, personality and emotions of man. These are the main driving forces that interact with organs of perception to give a suitable response. Intellect is the primary determinant faculty. The mind without intellect is like an uncontrollable mad horse or an untrained novice teenager who is driving a car for the first time. The wisdom is derived from mind-intellect complex that helps the mind to act with caution and discrimination and is influenced by collective past experiences and knowledge.

The world is dynamic. Nothing is permanent as everything is constantly moving with only an illusion of stability. No two moments are the same. The wise ones can easily adapt according to the shifting circumstances instead of being a slave to them. Persons who have equanimity of mind are neither elated by success nor depressed by failure. Buddhism teaches that reality is a coin with two sides: 'anicca' (impermanence) and 'anatta' (emptiness, non-self, ego-lessness, soul-lessness) and mind has to learn to live by it.

Mind can easily be polluted by greed, unending cravings, desires and jealousy created by self-centered ego. Mind when full of impurities is covered by dust of ignorance. One must clean one's mind and infuse it with wisdom that is derived from intellect and knowledge. One should not only clean physical body every day but also clean one's mind. It is wise to spend a few minutes every day for self-assessment when you wake up in the morning and as you go to sleep and purge all bad thoughts and desires. Company of good wise people influences one's mind and directs its behavior in the right direction.

There is a beautiful analogy of mind and body in Katha Upanishad[17,90] 'Where self is the rider of the body that is the chariot, intellect is the charioteer and mind is the reins for the horses that are the senses, which travel on the road filled with web of desires.' Charioteer (intellect) controls the mind like the reins of the well-trained horses that obey the commands by faculty of discrimination. On the other hand, an uncontrolled mind runs wild towards the temptations. In a wise man, senses obey mind, mind obeys intellect, the intellect obeys his ego and the ego obeys the Self.[17,90]

It is very easy to write or to teach but very difficult to practice continence of mind as it runs astray at the first sight of sensuous vulnerable moments. This vulnerability can befall on any individual at any moment, not only on the young who lack maturity of their character but also on the wise and the elderly. At times even the most learned and the revered ones fall prey to their desires thus losing self-control and making a mess of their lives forever. Sometimes you do unwise and sinful deeds when no one is watching, forgetting that your soul is the witness and if you are a believer, the Creator is seeing it all the time. He is omniscient and does not even need to open His proverbial third eye. Many deeds done in that state of temporary insanity can change your life and you end up living with that scar forever.

We have to control our mind by determination. Our mind cannot be controlled by anyone else, as we have free will. 'You are your own master' preached Buddha[64]

One who has the power of self-control is the wisest and the most powerful. One should focus one's mental energy towards positive, pious and virtuous thoughts after eradicating negative destructive thoughts from mind. One can control one's mind by gradual transformation. To practice one needs a quiet place and a mind at peace without any kind of agitation. Best time to concentrate, contemplate and meditate is preferably dawn or dusk. In the beginning it may seem to be difficult to contemplate and meditate. To start with, one should do this mental exercise a few minutes each day. You can control your mind by a single pointed focus after eliminating all distractions. Yoga of meditation brings discipline and harmony in life with inner peace, tranquility and true happiness.

There is an interesting story in Brihad-Aranyaka Upanishad [17,105,113]: Once three groups of people 'devas' (godly men), 'manavas' (men) and 'danvas' (demons) wanted to better their lives and make progress so they decided to approach 'Prajapati' (chief preceptor) to ask for his pearls of the supreme knowledge for betterment of their lives.

First a group of demons ('danvas') approached Prajapati and asked, "O Master! How can we make our life better and worth living?"

Prajapati said, "Da" and asked, "Do you understand?"

To this 'danvas' replied, "Yes, we have understood. Da, means 'Daya' –to be kind, merciful and compassionate."

"Good, now you can go and practice 'Da' in your life." Said Prajapati.

A few days later the group of men ('manavas') came and asked, "Please oblige with your valuable teachings so we can succeed in life"

Prajapati said, "Da" and looked at them inquisitively.

They answered, "Yes our master, we understand. Da stands for 'Daan' -to be charitable."

Prajapati said, "Excellent now go and pursue 'Da'."

Lastly a few days later Godly-men ('devas') arrived and asked the same question to Prajapati.

"Da" said Prajapati. He looked at them and asked, "Did you understand the meaning of 'Da'?"

'Devas' had understood the meaning and nodded, "Yes! Da is for 'Damayata' or 'Daman' meaning -to have self-control."

Prajapati was very pleased and said, "Correct, go now and practice 'Da'.

This mythological story goes, there was a thunder from the clouds proclaiming voice echoed, "Da! Da! Da!" "Practice Daya, Daan and Daman-Mercy and *Compassion, Charity and Continence.*"

In this story everyone interpreted 'Da' according to their weaknesses to improve themselves.

One must strive to get rid of worldly desires and passions from the mind and by contemplation fill up that void with virtuous and compassionate thoughts. Like a bird you are tied by a rope, you have to cut this rope to be free from desires (kam), anger (krodh), greed (lobh), attachment (moh), and most of all pride (ahankara) and hatred (grinah). A mind under control is tranquil and at peace. Penance is to keep your mind calm, cool, collected and controlled, and devoid of jealousy, anger and apathy. Let there be no harsh words in your speech, no vanity in your mind, no conscious sinful acts by your deeds and thoughts and no backbiting echoes in your heart. Control your mind to reach your destination; don't let your mind be a slave to your desires. Continence of mind opens the gates for inner peace by curbing ego and illumination of the Self for an everlasting bliss.

> *'The mind is the instrument, the flywheel, and the thickest comrade of man. Through it, one can ruin oneself or save oneself. Regulated and controlled, channeled properly it can liberate; wayward and let loose, it can entangle and bind fast."*
>
> ~ *ATHARVA VEDA*

CHAPTER 28

Mind at Peace is Happy

'We can never obtain peace in the outer world until we make peace with ourselves.'

~ *DALAI LAMA*

PEACE IS A state of harmony with the absence of violence, conflicts and hostility, and freedom from fear of the aggressive violent behavior. A healthy peaceful co-existence in relationships eliminates conflicts and boosts happiness for everyone.

Mahatma Gandhi strongly believed in the philosophy and practice of non-violent peaceful resistance and coined the term 'Satyagraha'. He started this successful movement for India's independence from the British. This philosophy influenced Martin Luther King Jr. in the civil right movement in the United States. Peacekeeping missions are in the charter of UNO that has helped end many conflicts to preserve international peace.

Peace and tranquility of mind brings a state of happiness. Agitations and fears of the wandering mind get transformed into the one, which is reassured, still, quieted and satisfied and which is kind and considerate in all aspects in mind, the thoughts and the deeds. Long ago at the dawn of civilization Rig Vedas taught and helped us as how to lead a refined pious life in an orderly society wishing for peace in every corner of world. The *Shanti path* is a mantra for universal peace, harmony and happiness:

'Om Dyau Shanti Antarisksham Shantih Prithvee...
...Om Shantih, Shantih, Shantih, Om'

The spiritual meaning of the 'Shanti Path Mantra' is:

'O Supreme Lord, bless thy celestial regions full of peace and harmony, let peace reign everywhere on Thy earth and waters. …Let everything in the universe be peaceful. O Lord thy bring peace to me! Om Peace, Peace, Peace, Om'

Body, mind and intellect as perceiver, experiencer and thinker are connected with objects, emotions and thoughts.[3,20] Desires arise and prosper by perception and thought of objects perpetuated by memories of the past experiences. There is a surge of burning desires (cravings, 'vasanas') to get the desirable objects and get rid of the undesirable ones. These desires are endless and perpetually growing in an uncontrolled mind. Attachment to desires makes one angry and agitated if one is unable to fulfill these. One might imagine and erroneously perceive that other people are creating hurdles and are conspiring against him. This clouds his vision to discern right from wrong and he becomes totally irrational in his anger filled self-centered agitated mind and ends up making his own life miserable. On the other hand, a self-controlled mind is steady and devoid of agitation, and is tranquil and at peace and thus full of happiness. Mental purification in a controlled mind brings equipoise in pain and pleasure. Self-control is secret to pace of mind.[20]

Inner-peace is the peace of mind when one is mentally and spiritually at peace that brings happiness and bliss. Inner calm and clarity silently exuberates mind with joy. Mind is the most powerful entity in the cosmos. It can make or break the human dignity. Mind-in-turmoil is like an earthquake that unpredictably roars, shakes and erupts lava of uncontrolled anger, fear and agitation, whereas, mind-at-peace is the fountain of love, happiness and contentment.[19] An uncontrolled mind is like an untamed wild horse, on the contrary continence and self-restrain brings an orderly thought process. One needs to look inwards to seek happiness and learn to enjoy it. When one uses one's positive energy of the mind at peace to deflect anger with love, greed with gratitude and replaces apathy with empathy, one is left with plentiful joy and happiness. The reward of a peaceful contented mind is greater than all the riches in the world. Wealth, as we all know, can neither provide the earthly comforts for good nor brings inner peace.

Mind is never still. It is always engaged in thoughts and deeds. It is never satisfied and is always seeking and pursuing desires. Some desires are, however, good for human growth and are natural. Overindulgence in desires erodes human values. Peace or agitation, pain or pleasure, sorrow or happiness all result from lack of coordination and disturbances in the equilibrium of mind. A well-balanced content mind always stays peaceful and happy.

Peace of mind comes from within, from understanding self and following your heart and doing the right by following your conscious. When you truly follow your inner voice there is everlasting peace as there is nothing to fear.

Inner peace cannot be destroyed by the behavior of others as long as you are in control. If you are facing a competition or are to appear in a test, so long you have prepared thoroughly and done to the best of your ability, don't worry, and leave everything to destiny.

Buddhists believe that end of all sufferings leads to peace. Sufferings stem from craving, greed, aversion, fear and delusions. 'Peace comes from within. Do not seek it without,' preached Gautama Buddha.

Forget and forgive: Make peace in your mind by forgetting and forgiving others for their shortcomings and other bitter negative experiences in life. If you ever want to be forgiven, you must be courageous and kind enough to forgive others. There is no one on earth who is free from defects, inadequacies, mistakes and misunderstandings. One ethical way is in the doctrine stated in Kaivalya Upanishads, '...to see self in all beings and all beings in the self.'[72] This is well illustrated in other religions and atheistic faiths as well. 'You shall love your neighbor as yourself.' (Matthew 22:39) When you start treating others, as you will like to be treated, you will become considerate, compassionate and charitable; and all the agitations of whirlwind mind will be replaced by quietude and tranquility. A total transformation of your mind is essential to bring it under control, at ease and at peace to bring lasing happiness.

'If you want peace stop fighting.
If you want peace of mind stop fighting with your thoughts.'

~ PETER MCWILLIAMS

CHAPTER 29

The Art of Positive Thinking

'Character is the ability to carry out good resolution long after the excitement of the moment has passed.'

~ CAVETT ROBERT

A MIND IS the master of wonders and mysteries and is the most powerful weapon that is capable of accomplishing the impossible and shapes the destiny. Secret of happiness is a positive mind, capitalizing in its' strengths and not dwelling on its' shortcomings. One should start the day with positive thoughts that bring positive attitude to the forefront. Negative thoughts, on the other hand, breed negativity and bring jealousy hatred and agitation in the mind and can ruin your entire day.

Hallmarks of a happy mind are positive thoughts like kindness, forgiveness and humility, as well as goodwill, empathy and compassion, which in turn bring harmony, peace and tranquility. Positive thoughts are soothing and bring love, joy and comfort, whereas, negative thoughts bring anger, hatred, agitation, hostility and confrontation. Positive mind is devoid of anger, jealousy, hate, greed and suspicions.

Great scientists, discoverers and entrepreneurs have a powerful positive mind and they are seldom discouraged by their failures. On the contrary failures further fuel their energy and bring unparalleled zeal in their endeavors. Powerful men with twisted minds have negativity as a dominant trait: Men like Adolph Hitler and Pol Pot will remain a disgrace to the history of mankind forever.

The metaphysical analysis of the world needs an open unbiased positive mind. The complexities of the world need to be approached with a positive pluralistic vision as in the absence of this vision the void is filled with negativity. Negativity is a powerful destructive force and is much easier to acquire than hope. If one inculcates habit of looking at positive side of things, the mind continues to develop positive impressions. On the contrary if one is always looking at negativity, the mind gets filled with more and more negative undignified impressions.[52]

You are slave to your thoughts. You can often see reflection of your thought processes in the mirror. You have a choice to project yourself as: a joyful, happy, giggling and laughing face or as an angry, confused, incoherent, out of control hateful person. Determine what you want to be in your life, how you want to see your-self in the mirror: happy and at peace or angry and in turmoil. When you are happy, your reflection is happy.

Now imagine the mirror you are standing in front of is another person. Happy positive mind reflects positive responses from that person. Now considering the opposite scenario of negativity, one of the two things will happen: 1), Hurtful negative comments from you will be reflected back with double the intensity from that person, like arrows or bullets ricocheting back at you. Like you other person may also lose control, a fight may start, further negating your mind with disturbing disastrous consequences. 2), It is possible that compared to you, other person has sound judgment and is mature and non-confrontational and just walks away. He doesn't want to lose his patience and peace of mind with an irrational person.

During private practice as a physician, occasionally we come across irrational patients or their relatives. Seriously ill patients and their relatives are bound to be under lot of stress and agitation because they are facing life and death situations. In that critical juncture someone may lose control and possibly become irrational abusive and hostile especially when outcome is not favorable. Our response as a medical personal should always be polite, compassionate and full of empathy.

Happiness prolongs life. Positive psychology improves individual and collective functioning, well-being and physical health. People who think positively and feel good actually live longer.[34] Life is prolonged up to 10 years in another study. Optimistic positive attitude can reduce the physiological damage that exists in negativism. Negativism has toxic mix of envy, resentment and hatred.

In one study people with a negative mind-set with unpleasant views of growing older showed hippocampus decline in 3 years, compared to its decline in 9 years in positive mind-set individuals. Loss of hippocampus volume is seen in Alzheimer's disease.

People who have positive belief about old age early in their life have 7.5 years more life span compared to ones' with negative beliefs –Becca Levy (Time Magazine March 6, 2017).

The key to happiness is to replace negativity of mind with the positive attitude. It is not that simple, as it needs patience and perseverance. Negativity is like a cancer that erodes your mind with poisons. One should always be on lookout for one's own negative behavior. Look for the appropriate alternative amongst the pair of opposites like pleasure and pain, love and hatred and attachment and aversion. One should make an effort to substitute your negative feeling with suitable positive one. One needs to replace hatred by feeling of love, aversion by attachment and resentment with kindness. Modify to redirect your negative thoughts to positivity. It needs focus and control of your mind to contemplate and transform it by positive psychology.

You have to do abnegation of negativity in mind by looking for positivity in every situation (look for good qualities in a person whom you perceive to be bad) and fill the void with positivity. This rechanneling of mind needs its determination to substitute negativity with a positive psychology. And finally you must retain positivity in your attitude.

Positive mind is a fountain of love, joy and happiness. On the other hand, a negative mind can turn into deadly venom, which can destroy not only the victim but also one-self as well.

Serenity, contentment and a positive emotional demeanor are fundamental to happiness as positive thoughts illuminate your intellect to make sound choices that bring peace and immense joy to your mind.

'*Watch your thoughts; they become words,*
Watch your words: they become actions,
Watch your actions, they become habits,
Watch your habits; they become character,
Watch your character; for it becomes your destiny!'

~ FRANK OUTLAW

CHAPTER 30

Emotional Balance Preserves Happiness

*'Anivat means a soft answer to a harsh challenge; silence in the
face of abuse; graciousness when receiving honor, dignity in
response to humiliation; restrain in the presence of humiliation;
forbearance and quiet calm when confronted with calumny and
craping criticism.'*

~ RABBI NORMAN LAMM

ONE OF THE most complex features of human life is its emotional aspect.
Different kind of experiences in life results in expression of different kind of
emotions. Emotions are the subjective conscious experiences characterized by
physiological expression and reaction of our mental state. Emotions lead to
arousal of nervous system with secretion of neurotransmitters and hormones:
noradrenaline, dopamine, oxytocin, serotonin and cortisol. The type and
the extent of the emotional distress leads to various physiological responses.
Apprehension and fear on cognition of real or perceived danger and threat
reflexly stimulates nervous system causing sweating, palpitation with rapid
heart rate and breathing and muscle tension.

Limbic system, left pre-frontal cortex, motor centers and other areas of
brain are involved in perception and response of emotions.

Historical stress and coping theory presently speaks less of stress and
more of emotion.[66] Cognitive and relational principals concerning coping and
emotional process are interlinked. Presently cognitive-motivational-relational
theory of emotions is well respected.[66,67] Psycho-physiological responses to an

event or confrontation leads to a positive or negative emotional state with corresponding facial, vocal and other expressions.

Emotions are a way of expressing oneself and how we relate to other human beings in life. These are the connecting links to other people. Awareness of our feelings gives us ability to control our emotions without being overwhelmed by them and makes our thinking clear, positive and constructive. This 'awareness of our feelings' enables us to manage stress and challenges in our life more effectively. As a result, we are able to communicate clearly and effectively and we can better understand others and empathize with them.[48]

Emotions are integral part of our life. It is normal to be emotional so long as emotions do not unduly overwhelm you and are thus of short duration as you are still able to control and overcome them.

Positive emotions are: love, joy, empathy, affection, attraction, happiness and laughter. Positive emotions lead to compassion, generosity and forgiveness, and contentment and calmness.

Negative emotions are: hatred, aversion, repulsion, anger, jealously and selfishness and these in turn leads to sadness, fear, shame, grief, doubt, worry, guilt, apathy and depression.

Negative thoughts lead to indifference, apathy and conflicts, whereas, being positive, acting concerned and empathizing builds and preserves your relationships and secures happiness.

According to Buddhist teachings,[63] negative emotions are 'disturbing emotions' that emanate from lack of clarity, poor judgment, bad intentions, low self-esteem and lack of compassion. These 'destructive emotions' cause inability to keep relationships and are harmful to the individual, as well as to others.

'There is aversion to an event or a person who opposes 'I' and attraction and love and attachment to one who pleases and reassures 'I'.'[63]

Jealousy is inability to rejoice in other's success or happiness. Whereas, hatred is when you want to destroy someone else's happiness. Pride comes with false high self-esteem when you think you are superior to others or when others are too low to match you. Anger can even be virtuous at times like when you see someone abusing others without any provocation (like abusing innocent children or the weak or the elderly). You can't make any one angry by just telling him to be angry. But when you challenge his 'I'ness by calling him names, adding the fuel to the fire he can suddenly become angry.

Happiness can be achieved by purging negative emotions. In Bhutan's study on Gross National Happiness Index (Chapter 18, Page 68: Quantification of Happiness) in 2010, 74.3% of respondents were not suffering from disturbing or negative emotions.

Inability to control emotions results in confusion, isolation and negativity.[48] Many times an uncontrolled torrent of emotions like monsoon clouds triggers imbalance of mind. Negative emotions are 'exclusive' in nature and result from underlying fear of confrontational actions of others and fear of the unknown. Positive emotions on the other hand are 'inclusive'. One should be able to control and contain one's negative emotions to avoid their harmful effects by transformation of mind. Lastly 'patience' is the key to control agitation and anger and to make the mind peaceful and happy.

Prioritize events: There are so many scenarios in life that can snatch away patience and peace of mind. Controlling these events with careful analysis and time management is essential. One must have adaptable mental outlook to circumvent changes in life. For self-management one should create some personal guidelines for assessing an event (pleasant or unpleasant) with arbitrary time allocation. We should prioritize as to whether any particular event in our life is worth responding to or not, and if is it important or urgent? All tasks for progression (for example reading, entertainment etcetera.) are important, whereas, tasks for maintenance (for example food and other bodily needs etcetera.) are urgent. At times one should learn the art of saying 'no' in a positive and polite manner. On way to be polite is to say, "I will love to get involved but as I have so many other projects to complete…Sorry, I will not be able to give your project the commitment it deserves."

One never loses hope amidst 'positive thoughts'. 'One who has hope has everything.'[110] One should not be a slave but the master of ones emotions. Let the reason rule over emotions.

However, emotions keep the wheels of life in motion. A man without emotions is like a body without a soul. It is like wearing an expressionless mask inside out. Both negative and positive emotions play a dynamic role in our inter-relationships. We are happy on festive events like birth of a child, weddings, passing an exam or getting a promotion etcetera. We suffer pain and sorrow with negative emotions when we are faced with a failure in an endeavor, death of a near and dear, after being fired from a job or when we fail to land a job etcetera. Joys and sorrows are passing phases of life. One way of closure is to genuinely feel sorry on negative events occurring around us and take time to sympathize with the people affected.

Everything, good or bad, is impermanent ('anicca') and thus finite and perhaps transitory in nature. Sooner or later things are going to get better. You are not the only unlucky person in such a mess. Don't panic and get frustrated by your sufferings, there are always many people worse off than you are. Pain and sorrow, like joy and happiness are not going to last forever. Gear your mind in other directions like physical exercise, reading a good book or watching a comedy movie, TV show or even keep your mind occupied solving a Sudoku or a puzzle. Too deep, persistent or sustained involvement in negative emotions can lead to depression with all the negative consequences

'We should remain equanimous in joy and sorrow.'[19,21] Such a blissful state is not possible for most human beings. Emotional responses need to be balanced; brief and contained where we neither jump excessively with exhilaration on a joyous occasion nor cry excessively on the tragic one.

One needs to gear one's mind to learn the art of positive thinking and always look for the light of hope. 'Positive emotions now, feel good at the present moments and in the future.' Good feelings, positive thoughts and 'a focus on goodness in others can not only change your life but also life of the people around you.'

'The mind is its own place, and in itself can make a heaven of hell, a hell of heaven.'

~ John Milton

CHAPTER 31

Anger - an enemy of Happiness

'Holding on to anger is like grasping a hot coal with intent of throwing it at someone else; you are the one who gets burnt.'

~ BUDDHA

ANGER AND HAPPINESS are two opposing states of mind. An angry mind is always agitated and unhappy and never at peace. The first step to attain happiness is to control ones' anger.

Anger is a normal psychosocial response to an untoward event, conflict or an outcome. Usually despite a momentary outburst of anger the individual is able to have a full control over his or her faculties and behave normally. However persistent or recurrent episodes of undue anger can be a symptom of underlying causes such as neurologic impairment, substance abuse or both.[26] Presently there is an epidemic of disturbing and growing phenomenon 'of anger-driven violence.[26]

Occasional trace of mild anger is normal physiological response and is healthy. To tell someone you are angry is all right, however, anger driven people are at a higher risk to develop cardio-vascular disease: coronary artery disease, high blood pressure and heart attack. A recent meta-analysis of anger in 2014[78] found that within 2-hours of an angry outbursts there is 5-fold increase in heart attacks and a 3-fold increased risk of stroke and cardiac arrhythmia (irregular heartbeats). Our teacher Doctor R. P. Malhotra, Professor of Cardiology, who was a heart patient to begin with used to say, "My life is in the hands of a fool who can make me angry."

Angry individuals have aggressive, violent and self-destructive behavior due to underlying chronically repressed rage. It results from a long-term mismanagement of anger. It needs to be addressed and managed especially if it is a childhood problem, before it becomes dangerous and pathological.[26] This disorder is increasing at an alarming rate, affecting more than 15 to 20 million people in United States.

When anyone is faced with frustrating, unexpected, untoward outcome or any other negative event, anger takes the center stage with a natural outburst of human emotions. Anger to an extent is unavoidable, valid and appropriate emotion. It is the normal emotional response when one is confronted with hatred, hostility and failure or bullying. Other events such as divorce, losing one's job, unexpected inconsiderate behavior of trusted friends or when one finds out that he or she has a cancer or a terminal disease is equally devastating. You are angry with anybody and everybody, you are angry even with God as to why you are the chosen one to suffer. A majority will temporarily get angry and then be able to control themselves. In some people the response could be extreme and they may lose their composure and behave inappropriately.

Anger has an important physiologic function by helping body prepare to fight-or-flee from danger with rush of hormones like adrenaline and cortisol. Consequently, face turns red and is perspiring, there is muscular tension, and your heart rate and blood pressure shoot up. You can lose self-control, become combative and hostile, and may start shouting and even end up in a fight. This extreme response is rarely exhibited; anger needs to be avoided, controlled and constrained.

Anger management is an art to recognize that you are angry and learn the tools to calm you down and deal with the situation with a positive cool mind. You have the right to be angry and frustrated so long as you can control your outbursts and restrain your provocative feelings. Let us assume you have confrontation with someone who is completely wrong and out of line. He uses foul language and insults you and even tries to hit you. Arguing with such an unreasonable person will be absolutely foolish. Insulting him back will only make the situation worse as it will make you both even angrier. Under these circumstances it will be most appropriate for you to just walk away from that unreasonable person and keep your honor and dignity.

Sometimes you have reason to be angry when all the pain-staking work that you have done in the past in a society or a community project is blown away at the whims of new officers with a different perspective. About 20-years ago I was very angry and frustrated in a similar quandary and vented out my frustration in the board meeting. After the meeting a friend of mine took me aside and advised me to stay calm. He asked me to imagine that I am at a beach, trying to 'stop high tides of storming ocean in vain.' "You did your job to the best of your ability and you knew how to do it. Now let the future take care of itself as your role is over." His advice made me calm, though reluctantly and my anger and frustration eventually subsided.

Spiritually speaking anger, hate and other doshas (inadequacies) are defects that are suppressed virtues in an obstructed state. Just like short-circuited electric lines, which are dangerous, a locked up virtue becomes a vice. There is sublimation when you remove the cause of degradation. Cosmic love emerges when anger is gone and humility emerges when pride is gone. In essence by destroying the twisted aspects of mind the essential divinity of the soul may be revealed.[52]

ANGER AT WORKPLACE can generate additional stress in your life. You may have triggered anger because of your own fault, your shortcomings or work-performance. You need to calmly and carefully introspect as to whether your actions or work needs to be blamed? Does your performance and work ethics need to be improved and rectified? If you are angry with your unreasonable boss, don't pick a fight, think overnight or even over the entire weekend, and consider other options. When your anger has subsided, explain yourself in a cool and precise manner. In case of repeated confrontations, it might be helpful to keep a record for future reference. Anger is detrimental at work place as it decreases self-esteem and moral of everyone in the workplace. It is possible, on the other hand, that there is a hostile environment and everyone there needs anger management counseling.

If and when you face an unexpected challenge or a problem, neither get angry and get overwhelmed by it nor underplay and ignore it. Instead face it boldly with a cool mind and find the solution with an un-agitated balanced mind.

Thich Nhat Hanh beautifully dealt with storm of emotions in his book 'How to be Happy and Free, Under the Banyan Tree.'[41] He described the storm of strong emotions metaphorical to a tree during a storm. You should not fight the storm by remaining engaged in your brain, the mind or the heart. The technique of 'mindful breathing meditation'[41] is to try to bring your storm of emotions like anger to your naval (metaphorical to strong trunk of the tree, not the leaves or the branches) and breathe deep, in and out, concentrating on this awareness in the rise and fall of your belly. Focus on air going in and out through your nostrils into your lungs and rise and fall of your abdomen. Eventually anger will melt away in 10 to 15 minutes as the mind and the body relaxes and you are at peace.

Some basic guidelines to manage Anger are:

1. Anger is acceptable emotional response. It becomes a problem only when it is out of proportion to an event or is difficult to control.
2. Diffuse your anger. Be empathetic and forgiving and try to understand 'other's point of view'.
3. Be humble and polite. Don't be argumentative or confrontational or hold any grudge.
4. Agitated mind can't focus and is unreasonable.
5. Calmly solve the issues as solutions evolve with time.
6. Learn how to say sorry with genuine remorse.
7. Develop a habit of listening instead of arguing.
8. Don't repress anger, manage it or walk away.
9. Deep breathing and Mindful meditation reduce stress, anger and anxiety and it relaxes the mind and the muscular tension.
10. If anger dominates your life you may have to consult health professional for Anger Management Therapy

> *'Anger is an acid that can do more harm to the vessel in which it is stored than to anything on which it is poured.'*
>
> ~ MARK TWAIN

CHAPTER 32

Addiction Robs Happiness

'Addiction is the shortcut to happiness or a fast-track to self-destruction.'

~ REV. DAVID B SMITH

HAPPINESS IS NOT only an individual right but has become the national obsession. Quest for happiness and to acquire it instantly one runs the risk of addiction by chasing easily available ways of instant gratification of pleasures through brain reward circuitry. These 'feel-good chemicals' like dopamine, serotonin, norepinephrine and endogenous opioids quickly give us a sense of euphoria and pleasure. But don't forget it is a cycle of short-lasting pleasures. This opens the gates for addictive drugs like crack, heroin, prescription pain-killers, Fentanyl and other illicit drugs. Boredom ensues when level of these chemicals fall and we end up seeking more and more of the addictive substance or behavior. Real happiness is lost in this misguided attempt to seek pleasures of life. Addiction ends up ruining lives, both your own and of the near and dear ones and ultimately robbing happiness of everyone around.

Accounts of use and abuse of addictive substances have been known for thousands of years since the beginning of civilization. Alcohol, cannabis (marijuana), betel nut, opium, coco (cocaine) leaves and ingested psychoactive mushrooms have been addictive elements for generations.

Historically for a long time Chinese were known to use opium for its' medicinal value. Drug addiction in China began with importation of opium by British East India Company in late 1700's. Opium export became a profitable commodity of the British trade and colonization in 1800's. Two Opium wars in China are well illustrated by historians. British imported Chinese tea and exported opium (cultivated in India under British rule) to China. The British paid the persistent trade imbalance by the precious silver to China. Opium trade was legal under British banner at that time. Persistent opposition by the Chinese to stop opium trade led nowhere. Emperor of China ended up enacting new strict laws against opium use and trade. The nation continued to suffer, as more and more Chinese were becoming addicts, lazy and unemployed. China was ultimately compelled to sign The Treaty of Nanking in 1842. According to terms of this treaty China paid indemnity of $21 million and ceded Hong Kong to the British to get rid of opium trade. This trade became confined to China's Hong Kong territory. Hong Kong became a free port for opium trade, gambling and prostitution. Ultimately it flourished into a big modern commercially successful free port. Hong Kong was finally ceded back to China in 1997.

Chinese immigrants came to USA in 1870s for a better life. Along with, they brought habit of opium smoking. Laborers and Afro-American people working long hours of hard labor got addicted to opium as an escape. Most of well-publicized 'potion' in United States had opium or cocaine in it. Potions were geared to the rich white women.

So much for the history, addiction to other substances like drugs has escalated in the last 50 years. Presently it has become a worldwide problem with no geographical barriers. It is fast becoming a major problem in the developing countries. Major tobacco companies have faced stricter antismoking laws in the West particularly in the United States with a decreasing incidence of smoking due to public awareness. However, tobacco companies are carrying out major advertising campaigns in the developing countries, and getting rewarded with more smokers worldwide. Presently the new fad of smokeless e-cigarettes is in the horizon that has created new challenges for the future. Recently legit use of medical marijuana in many states in USA has opened new gates of substance abuse that will need to be tackled in future decades.

United States is the leading consumer of illicit prescription drugs and it is the largest consumer of pain-killers (71 % of world's oxycodone and 91%

of hydrocodone use). In 2007, 23.2 million people (age12 and over) needed treatment for the substance abuse in the United States.

The use of synthetic opioid Fentanyl, which is 50-times more potent than heroin, has overwhelmingly increased fatalities in United States. A bootleg version of potent painkiller Fentanyl is commonly made in China. Its chemical analogs are also on the rise. There were over 50,000 deaths from drug overdose in 2015; over 2/3rd of fatalities resulted from opioid drugs.

Amphetamine type of stimulants (speed and crystal meth) and date-rape drug Ecstasy are increasingly being abused. In a 2009 report: 15 to 56 million people (15 to 64 years of age) used these stimulants, and approximately 149 to 271 million people in world used an illicit drug at least once in the year 2009.[107] Worldwide prevalence of alcohol abuse is 1.7 percent. It is 5 percent in North America.[22] Drug addiction is increasing at an alarming rate in many parts of World. India has around 70 million (5.6%) addicts and these numbers are alarmingly getting worse.

In the past the addiction was considered a moral flaw. American Society of Addictive Medicine came up with a new definition of addiction in 2011 considering addiction a chronic brain disorder and not a behavior problem (or bad choices) like smoking, drugs, gambling and sex.[4] However, many psychiatrists don't accept this etiology of addiction.[94] About half of the addicts have genetic predisposition affecting many members of the same family.

As goes the story of Mahabharata, even Dharamraj Yudhishthira, the eldest most revered of Pandavas brothers, had the weakness and addiction to gambling. Duryodhana, his rival Kaurava, knew of his vice and challenged him into a game of dice. After losing his kingdom Yudhishthira put on stake not only his brothers but also Draupadi, their wife and lost them all in the game. That was one of the prime reasons for the start of the seeds of bloody war fought between Pandavas and Kauravas in Mahabharata. Addiction can destroy families and be a cause of their total destruction and disintegration from which they may never recover

Frontal lobe morphology of the brain is implicated in addiction as it normally inhibits impulsivity and delays the urges for gratification. Exposure to substance abuse during early formative years of life is detrimental to addiction. Disease affects the neurotransmission as well as the interactions within the reward structures of the brain. The neurotransmitter dopamine stimulates the cells in the 'pleasure center' of the brain to elicit pleasurable sensations that we get on taking cocaine or marijuana and even on eating a delicious meal. This region of the brain that governs impulse control and judgment is altered and diseased in addicts, leading to compulsive nonsensical desire for 'rewards'.

Repeated use of addictive drugs over time leads to fundamental changes in brain structure and function. Long-lasting changes in the brain lead to distortion of cognitive and emotional functioning, and compulsion to use drugs. In essence, it is 'a disease' of the brain but an addict cannot be absolved of his actions and is responsible for his behavior.

The addict has a progressive, persistent, compulsive dependence. He becomes progressively dysfunctional in society.

Addicts are escapists, devious, impulsive, manipulative, self-centered and dependent individuals. They engage in denials and are self-destructive with flawed social learning.

Treatment for addiction needs to be persistent and aggressive. It is tailored to individual's needs, involving combination of drug and behavior cognitive therapy including group therapy and AA (Alcoholics Anonymous) and NA (Narcotic Anonymous). Opioid detox facilities are opening up through out the United States.

However, 50 to 90% of people relapse after a period of successful recovery. This statistics is an on-going frightening challenge further complicates the equation.

Providing opioid antidote Naloxone and clean needles etcetera are additional burdens.

Addiction brings short-lasting pleasure at the expense of real happiness. One must prevent addiction with a firm resolve. Only prevention, treatment and rehabilitation of addicts can lead to real happiness of society at large.

'Nobody can go back and start a new beginning, but anyone can start today and make a new ending.'

- MARIA ROBINSON

CHAPTER 33

Depression Steals Happiness

'Depression is like war. You either win or die trying.'

~ UNKNOWN

THE PURSUIT OF happiness is endangered by a state of melancholy and depression. Happiness and depression are the opposite ends of a pole. The mind must be positive and determined to steer away from the shores of sadness and depression during ups and downs of life.

Depression is a major cause of morbidity and to some extent significant mortality worldwide. Depression affected around 5 percent of world's population, around 350 million people in 2012.[122] Lifetime prevalence of depression varies from 3 percent in Japan to 17 percent in USA. Incidence varies from 8% to 12% in other countries of the world. It is about 10% in India.

Clinical depression, as per Mayo Clinic, 'affects how you feel, think and behave and can lead to a variety of emotional and physical problems. These individuals may have trouble doing normal day-to-day activities...and feel as if life isn't worth living.' Depression is a common mental disorder. The person is lonely and sad with decreased energy, a low self-esteem and a feeling of guilt, with no interest in joyful and happy activities.

In clinical depression individual feels like in an abyss, metaphorical to being sucked into black hole gravitating into an unending black tunnel. The individual is unable to concentrate and feels miserable and is unhappy, angry, and helpless and his appetite and sleep are disturbed. According to National Institute of Mental Health major depressive disorder is a mood disorder characterized by combination of symptoms that interfere with person's ability to work, sleep, study, eat and enjoy any pleasurable activities.

Everyone feels depressed at one time or another for a short period. 'Reactive depression' develops secondary to an external stress and is usually mild and self-limiting.

On the other hand, 'endogenous depression' is a major clinical depression where a person is unresponsive (non-reactive) to the environment regardless of its nature. It is of a greater severity with more sense of guilt and loss of interest and has decreased appetite and sleep.[29] There is impairment in every day functioning that lasts for at least 2 weeks. This is also called 'unipolar depression' or 'unipolar disorder'. Episode may occur only once or such episodes may recur throughout life.

'Chronic depression' is less severe than major depression and an episode may last up to 2 years. These patients at times can also have episodes of major depression.

'Bipolar disorder' or 'manic depression' is a complex mood disorder associated with alternating clinical depression with periods of extreme elation or mania.

Exact etiology of depression is not known. It runs in families. Chemical changes in brain and genetic predisposition alone or in combination have been implicated.

Depression can afflict anybody, even small children without any family history. Social isolation is a major cause of depression in the elderly. Depression is 50% more common in females.[122]

Almost any negative event in a predisposed person can trigger a bout of depression. It can be precipitated by anything like loss of a job, a domestic fight, a divorce, a breaking-up of a relationship or a death or an illness of someone close. Alcohol and substance abuse, cancer or persistent long-term pain or illness also makes one susceptible to depression.

Pessimism: Depressed people have negative attitude in life; the glass seems always half empty in their mind. They lack a positive outlook in life and that snatches away their happiness. There is a loss of interest or pleasure in activities they once enjoyed and they are lonesome and sometimes suicidal. In

United States 3.4 percent of patients with major depressive disorder commit suicide. About 60 percent of persons who commit suicide have major depression or other mood disorders.[6] Worldwide there are about 3000 suicides a day and about I million annually. For every suicide there are 20 or more depressed persons who unsuccessfully attempted to end his or her life.[122] People with depressive disorders have shorter lifespan, because of higher suicide rate and in addition they have an increased risk of other medical disorders like heart attacks.

Depression is a part of PTSD (Post-Traumatic Stress Disorder). Lance Cpl. Williams of US Army was the last marine standing as the sole survivor of his 12-man squad in Iraq. A roadside bomb wiped out his comrades in 2006. He suffers PTSD as his life is tormented by survival guilt while others around him died. He lives a life of emotional isolation and smokes marijuana every day. On a bad day he is tortured by guilt for having gotten out of Iraq alive. On a good day he feels guilty for not having a bad day. (Time Magazine)

Treatment options for depression consist of basic psychosocial support combined with antidepressant medications or psychotherapy. Psychotherapy includes cognitive behavior therapy; talk therapy, interpersonal psychotherapy or problem solving treatment.[122] 'Most people with depression feel better with medication or psychological counseling or both.' (Mayo Clinic). Mild cases need only one of these therapies while combination is essential in established serious cases. Patients with suicidal thoughts need in-patient treatment in a psychiatric facility.

'Cognitive behavior therapy' teaches a patient how to fight negative thoughts, spot symptoms and other triggers of depression and attain problem-solving skills.

'Light therapy' which is very affective in SADs (Seasonal Affective Disorders) can also be used in depression.

Chances of 'relapse' after stopping antidepressant medications is high. It is 50% after one episode of depression and 80% after two episodes. This risk is half if you continue medications with no interruptions.

If one thinks that he has depression with suicidal thoughts, one must call hot-line if available and seek professional help immediately.

Prevention

The art of 'positive thinking' is essential to keep one's composure in ups and downs of life. Happiness can only be preserved and sustained with a positive attitude. One must learn to live and maintain a high self-esteem by believing in one-self. It needs a positive enforcement of mind like: 'I am the architect of my own destiny, I have infinite resources of hope and spirit within me…I am gaining more will power everyday…I am master of my mind and intellect and senses… and peace and happiness belongs to me.'[51] One should gradually bring positive thinking in forefront of one's mind.

One should get involved in a 'volunteer job and in-group activities' like sports and exercise that almost always bring happiness. Being around caring and positive people who will stick by you and help you through tough times is essential to prevent and combat loneliness and depression. One should 'avoid alcohol and other addictive substances' as these almost always make the situation worse. One must also avoid and reduce undue stress in one's life and maintain a healthy life style with nutritious food, exercise routine and good sleep habits.

Positive psychology helps in preventing depression. Remember, if you look around, you are not the only person entangled in the cobweb of difficult circumstances. One should try to free oneself from negative thoughts to gain freedom of mind and attain peace and happiness.

'I don't want you to have to save me. I want you to stand by my side as I save myself.'

~ Unknown

CHAPTER 34

Live Life a day at a time

'Each night of your life is a wall between today and the past.
Each morning is the open door to a new world, new vistas, new
aims, new tryings.'

~ LEIGH HODGES

ONE OF SIMPLEST way of living a happy life is to stay in here and now, living life in the present moments one day at a time. Time is the essence and right now is what matters the most. Enjoy today as a most precious gift. Resolve to deal with the problems that confront you today.

Don't lament on the lost opportunities or the good old-days or as to what went wrong yesterday or what tomorrow will bring! Today's lost moments will become tomorrow's lost window of opportunities. Today, there is no past and no future; only today is the day to deal with. Avail and enjoy what you have today and what is within your reach. As Jim Rohn defines it: 'Happiness is not something you postpone for the future; it is something you design for the present.'

However, it is prudent to plan for tomorrow, for the needy days or for when one is retired and can earns no more because of old age or sickness.

Many people just sit idle and brood and are full of worries reminiscing as to what went wrong in the past by looking inquisitively through the backyard window. This makes the precious present moments fearful and non-productive. Such people spend the nights awake looking at the darkness through the window in the front yard, waiting with the hope for sunshine tomorrow. They are worried as to how they will deal with the new day with newer set of problems and thus end up losing the precious moments of today. Only by shutting the front and the back windows of the mind, which are pointing to the future and the past, we can happily live in the present moments.[102] Living in the past or worrying for the future only brings anger, agitation, anxiety, fear and frustration.

Presentism is the unique philosophy of living in the present moments of today as objects and values exist only in the present time and there is no past and no future. Only it is the present moment that matters. One can make it full of worries and unknown fears or one can make this moment full of joy and happiness. Each moment of today is waiting to be explored, make it happen now, as now is the moment that can solve all the mysteries of life and has the keys for the future.

One should try to remain positive all day long from the moment one wakes up. The pattern of ones' attitude for the entire day is determined by mind and thoughts from the moment one wakes up. Try to wake up with a smile, not with a frown and be thankful for the gift of another day. I used to have a very pessimistic friend. I frequently ran into him (on hospital rounds) at work around 7-7:30 in the morning. Almost always he started the conversation in a negative way: as to how selfish the people are, how discriminatory hierarchy is and how bad so and so is etcetera. He was mostly correct as he was analyzing everything from his own negative prospective. I will have a cup of coffee and empathize with him. He used to feel a little better but I often ended up in the vicious cycle of negativity for at least a while. After few years I decided to change my course seeing him from a distance and trying to meet him less often to keep my psyche positive.

Lastly one must learn to be positive to enjoy every facet of the present moment. It does not make sense to run away from it. According to Buddha's philosophy you can attain nirvana in the present moment without worrying about the past or the future. Past and the future meet at todays' present moment. Thich Nhat Hahn recommends practicing 'walking meditation'. It is when one mindfully walks without any destination, enjoying one step at a time.[41] Happiness is already here in this very moment, it is enough for everyone to enjoy and behold.

Many Christians believe that God is viewed as outside of time and from the divine prospective past, present and future exist in the 'now of eternity'. Thomas Aquinas offers a metaphor of a watchman, representing God looking down on the crossroads where past, present and the future meet.

Idleness brings loneliness and unhappiness. 'Every hour must be accounted for and one must enjoy everything one did.' Theodor Roosevelt said, 'Get action, seize the moment.'[74] 'Inaction belongs only to the living dead.'[110]

When the present is challengingly difficult and there seems to be little hope for the future, one wishes to live in the past forever. However, one must passionately pursue to make the best in everything that one has. Past is full of memories, future is full of thoughts, plans and ideas, but the present is real.[62] Do some deeds for posterity in the moments of today.

In his book 'The Five Supreme Secrets of Life'[102] Sirshree describes that life has three windows with a vision of the Past, the Present and the Future. We should learn to live in the present. We must get liberated from the past memories of hatred, guilt and remorse. We unnecessarily search for 'cues to our miseries in the future', forgetting that this 'beautiful future can be created only in the present.' Don't let the opportunity of the present slip away in hopes of tomorrow.[102] 'Forget about success and failures that belong to the future.' 'The hope is the child of unborn future and ego is the lingering memory of the dead past. Don't miss but live in the dynamic 'present', which is a noble chance given to us to create, to advance, to achieve and to enjoy.'[19]

'Worry does not empty tomorrow of its sorrow, it empties today of its strengths.' Rightfully said Corrie Ten Boom. Every moment presents the opportunity to rectify the past and reinvent the future. Today is only the extension of yesterday. In present we can create blueprint for the future.[19]

Past is the memory of the germinating seeds and the flower buds, today flowers are in full bloom and tomorrow many of these flowers will wither and blow away without any trace of their beauty and fragrance. The wheels of time move at their own speed so never wait for it; the time spent worrying is worthlessly gone forever. The winds of the future could be more invigorating in our vision of hope.

Listen to the exhortation of the dawn
Look to this day! For its life, the very life of life.
In its brief course lie all the varieties and realities of your existence.
The bliss of growth,
The glory of action,
The splendor of beauty,
For yesterday is but a dream,
And tomorrow is but a vision:
But today well lived makes
Every yesterday a dream of happiness,
And every tomorrow a vision of hope.
Look well therefore to this day!
Such is the salutation of the dawn!

~ KALIDAS

CHAPTER 35

The Atonement of the Sufferings

'To live is to suffer, to survive is to find some meaning in suffering.'

~ FRIEDRICH NIETZSCHE

TRUE GOAL OF life is not the pursuit of pleasure and happiness but a quest for knowledge to understand the true meaning of life. Pleasure and pain, good and evil, joys and sufferings are like shadows chasing our life. Their combined impression leave imprints on our mind forever transforming and building our character and integrity. Foundations that build our character are poverty and miseries more than wealth and happiness. Sufferings and poverty ignites the inner fire with far more intensity than pleasure and praise.[115] Sufferings catalysis human transformation and bring it to the shores of new hope to make the life more meaningful.

Pain and suffering are part of life. Buddhism takes a realistic view of life and the world. 'Dukha' is a Sanskrit word for the suffering, and in Pali, it means 'what is temporary, limited and imperfect' conditioning. Anything that is limited and temporary is dukha and it includes short-lived happiness. It takes a central stage in Buddhism. One of the famous saying of Gautama Buddha is, "I have taught one thing and one thing only, dukha and the cessation of dukha." Physical and mental suffering are a part of birth, growing old, illness and finally death. Suffering results from desires, temporary pleasures and disturbing thoughts from an impure negative mind. These destructive thoughts lead to a cobweb of sufferings: anger, jealousy, dissatisfaction, loneliness and depression. You not only worry about securing and sustaining satisfaction in desirable objects but also in trying to get rid of undesirable objects.[62]

Sufferings result from self-centered behavior- the root of all miseries. Nirvana is to know and experience self correctly, whereas, a distorted view leads to 'Samsara'- the cycle of re-births (Buddha). Sufferings lead to mental and physical pain. 'Only compassion can bring true inner peace and inner strength.'[64]

Many times we are faced with desperate situations. There is no justification when innocent people are punished, when a near and dear one dies or is disabled for life or when one finds out that one has terminal progressive disease or a deadly cancer spread in one's body. In these types of catastrophes these elementary questions have been asked innumerable times: 'Why God is so unfair?' 'God where are you?' 'Why are you inflicting all the pain and suffering on good innocent people?' We are helpless and angry watching the sufferings of the nice people and witness dying of poor innocent children even before they learn to talk or walk on this earth. When all our prayers remain unanswered, and all our pleas remain unrequited, we may even say, "God I hate you!" We are perplexed and confused even more when we see thugs, liars and other criminals prospering at the same time.

Death of a loved one is a universal stressor. Sickness, old age, suffering and death are part of life.[15] Death of a loved one is always very painful. There is 'acute grief' in bereaved individual with a wide range of emotions like shock, disbelief and separation distress. Memories, images and thoughts of loved ones occupy ones' mind. Grieving and mourning are natural outcome. Acute grief can last up to 6 to 12 months.[101] One has to adapt and learn to live ones' life without guilt feeling and self-blame. 'Integrated Grief' is described as when mourning process is less intense and shorter when reality and meaning of death are assimilated with return to normal life. One feels sad, but the loved one is not forgotten, and it is not constantly occupying one's mind and thoughts. It becomes 'Complicated Grief' when there is inability to live a normal life as intense grief persistently occupies the central stage.

In Posttraumatic Stress Disorder (PTSD) persistent and generalized fear dominates, whereas, in 'complicated grief' (also called Post-Loss Stress disorder) prominent emotions are longing and sadness.[101] There can also be suicidal ideation.

According to Old Testament, the very first Jew, Abraham asked God at the dawn of creation, "Why the judge of our world would not act fairly? Would you also destroy the righteous with the wicked?" Moses was an early leader of Hebrews and the most important figure in Judaism. He inquisitively asked God with devotion, "Why have you treated these people badly?" Why God, why have you been unfair? This 'Why to God' has remained a lingering question ever since? Why bad guys are enjoying the life to the fullest while the innocent suffer? Different religions have tried to explain it differently. In Hinduism it is the central core of laws of karma.

Adverse circumstances are often a litmus test of your faith and convictions. A painful event or a tragedy somehow first brings courage to deal with the situation. This is followed by a period of anger as to 'why it occurred to me?' Then gradually you rationalize in your mind as to 'why not me?' and cope with it learning to live in peace. However, there are some people who lose their faith in God and His Justice.

Non-believers think that life is everything, enjoy it to the fullest, as there is nothing after death. They fail to understand that consequences of our actions reverberate for a long time. Sooner or later many of these non-believers make 180 degree turn in their thinking like 'born- again Christians'. Untoward events and catastrophes should neither dampen our spirits nor weaken our faith. On the contrary it only should strengthen our resolve and our faith and brings a new zeal of compassion to help other human beings in need. 'The hope of happiness rises from the ashes of tragedy.'[110] These negative events can bring a new transformation in our lives.

Painful suffering or abundant happiness is reaping of the fruits of our past Karma. When there is a natural calamity like an earthquake, hurricane or a tsunami, thousands may die instantaneously and many more suffer from injuries and consequent epidemics. The victims are both good and bad, adults as well as helpless elderly and innocent children. We fail to comprehend as to why the innocent and the blameless suffer? How do we explain? May be God makes laws of nature and His universal rules of creation and does not micro-manage each and every incident.

We bring all the accusations of unfairness to God, who is supposed to be fair and just. Why does the God allow all this to happen to the innocents? If you go to observation deck of the Eiffel Tower or the Empire State building and look down, on a gross distant view men and women look like ants or small children driving mini cars. It seems that God high above in the sky or in heaven is watching his creation and to Him we are like toys, running, jumping, loving and fighting and creating and destroying at our 'free will'. God gives us ability to think, to discern and to act according to our own free choices but He does not micromanage.

Resilience germinates from the ashes of pain and sufferings. Hope brings some respite from suffering. Negative painful events remind us to empathize and help others in need. There is happiness in giving and sharing. We can forget our sufferings on seeing happiness on the faces of others. If you are in pain help those who are in pain, and happiness is your reward. We can lessen our pain by openly talking with others and sharing in their grief. Depression can result from pent-up feelings. Our faith guides us through this difficult path and brings us closer to the edge of happiness. A positive will power in adversity is the shining light that can illuminate and guide us to the gates of happiness.

'Out of sufferings have emerged strongest souls; the most massive characters are seared with scars.'

~ Khalil Gibran

CHAPTER 36

The Spirit of Freedom

'Better to die fighting freedom than be a prisoner all the days of your life.'

~ BOB MARLEY

THERE CAN BE no true happiness without freedom. The human spirit likes to be a 'free bird' that can fly anywhere in freedom to explore and discover joy and happiness. There is still discrimination at many levels in many parts of world depending on race, sex, age, religion, color, cast and creed. Freedom of individual expression and movement is curtailed in many authoritarian regimes. People are ridiculed, mocked, ostracized, wronged and persecuted without any recourse. Debating the issue for freedom of press, 'government without newspapers' and 'newspapers without government' Thomas Jefferson chose later as it represents true freedom of choice.[73] Freedom is not free as it comes at a great cost of personal or national sacrifice.

Last century witnessed a wave of independence for many nations across the globe that got freed from clutches of foreign rule. In some cases, this lead to many improvements across the board like better living standards, higher life expectancy and limited progress in economic front. Freedom from poverty, illiteracy and mortal illnesses needs persistent endeavors. Individual freedom is curtailed in many parts of world on account of diverse political and religious views.

China invaded Tibet in 1950. During 1959 Tibetan uprising, 14th Dalai Lama, a young man of 24 at the time and presently a world leader, fled to

India and setup Tibetan Government in exile. He has been trying in vain to kindle sprit of religious tolerance in Chinese rulers by peaceful means. Buddhist Tibetans struggle to preserve their heritage and religious freedom continues. He has become a beacon of hope for freedom in every aspect of human existence.

Freedom and to be free will always need personal, moral and spiritual introspection in relation to time and space with different standards and interpretation in different eras of human existence. The same issue might have altogether different interpretation in different parts of the world. There was hardly any personal freedom in barbaric era, in dictatorships and in other authoritarian and autocratic rules. Kings and the queens as rulers of the world enjoyed everything at the expense of the common masses. There was hardly any personal motivation for the common man except to work for the bread and butter and be subordinate to and get abused by the governing forces. Genghis Khan, Attila the Hun, Timur, Vlad Dracula and Ivan the Terrible are just to name a few cruel rulers in recent history. Ivan crowned himself as first Czar of Russia in 1547.

Amongst the modern day notorious clans of killers of mankind, the committers of the most heinous acts are Adolph Hitler, Joseph Stalin, Idi Amin, Pol Pot of Khmer Rouge to name a few. They executed millions of people. Their inhuman acts of barbaric oppression, brutality and persecution can never be erased from the history of mankind.

'The cause of freedom is the cause of God!", said William Lisle Bowles. Thought of freedom ignites the human spirit. Slave trade was rampant in 16th to 19th century. It was a lucrative business trading up to 12 million slaves from Africa. The struggle for freedom can be a very slow process encompassing generations. Thomas Jefferson envisioned and ignited the struggle for emancipation from slavery in 1770s, but finally President Lincoln signed Emancipation Proclamation in 1865. However, discrimination continued to exist and propagate to this date. It was Civil Rights Act of 1964 enacted by President Johnson after violent riots in Detroit and other places in the United States that brought true sense of equality, justice and freedom. 'All men are created equal' despite being true in any ethical, moral, spiritual and political sense, it has remained a controversial issue. Unfortunately, it has never been adopted in true sense since the dawn of civilization.

According to UNO,[121] '...a quarter of a billion children age 14 and under, both in and out of school, now work, often in hazardous or unhealthy conditions.' Child labor is exploited most in Asia (61%), Africa (32%) and Latin America (7%). This tragedy is replicated despite protection from economic exploitation by recently enacted International laws to protect children from child labor. Children are sold as slaves and used for pornography, prostitution, debt bondage, and begging, forced labor in sweatshops, drug trafficking and children are recruited in armed-conflicts.

Present day curse of modern slave trade involves buying and selling humans, especially children. Presently there are 20 to 30 million people in involuntary servitude against their will or through deceit. Women have been exploited as sex slaves and in sex trafficking due to poverty. Mail order brides are available in many parts of world. A wealthy Sheik buying a woman-bride in South-East Asia is well known. Bride trafficking has emerged as a profitable vice in many parts of the world. In some parts of India like in Haryana, it is cheaper to buy a bride from Kerala or Assam than raising a girl in the local community. Sex selection and female infanticide (although illegal) have changed sex ratio in many parts of India: 1 male: 1.08 female Kerala, 1 male: 0.87 females in Haryana and 1 male: and national sex ratio is 0.94 females in India in 2011. This ratio is 1.01 male: 1 female worldwide and 0.97 male: 1 female in United States.

However, ways to bring freedom of mind, body and soul are essential for true and lasting happiness. The freedom of choice is individuals' right to exercise his or her freedom in any manner or choice except where such an act hinders or prevent others from exercising their freedom. The state of being free and at liberty to do what you want and when you want, and make choices without any constraints is the only real freedom one strives for. Freedom of speech and freedom of press is of paramount importance in a free society. Some of the famous quotes by well-known people describe freedom as: "Freedom to reject is only freedom." (Salman Rushdie). "Freedom lies in being bold." (Robert Frost) "Freedom is not worth having if it does not include freedom to make mistakes," said Mahatma Gandhi. Dwight D. Eisenhower said in State of Union Address, February 2, 1953: "To be true to one's own freedom is, in essence, to honor and respect freedom of all others."

All men are created equal in the eyes of God, as we are all his children sharing the same love. Equality is the essence of humanity. Egalitarianism is the key for real happiness in this pluralistic society. Despite moral and ethical pursuit of equality there is still a persistent, widespread discrimination based on cast and creed, between rich and the poor and on racial divides. Martin Luther King, Jr. words on the day of freedom march more than half a century ago will echo forever: "I have a dream that one day this nation will rise up and live out the true meaning of its creed. We hold these truths to be self-evident: that all men are created equal... I have a dream that my four little children will one day live in a nation where they will not be judged by the color of their skin, but by the content of their character." Those historical words challenged and awakened conscious and morality of the people all around the world and still reverberate in the depth of our hearts. That brought a fundamental change not only in United States but ignited the flame of equality and freedom in all corners of the world.

"Never, never and never again shall it be that this beautiful land will again experience the oppression of one by another." Eloquently spoke Nelson Mandela in his inaugural address as President of South Africa in 1994.

Freedom of expression is the real freedom including right to dissent and to peacefully demonstrate, so long it does not infringe on the rights of others. Freedom in a free mind is always in a state of bliss.

'Caged birds accept each other but flight is what they want.'

~ TENNESSEE WILLIAMS

147

CHAPTER 37

Technology Impacts Happiness

'People who are crazy enough to think that they can change the world are the ones who do...Let us go invent tomorrow rather than worrying about what happened yesterday.'

~ STEVE JOBS

PRESENTLY HAPPINESS IN the modern day life is increasingly connected to technologic advances by enhancing our well being in numerous ways. There have been major incredible innovations that have affected almost all aspects of human life: from electricity to telephones and television and from automobiles to airplanes. Better understanding of physiology of human body, pathophysiology and genetics of diseases and the newer diagnostic and therapeutic techniques, and immunizations, antibiotics and blood transfusions have more than doubled the life expectancy in the last 100 years. Last few decades have witnessed an unimaginable spurt in technologic achievements that have revolutionized our day-to-day life styles. We have become quite dependent on many of these innovations.

Presently it is impossible to imagine life without some of these newer technologic aids. Computers and other multimedia devices, smart phones and televisions and social media like Facebook, Instagram and Twitter are affecting all aspects of our life. Google can answer any question in seconds. We can instantly have real time video chat with near and dear ones' thousands of miles away with Skype and Face Time.

Gone are the days when we used to write letters in beautiful cursive handwriting and eagerly awaited the mailman to come with a reply. Presently most

148

of our mail is junk mail. No one write letters. It is replaced by instant texting and emails written by many in unconventional abbreviated words where 'u r' stands for 'you are' and '4U' stands for 'for you'.

If you don't change your habits and learn about newer gadgets, you lag behind like you belong to the middle ages. I felt that way when I got my first smart phone in place of a regular cell phone. You have to advance with newer gadgets, learn from your children and everyone else who knows more than you including your grandchildren who may not be more than 5-6-years old.

Technologic innovations have improved human life in almost every aspect. Everything is expediently and easily accessible due to modern technology. In many ways life is better, quicker and more interactive. It is difficult to fully comprehend all the technologic advances.

On the other hand, nothing in the world is more exciting than turning pages of a real book. We are losing writing skills. The beauty of handwritten manuscripts in calligraphy in the museum can't be described in words.

Negative Impacts: Technology helps make us happy in many ways. But it is also a major cause for lack of physical touch and, in many ways, lack of enjoyment of meaningful sense of work. It has made our life very busy, complex as well as flat and emotionless. Are we just a human machine without a soul? Yes, we can interact by social media but it is one-dimensional approach. It is too fast and too impersonal. We project only positive side of us with bragging and are hungry for the 'like it' comments that fulfill our ego. People like to portray themselves as looking more attractive, more successful and happier than they actually are. There is a constant effort to impress other person with false displays that create a genuine conflict in mind with negative effects and low self-esteem.

Unfortunately, recent research have found that a majority of people feel worse about their personal life after spending time on social media sites where life is unnecessarily exposed like an open book. Easy Internet access can unduly expose a person to distractions like indulgence in gambling, visiting porn-sites, bullying and other vices. (The Wall Street)

We often display our illusive luminary and pretentious existence in digital scrapbook, where dignity takes a back seat displaying disgusted images of human heart exposing secret passions and desires. Most of us fail to realize that at times we display most mundane and often embarrassing private moments in social media.

One of the negative impacts of blabbering on social media has been on the employment opportunities as many of employers look to social media sites to know more about you, which can influence their opinion in negative ways more than the positive ones.

Screen time and multitasking affects children and teenagers' ability to focus and learn. Many children are too busy wasting time on computer games and ipad and on social media and are addicted to it. All of us have seen 1 to 2 year old children running around with iPhones trying to talk to Siri.

There is a four times higher risk of road accidents in distracted driver by use of cell phone and this incidence is at par with driving while intoxication. *Texting* while driving can increase the incidence of accidents up to 23 times higher.[98]

We must adjust to the waves of new technology and somehow abolish the divide between scientific progress and our ethics and morality. Our actions need to be in tune and in harmony with all aspects of life. Real-time videos on Facebook and Instagram have become new methods of news reporting. Smartphones have become eyes and ears for free press in uprisings and to highlight plight of disadvantaged people and authoritarian brutalities.

Artificial Intelligence will change world in the future. It may surpass humans' limitations. Imagine human brain and mind embedded in the computer chips. It seems that newer 'robomen' will probably replace entire workforce in future. Will it be 'awesome' or 'dishearteningly wearisome' for the human race? Only time will be the judge.

Despite triumphs of modern achievements in every sphere of life, one should keep on walking proudly to seek inner peace and happiness. Instead of getting disappointed by selfish modern day culture of being totally absorbed in texting, iTunes and iPads one can use modern social media in a positive way to find newer methods to reach and help all segments of society even in remote corners of the world and bring real joy and happiness by improving their life.

'I fear the day when the technology overlaps our humanity. The world will only have a generation of idiots.'

~ ALBERT EINSTEIN

All of us have seen many of such intellectuals (?) who are absorbed in their iPhones in social gatherings and in the parks (instead of admiring the nature and the surroundings).

CHAPTER 38

The spirit of Migration

The Lord said to Abraham, "Go from your country, your
people and your father's household to the land that I will
show you."

~ GENESIS 12:1

THE SOLE PURPOSE of migration is betterment of life to pursue happiness by
seeking new vistas and opportunities. Migration of civilization across the globe
has remained one of the significant aspects of human behavior dynamically
transforming the landscape with assimilation of different cultures, traditions
and values. This has been the story of humans from the times immemorial. Noah's Ark is the earliest migration story of creation in Genesis when
Patriarch Noah saves the world at Gods command.

Migration is well documented by historical, archeological, linguistic,
demographic and genetic methodology. Human migration individually or in
large groups from one place to another, many times long distances (across the
countries and continents) used to be a big challenge that has become easier in
the modern era of transportation and information technology.

Migration can be both voluntary and involuntary. It occurs constantly due
to changes in climate like draughts and inadequate distribution of resources
and services and opportunities. Besides man by inquisitive nature has the
natural instinct to explore the distant lands and oceans and settle temporarily or forever at the suitable area around the fertile shores of a river (full of

resources including easy transportation). Major civilizations had flourished around landscapes of rivers.

Forced migration due to human depravity, political and religious persecution and ethnic cleansing like Exodus and migration of Jews, bloody migration on India's partition in 1947 and displacement of Jews and Palestinians are some examples that leave a bitter taste that lasts forever. Other examples of forced involuntary migration include slave trade and trafficking of human beings for sex trade and prostitution. Around 59.5 million people were forced to flee from their homes due to war or persecution in 2014. Political refugees from war torn Middle East are swarming in thousands to European shores. In one estimate approximately 700 million people want to leave country of their birth; 13% of these want to immigrate to United States.

The Biological bases of Migration
Optimism is the key ingredient for settlers, whether voluntary or involuntary. They have to work hard to survive and excel to get accepted in order to blend with the newer lands and its cultures.

Migrating population has genetic predisposition to take challenges, whereas, sedentary non-migrating populations are in the habit of taking things for granted and passively accept their lot. Earliest pre-historical migration of our ancestors Homo sapiens began millions of years ago from the cradle of Africa across Eurasia, Asia, Europe and the New World.

The 'novelty-seeking genes' are involved in behavior genetics that transpires the spirit of adventure. Dopamine and Serotonin are feel-good neurotransmitters.[53,54] DRD4 (Dopamine Receptor –D4 subtype) is responsible for neuronal signaling in the mesolimbic area of the brain that regulates emotions and complex behavior. It is one of the most polymorphic DR genes studied.[18] These gene codes are responsible for even-temperedness and reflection, exploratory and impulse behavior, risk-taking and novelty tolerance. Population with repeated migration continues to possess genes favoring exploratory behavior. People with this forward-looking behavior with optimism seek fulfillment and happiness. Africa model is 4R allele and decreases in frequency as you move away; 2R is more frequent in East Asia, whereas, 7R is very frequent in some tribes in the New World.[54]

Another gene 5HTTLPR of Serotonin transport is responsible for development of stress-related disorders.[75] This genes frequency is less common in individualism versus collectivism cultures like United States versus Eastern cultures. Migrants in the New World have genetically optimistic temperament essential in the biology of happiness.

Genetically or not like other immigrants we are happily living in the United States, the land of optimism and opportunities. Our genetically driven novelty seeking, risk taking exploratory behavior has constantly pushed us to work hard, remain optimistic, and educate our children to the best of their abilities and potentials.

This is the story of you and me and every human being who ever crossed the boundaries of their confines. This is the story of generations that dared to seek the unique challenges in faraway foreign lands, assimilate in different cultures and values and found a newer place called 'the happy home' for their children and children's children.

In ancient times, we as migrants used to walk miles and miles on foot, or in carriages and on donkeys and horses, crossing rampant rivers and challenging oceans. Now are the easy times of technologic improvements where all information is on our fingertips, a few clicks away in our computer and foreign lands are unknown no more, distances are not measured in weeks and months but in hours of air travel. These are the dreams of forward looking hard working happy people that makes this country great and this world richer in its heritage. Franklin D. Roosevelt inspiringly said, "Remember, remember always, that all of us, and you and I especially, are descended from immigrants and revolutionists."

Endless global migration occurs at different times from different regions for different reasons to alight in adopted lands during their long journey of life to make a better place worth living happily for themselves and everyone else.

'The land flourished because it was fed from so many sources- because it was nourished by so many cultures and traditions and peoples."

~ Lyndon B Johnson

CHAPTER 39

Goodness, Good, Better and Best

'True religion is real living; living with all one's soul, with all one's goodness and righteousness.

~ ALBERT EINSTEIN

GOOD CHARACTER AND good qualities of a person brings one to the doorstep of real happiness. The word goodness stands alone for a great variety of gracious deeds and moral values. It stands for excellence of quality in any sphere of life for example, goodness of workmanship. It also can depict the best aspect of anything, reflecting on the essence of values and strengths. It can be part of a humble and pious act of graciousness, for example even if you don't agree with someone you have the goodness in you to be polite!

Good and the goodness touch the very moral fabric of human behavior. Goodness means a lot: your virtues, your character, your decency and integrity and your honesty and morality. It is an absolute term and cannot be compared. Many miseries in life are self-created from one's ego and jealousy. One becomes miserable when satisfaction and contentment of mind is disturbed by sharp pangs of jealousy and unnecessary comparison with others. Everyone is busy in having more and more materialistic possessions: better homes, better cars and more bank balance than others around him and in this process becomes miserable in pursuit of 'material things'.

Being good can be an absolute fulfilling and wholesome experience in life, bringing goodness in you to the forefront by exposing the hidden qualities in you. It is the realization of the fact that majority of the people are good and honest. By concentrating on good of the people you overlook their shortcomings that creates a feeling of love and compassion.

I have a long standing friendly dialogue with a friend of mine regarding the word 'good versus the best.' He always argues that good is an absolute term and is better than best, which is a comparative term. On the other hand, I believe in trying to be the best in everything as it is better than good. It is a no win situation for both of us. Once laughingly in a social gathering I confronted him in the presence of his newly wed daughter-in-law and said, "Won't you agree that your daughter-in- law is more than good, she is absolutely the best?" At this juncture he agreed with me and there was a huge laughter from all around. Hence I won the argument with him for the first and the only time.

Leaving this argument as a sideline issue, I was intrigued by the subject when I came across Zig Ziglar's book 'Better than Good- Creating a Life You Can't Wait to Live'.[124] Does it mean that there is something better than good and only word I could find in the dictionary is the 'best'? Ziglar advocates passionately pursuing everything in life and trying it hard and to not only being good at it but better than good. You constantly endeavor to uplift your course of action and thoughts beyond the point of goodness. Try to do better than good at all times.

The word 'goodness' is a virtue that stands for decency, excellence, graciousness, kindness, integrity and virtually best of anything and everything. It is an inclusive wholesome term without comparison, whereas, good, better and the best are comparative terms that can cause conflicts. Comparison is necessary for such things like judging competitive sports and academic achievements. Even looking at the better of the two football teams like Michigan versus Ohio State can start an unending debate.

Comparison of values and possessions emanates from self-pride that is egocentric. On the other hand, can anyone quantify kindness, compassion, love and selflessness? We are slaves to our egoistic thoughts and are inherently envious in our behavior.

A few years ago my four-year old grandson innocently asked, "Grandpa! Isn't my home bigger and better than your home?"

"Yes! Of course." I said with a smile.

"Grandpa, our television is bigger than yours?" Said my other grandson. Of course I nodded with a smile.

Well this is not only the present day culture but it has been inherent to human race forever. Young and old, innocent and the intellectuals are all the same. We need to improve our thought process and stop doing comparisons. It needs discipline of mind to learn to appreciate and to be kind and considerate. Our vanity and nasty vindictive remarks and showing off our possessions can remain hurtful to others forever. On the other hand, one never forgets the kind help that you give to someone in need. Even your polite sympathetic words of empathy are never forgotten.

Inculcating goodness in one's trait is the noblest quest. Goodness is of paramount importance in any sphere of life but most desirable in the medical profession. Physician's attitude is more valued than the medial degrees and scientific chutzpah.[9] He or she needs to be dedicated, compassionate with flawless understanding of patients concerns and should have an interminable desire to help and relate to their fears. Physician should work ethically and tirelessly in hope of their cure. This unique art in a good physician is gained by experience and is best displayed through humble self-reflection. During my practice as a trauma surgeon I have touched many lives in life and death situations and have experienced with tears of joy and of failures. I learnt my lessons every day to be humble and polite and hopefully have done some good to the others.

One should strive to be good to others. Humility instead of vanity and arrogance is virtuous. Whatever you do, do with enthusiasm, passion and concern and be considerate to others. A good hardworking farmer or an honest laborer is as valuable as a good banker, an engineer or a doctor or an astronaut. Passionate hard work of any kind that does not hurt anyone is essential goodness. What you think is good for you is good for all beings?

Random acts of kindness are most rewarding. Acts of goodness by strangers like helping the flood, tornado or earthquake victims are never forgotten. Even helping someone stranded with a flat tire is a very compassionate act. Helping the blind or the disabled person cross the street or offering them your seat in the bus or the train are good karma. Any act of kindness or goodness, even a small one can make a big difference. You can make the difference and brighten somebody's day by some kind, thoughtful, nice and caring act.

Everyone should inculcate the habit to pass-forward the good acts of love, kindness and compassion. Goodness is innate trait of all human beings. We are all born perfect as we see the reflections through the innocent eyes of a baby, and then gradually imperfections seep into our character invading our mind with impure thoughts, narcissism and ego. One needs to stop making comparisons and feel good or bad about oneself. Be good in your thoughts and actions. Be good at your work. Be good in following your goals. Be good and honest in your habits. Be good in whatever you do. Be good to your neighbor, your community, your nation and even the whole world. If you are good you will evaluate every one not with a myopic vision but with your kind and broader vision when the whole planet will look good. The human race needs to be defined by these magnificent acts of goodness and not by its worst composites. Goodness germinates happiness.

'But the fruit of spirit is love, joy, peace, longsuffering, gentleness, goodness, faith....'

- GALATIANS 5:22, KING JAMES BIBLE

CHAPTER 40

Happiness at Work

'Chose a job you love, and you will never have to work a day in your life.'

~ CONFUCIUS

JOB SATISFACTION IS paramount for overall well-being as it brings happiness not only at workplace but also at home and in other relationships. Positive atmosphere at work results in high self-esteem. A satisfactory work place is where job is appreciated and work is to your liking and work has to be good for your growth and for better opportunities. Also it should include satisfactory remuneration and work hours should leave sometime for social activities. However, such work opportunities are hard to come by. A perfect workplace can only be achieved by your positive aptitude that can transform your mind to adapt to your work environment when you work passionately with good work ethics.

It is a blessing if profession you choose is to your liking as wrong choices sometimes can cause chronic unhappiness and even depression.

OPTIMAL WORK HOURS FOR HAPPINESS

Happiness can be eroded by stress at the work place. People end up spending majority of their daily active time at the work place. A full time job is 40-hours a week and two thousand hours of work annually. However, many work at two or even three-part time jobs to make both ends meet. Too many hours at work increases fatigue, lowers morale and interferes with family life.

Since the beginning of last century labor unions in United States and United Kingdom fought for a 'short workday' from 12 to 10 hours a day. In 1914, after years of close scrutiny, Henry Ford doubled the salary of workers and cut down working hours from 9 to 8 hours per day. It caused uproar in business circles but resulted in high moral, better production and increased profitability. By the end of the century many businesses found significant increase in production and profitability when working hours were cut and workers were happy.[92] Excessive overtime, tiredness and lack of sleep cuts down efficiency.

According to Sara Robinson's Salon article, 'Bring Back The 40- Hours Work Week'[92]: 150 years of research proves that long hours at work kill profits, productivity and employees.

Professor James Vaupel from Denmark gives a newer concept of work, where everyone will work no more than 25 hours a week but everyone will have to work till they are 80-years of age.[111] This will leave significant free time to spend with the family when they are young. 'Elderly who work part-time are healthier and happier.'

'The 4-Hour Workweek' by Timothy Ferriss has also been suggested to create a better life balance.(2007)[33]

For workers' genuine interest, about 6-hours a day, 30 hours a week is most appropriate to bring most efficiency and productivity with good time to spare for other activities. Surprisingly too many hours of overwork delayed Apple's Mac project.[92] 'Productivity experts estimate that we'd have probably had the Mac a year sooner if they'd worked half as many hours per week instead.'[92]

Too many work hours in medical training during residency is an obstacle to decision-making that potentially can put patients' safety at risk. During our residency days in 1970's, at times we thought we were doing a slave labor. Don't misunderstand it as hard work is paramount to gain experience and is a hallmark of any resident's and medical student's life in training. Misconception was that most peers always define hard work if they see you working at odd hours like very early in the morning or very late in the evening till 8 or 9 pm when you should have worked only till 5 or 6 pm. We were on in-house call every 3rd night and in some rotations every other night, in addition to the full day's work, thus working uninterrupted for 36 to 40 hours, and then to report again the following morning. Sometimes we found hardly any time to eat or snatch couple of hours of sleep while on call.

One incident stands out in my mind. Once my wife came to the hospital with our 2-year old son (she was on call previous day as a resident). She brought some home cooked dinner for me around 7 o'clock in the evening. She slipped on the stairs at the hospital, ended up having evaluation in the emergency department, had x-rays and was found to have a fracture of her ankle. She was given a cast and crutches (with hardly any training as to how to walk). My chief resident was kind enough to grant me *one-hour break* to take my family home, which was less than a mile away. I went home, dragged the crib next to her bed, put a glass of water with pain pills and two bottles of milk (for the baby) on the table next to her and hurriedly went back to work. I come back home to take care of them after 22 hours (next day evening). There are so many other stories and such incidents that I don't want to elaborate. I am sure all residents have their own similar stories to share.

Now the times have changed and the medical resident work hours have been reformed to some extent. The Accreditation Council for Graduate Medical Education implemented substantial changes to the work-hour guidelines in 2003 with 80-hour/week limit and newer better guidelines were implemented in 2011.

Long work hours, even up to 12 to 16 hours a day 7-days a week in many countries especially in private sector are alarming, Long hours' result in fatigue and lower their proficiency, competency, productivity and moral. The reasonable work hours are essential to preserve a healthy life style and a happier family life.

IMPACT OF WORKPLACE

Work in context of Karma is part of life as it occupies a center stage in our productive years. We get educated in various professions in younger age preparing for this lifelong passion for work and in relinquishing part of it in retirement years to partially renounce responsibilities. Work is the fuel that keeps the wheels of life in motion. There are so many ingredients to make workplace a happy media for fulfillment of ambitions.

Stress at Workplace: There are so many challenges at work like pay, working hours, demands complicated by availability, competition, jealousy, commuting distances, and work environment.[61] There is nothing black or white as everything is relative. There can be exploitation, unfriendly environment or element of injustice at workplace like overtime reimbursement.

Repetitive activities give rise to boredom unless you have the habit of being passionately involved in whatever you do. Challenges at work need be balanced: neither too little to cause boredom nor too much to cause anxiety. Challenges are willingly undertaken to tap newer opportunities. Work is more than earning wages. YOU need to make a mental connection to have a positive attitude at work to enjoy it and to succeed as well as to excel and to have job satisfaction and finally to be happy.[61] Twenty percent of American workers report total absorption in activities at work so as to lose track of time.

Stress at Workplace varies in different professions depending on work place culture, competitive environment and interrelationships between the co-workers and their superiors. It can be friendly and helpful or be competitive and cutthroat full of jealousy backbiting and favoritism.

Surprisingly a new research by Sarah Damaske from Penn State University published on line in Social Science and Medicine journal in May, 2014 revealed a lower level of stress related hormone -cortisol when at work compared to home. This finding was irrespective of type of work, whether they were single or married or liked their job or not. The difference was more in individuals with children. The cortisol level was same (at home and at work) for those earning more than $75,000 annually. Women are happier at work than men. Decreased stress at work may be related to many factors: you get paid at work, become more proficient with time, excel at work and are appreciated. Behavior etiquettes at work prohibit distractions that are common at home.

Work passionately to find 'happiness at work and work for happiness.'

'The best preparation for good work tomorrow is to do good work today.'

~ ELBERT HUBBARD

CHAPTER 41

Mind over Heart or The Heart over Mind?

'Educating the Mind without educating the Heart is no educa-
tion at all.'

~ ARISTOTLE

THERE IS A complex link between the mind, the heart, the soul and the happiness. This is further complicated by the ever-intruding selfish ego. There
are two voices, one of the mind and the other of the heart. Basically the mind
reasons loudly in our brain while the heart quietly suggests like a whisper.
The rational intellectual faculty is represented by the mind (head), whereas,
the faculty of emotions is represented by the heart. There is a conflict between
heart as to 'what we want to pursue' and the mind 'as to what we feel as practical'. Happiness lies in harmonious relationship between the two, our inner
feelings as to what we want and the discerning power of rationalization and
logic, while, their conflict results in indecision that snatches away one's composure leading to anxiety, pain, anger and frustration with uneasiness of the
mind (brain- headache?) and the heart (heartache?). We lose lots of energy
and time in this conflict of indecision that makes our daily life miserable and
worrisome.

There is frequently a dichotomy in our thoughts and actions and in our
choices posed by the heart and the mind. Indecision is the cause of many
inner conflicts that takes away our sleep, our composure and most of all our
peace of mind and happiness. How can one remain calm if the mind and

the heart are at odds having a recurring battle? Indecisiveness is the conflict between the cool mind and the warm heart or a 'calm mind, healthy heart.'

Mind listens to reason and logic and gives the options that are practical but may not always be perfect. It tries to assess pros and cons and give some direction that is loaded with multiple choices and thoughts. It portrays a multidimensional physical prospective based on past experiences. It rationalizes, organizes and interprets the physical reality of the present situation. It gives us choices and a practical plan of action. Mind is knower of the past. However, it has limited power over predictability of future. It can help suppress the emotions with some logic. It stipulates and warns about the consequences of our actions and can easily say 'no' to the heart.

Heart softly and calmly suggests what need to be done and simply asks us to 'do this' without giving any reason or logic. It follows emotions and feelings that make us feel good and happy irrespective of the consequences or the opinion of others. It reflects and mirrors the image of our inner-self. We need to have faith and a belief in our feelings as heart has an insight. It has the futuristic eye that can map and imagine in multiple ways. The heart is the source of a subconscious instinct that at times works as a compass to guide. Don't always ignore your intuitions. It is famously said, 'Follow your heart wherever it leads.'[110]

At a crossroad one needs a solution to find the right choice that is 'good and advantageous' to you. Best is to pick that choice, concentrate on that 'one thought' to arrive at your decision? Asking yourself as to what is 'best for you' usually brings that choice to the forefront. More often we are inclined to listen to our hearts even though it may be something simple and impulsive.

These conflicts between the head and the heart need to be resolved amicably to avoid tension and indecision. Heart silently puts the idea in our mind, which in turn pursues it. Take an example you happen to be around a food court in a shopping mall where the sight and smell of food entices your heart as 'I want to have two scoops of ice cream.' Mind tells you to go and get it to satisfy and please yourself. Now you have to make the 'right choice' as to what is best for you and to your advantage. Your rationalize as 'you know you are a diabetic, your blood sugar is already difficult to control and eating ice cream will only make it worse. It is not the right choice for you.'

You need to educate your mind to help follow the right choice and not necessarily be interference. While driving you have a tendency to over-speed to reach your destination quickly and in time while your logical mind tells you to obey the speed limit and to take is easy and take your time and stay cool.

Feelings of empathy, compassion, kindness, and humility are all the echoes coming silently like a whisper from the depth of your heart. Concentrate on your heart at the time of conflict and indecision to bring in all these feelings of togetherness to the forefront to resolve the issue. Seek the wisdom of your heart and the intellect to usher happiness.

In Kabbalah, the mind is cool and damp like 'water' and the heart is hot and dry like 'fire'.[49] The mind is objective and observes reality through five organs of perception, it is the 'perceiver' that oversees the body, it needs intellect to discern, whereas, the heart is the one that 'experiences' all the excitements and indulges in subjective feelings. There should be cohesive balance between the mind and the heart. A discord between these two forces in life lead to dissonance, confusion and imbalance akin to a divorce.

When you fall in love follow the cues from your heart. Mind has only a collaborative role. Unless you follow your heart you may suffer rest of your life as love is said to be blind with no rationalization.

'Broken-heart syndrome' mimics heart attack symptoms without any coronary-heart disease. Symptoms of heartache are triggered by strong physical or emotional stress like anger and anxiety or grief of death or terminal illness of near one's, according to Harmony Reynolds, MD. This results from autonomic imbalance due impaired parasympathetic nervous system (PNS). PNS helps body to calm down. Various deep breathing techniques, diaphragmatic breathing, pranayama, meditation and mindfulness can heal and prevent broken heart syndrome. Famous Hollywood actress Carrie Fisher of Star Wars fame where she starred as Princess Lela died on December 27, 2016 after suffering a heart attack. A day letter her mother, famous actress Debby Reynolds suddenly died. She probably died from broken heart due to sudden extreme grief.

'Heart is a conceptual center in the mind from where all positive and noble thoughts of love and tenderness, kindness and charity, devotion and surrender, constantly spring up. One should let the mind function in the dignity in the lotus of the heart.'[19]

It is mute question as to what is better, mind over heart or heart over mind? None is better than an amicable and pragmatic approach, where an individual makes the choice most suitable and advantageous to him or her. Treat the heart and the mind as equals and work synergistically with a pragmatic approach keeping peace of mind to preserve happiness.

'To be kind is more important than to be always right.
Sometimes all what we need is not an intelligent mind that
speaks but a patient heart that listens.'

~ Unknown

CHAPTER 42

Stress Disparages Happiness

'The greatest weapon against stress is our ability to choose one thought over another.'

~ WILLIAM JAMES

LIFE IS INTERTWINED with attachments and expectations that lead to host of behavioral changes gravitating to mostly myriad of negative attitudes. Every act or event in life has cause and effect relationship. The real challenge for the treatment of effects and effective behaviors should be to root out the causes rather than treat the symptoms. Presently we can't change the genetic predisposition, which modifies some behaviors. Resentment, anxiety, fear and anger as the major sources of stress need be eliminated. The stress needs to be avoided and remedied to remove this major obstacle to happiness.

The stress can be physical, mental or emotional strain or tension that easily results from variety of day-to-day challenges at home or at workplace or other everyday encounters. One of causes is when a person perceives that the demands exceed his or her resources; there is a lack of affordability of both personal and social resources that the individual is able to muster.

Physical stress is bodily reaction to various triggers like physical trauma or a recent surgery. Physical and emotional stress is interrelated resulting in insomnia, indigestion, stomach cramps, loneliness, low self-esteem and depression.

Stress in life can result from both pleasant (eustress) and unpleasant (distress) events or encounters. It is not uncommon to see 'fight or flight' response in *'acute stress'* with output of hormones catecholamines and corticoids that results in high blood pressure, palpitation with increased heart rate and rapid breathing, flushing of face, excessive sweating, trembling, weakness and fatigue.

Chronic stress on the other hand is a part of daily living with day-to-day challenges at home and at workplace. Euphoria of 'eustress' is motivational whereas negativity of 'distress' poses health hazards. Inability to adapt to challenges of stress erodes health in general affecting both the cardiovascular (high blood pressure, heart attacks) and immune systems. It can also lead to insomnia, depression, suicidal ideation and decreased life expectancy from various factors. Levels of bad cholesterol (LDL: Low Density Lipoprotein) increase due to chronic stress. All these lead to a cascade of health problems.

'*Stress syndrome*' elicits first alarm stage, then stage of resistance by the body and ultimately stage of exhaustion, when all overburdened adaptive mechanisms fail endangering life.

Desires and cravings emanate from a self-centered egoistic mind that clouds our wisdom to be oblivious to reality that 'You as being are no different from other-beings.'

We all have conflicts due to attachments and aversions, likes and dislikes and *expectations and demands*. When someone fails to do an act that we like and expect it leads to stress, anger and agitation of mind. When we fail to come up to other's expectations it also creates feeling of hurt and guilt leading to stress within our minds. It is difficult to read someone else's mind and their expectations.

Everyone tends to like the friends better as one expects little or nothing from them. This is in contrast to family members as closer the relationships higher are the expectations. In a way entire world is full of a spectrum of relationships bound not only by blood but also by friendships and different roles we play in the world.

We have to *accept the people as they are.* Love is always 'as-is' without asking for a change. We can change ourselves but can't change others. At the most we can kindle only the spirit of a change in others.

Every person is imperfect by any yardstick, a mixture of virtues and shortcomings or limitations. When our expectations remain unfulfilled there is anger and stress with resulting unhappiness. We have to have relationships without undue expectations. We have to learn to handle the element of dislikes metaphorical to gentle handling of the stem of roses that is always full of thorns.

Motivation at work place for self-advancement is a requisite for progress but try not to blame yourself when your expectations are not met, as it will lead to stress.

Failure to remove causes of stress lies in our inability to grasp true realities of life. A positive outlook and its adaptation in life can resolve stress. Negative attitude in life, on the other hand, increases and precipitate stress.

One should avoid Stressors that trigger stress. There are too many variable causative factors. It is helpful to keep a journal and try to avoid the tasks or habits that predisposes or triggers stress. It can be a hectic life style or a stressful job. Obsessive compulsive shopping and too many bills to pay increase stress. It can be some bad habit like smoking, drinking, gambling and procrastination. Bad driving habits, texting, excessive TV, drugs and other addictions and unhealthy lifestyles can lead to a guilt feeling causing stress.

Physiologically stressed individuals have autonomic imbalance with impaired parasympathetic activity. Parasympathomimetics relaxes mind and reduces stress. Yoga, meditation (chapter 56) and mindfulness (chapter 57) relax mind and reduce stress. Deep breathing stimulates the vagus nerve and by its parasympathetic action reduces heart rate and relaxes the mind. It is a simple way to reduce anxiety, anger and stress. Please see stress related 'Broken Heart syndrome' in the previous chapter 41.

Try to do one task at a time and do the tasks that you like if practical. Learn how to say 'no' gracefully and diplomatically if you don't have time or don't like to do certain tasks. Lack of free time due to too many commitments increases your stress.

Stress management must include elimination of causative factors of stress and a change of lifestyle with a positive demeanor. Other psychological therapies including mindful meditation and medications to help alleviate anxieties and stress and relax mind are also beneficial.

A *mental health evaluation* is desirable for stress management when it is persistent, recurrent or resistant to simple techniques of management or when confronted with depression with thoughts of harm to self and others.

SOME GENERAL TIPS TO REDUCE STRESS:
'*Practice Positive Thinking*' is the key to relieve stress. Once your attitude changes all your apprehensions will be replaced by a relaxed mind.

'*Avoid Stressors*' that trigger stress.

'*Simplify your life*'. Engage in healthy habits, balanced diet and physical activities.

Better Work Habits: Get organized, finish jobs in time, don't be late to work and don't procrastinate or clutter.

Quit bad habits to avoid undue stress.

Inculcate good habits and be positive. Instead of criticism learn to praise others.

Be a patient listener to understand others' point of view and learn to laugh and enjoy.

Build relationships and surround yourself with good company.

Be Compassionate and considerate and be humble, helpful, kind and soft-spoken.

Have 'Faith in yourself' as only then others will have faith in you.

Physical Activities and Free Time for Yourself is necessary to reduce stress and to be happy. Learn to enjoy a relaxed walk and leave time to read a good book.

Learn to 'relax and enjoy' and to have a good company.

Use Relaxing Techniques like yoga, meditation and mindfulness to relax mind and reduce stress. Participate in-group and social activities and try to help others.

Remember every problem will find a solution sooner or later. One must learn to ride the roller coaster of complex life laughingly to preserve self-esteem and happiness.

'The key to winning is poise under stress.'

~ *PAUL BROWN*

CHAPTER 43

Enigma of Myths and Superstitions

'Old myths, old Gods, old heroes never died. They are only sleeping at the bottom of our mind, waiting for our call. We have need for them. They represent wisdom of our race.'

~ STANLEY KUNITZ

HAPPINESS AND PEACE of mind is interwoven with various myths and superstitions. Psychological effect of certain myths, traditions and values can have changes in human behavior depending on intensity of one's beliefs. There is a connection between myths and happiness and also myths about happiness.

Connection between happiness and myths is a fine line depending on intensity of one's beliefs. So long it does not affect others negatively, holding on to your strong beliefs can be beneficial. To tell a young child that Saint Nicholas coming down the chimney with the presents on Christmas night is a pure myth will only dishearten a child and snatch away his or her happy anticipation.

Myth is named after Greek word 'mythos' meaning a story or a word. Ancient Greek mythology deals with study and teachings of its gods and goddesses, their religious practices and other traditions and superstitions. Paganism comprises ancient mythical polytheistic religious practices with Pagan gods and other beliefs. Modern scholars study myths in an attempt to understand religious and political practices of civilization, and to gain understanding of the mystery of myths.

The myths are collection of narratives of many aspects of human and superhuman endeavors dealing with the God, his creations, origin and nature of the universe. Myths can also be related to religions, civilizations and the cultures of olden days. These are historical elaborations evolving from truthful depictions, rituals, and traditions and these can be in part fictions, with or without actual or perceived supernatural characterizations of historical events. Many myths are considered to be sacred and true by their believers. Many myths are obviously supernatural that cannot be explained by any stretch of scientific methodology, as they don't follow the laws of nature. These can be eerie and disconcerting without any rationale or logic. Are the individuals with magical control over nature or other paranormal powers superhuman or pure myths?

The followers of the religious sects create many of these myths by giving them supernatural divine descriptions. Most of the myths can't be truly assessed by any scientific methodology or explanations. Many religious stories are narrated from generation to generation. Religious and educational values are interwoven in these stories. To make these stories interesting and absorbing many fascinating and colorful exaggerated imaginary incidents and fictitious characters are added. Many miracles and supernatural happenings are engrained in many stories that cannot be explained by the laws of nature and are illogical. With times these become our strong religious beliefs, immutable and true. Other open-minded people call these religious myths. Many call irrational belief in those unexplainable supernatural events and characters blind faith.

Mythology is considered by many believers to be true accounts and stories of the past, whereas, false stories are 'fables'. 'Legends' are true stories of the recent past. Many 'folk-tales' are fictitious or half-truths woven to create heroes for their cultural values. Sometimes, it is difficult to distinguish between myths and legends. When a religious myth gets disconnected from the religion that strong particular belief becomes a legend. People take offense when someone labels their strong historical religious beliefs as myths; they defend those as true revelations.

Can the quest of happiness be accomplished by blind-faith in religious beliefs? Are the myths essential for happiness in life? Without myths the study of the history and culture will not be fascinating or thought provoking. We have transformed myths into petals and a collection of these makes flowers that enriche the cultural landscape. Our religions and cultures are so much intertwined that sometimes disbelief in one aspect ends up shaking its very foundation. Most of us have strong beliefs and convictions, many of these can be totally false, but these are so much connected to our psyche that mere challenge to these leads to outrage and unhappiness of mind.

Sometimes it takes years and centuries to slowly build a myth about a belief that slowly becomes part of human acceptance and gets engraved in the mind as the truth. We know that many of our cultural and political myths are pure fancies like superiority of one race or cast over another, or athletic superiority of a race. Science and reasoning is unable to crystalize many of these concepts, only the time can demystify some of these erroneous beliefs? Human life is enmeshed in the web of our cultures that have taken eons to make. Right or wrong, we live and breathe in those values,. These are our realities and truths beyond any doubts. Myths, surely, can increase self-esteem and pride that help keep diverse cultures from disintegration.

Myths have been ascribed as 'the divine echo of the truth' that is 'fundamental' to the strong beliefs. We normally defend our own myths as true reflections of reality but question someone else's beliefs as unrealistic. Jesus walking on water or Moses crossing the red sea with his fellow Israelites is thought to be a biblical truth. Hanuman flying and bringing back big mountain with medicinal herbs in Ramayana is considered a truth in Hindu Philosophy.

Superstitions are false beliefs where one event supposedly leads to another without any logical or scientific bases, like things went wrong because it is Friday the 13th or because your path was crossed by a cat in the morning and similar other premonitions. These are irrational beliefs especially in regards to the unknown. These have nonsensical bases and create undue fright or expectations. Superstitions can be both good and evil and can be based on any concept in life. These include witchcraft, black magic, voodoo and also spirits and omens, haunted houses and other distorted traditions and beliefs that contradict factual science. These can vary in different cultures, traditions, religions and geographical regions. There are both good luck and bad luck superstitions like knocking on wood, crossing fingers, ringing of the bells on happy occasions to frighten evil spirits away, a black cat crossing your path causing bad luck or the Russian belief that bird-poop on your car or property brings riches. Many of superstitions are based on symbolisms and rituals but their origin and meaning is lost. Astrology is not a verifiable science that can cause undue hopes and unfair superstitions.

Are there ghosts? Do dead people haunt you as ghosts and evil spirits? Do they exist or are they part of fairy tales or fiction in books? Are they part of supernatural movies created just to entertain and frighten?

Superstitions are illogical beliefs that needn't be taken seriously. You don't have to confront others to argue about their false beliefs but a smile with or without telling them that you don't believe in theses fantasies is enough. Take it as an entertainment value without making fun of anyone. After all myths and superstitions are good topics to explore with light humor as long it does not harm others.

Personally one should free oneself of superstitions by acquiring knowledge and sound reasoning with a logical mind and intellect. Bad luck superstitions bring undue fear and fright and good luck superstitions bring false hopes and disappointment when they do not materialize. All you need is strong logical mind without transgressing other's beliefs.

Pursue your myths and superstitions so long these don't harm others. Don't make fun of others if they do believe in and you don't. Let everyone be happy in his or her conceptions and illusions.

'Fear is the main source of superstition, and one of the main sources of cruelty. To conquer fear is the beginning of wisdom.'

~ Bertrand Russell

CHAPTER 44

Habits are the Key to Happiness

'Motivation is what gets you started, Habit is what keeps you going.'

~ JIM RYUN

HABITS ARE A set pattern of the routines of behavior that are automatically repeated. These occur at subconscious level without a person's awareness. These more or less fixed patterns of habits are acquired sets of behavior reinforced in the mind by their repetitive use. Personal habits develop during childhood and constantly evolve in the beginning and then become a set pattern. Old habits are difficult to relinquish or replace and new habits are not easy to cultivate.

Basal ganglion in the brain is the site of habit-forming behavior. It is also responsible for development of emotions, memory and pattern-recognition. Pre-frontal cortex is responsible for decision-making. When decisions take an automatic routine pattern a sequence of habitual actions take place with little or no involvement of brain, which is spared and is free to participate in other activities.[30]

We perform so many routine activities every day that are a part of habits. We have learnt these habits by experience and by repetitive actions like driving, parallel parking, playing sports, writing or working on computer or performing other simple tasks as well as operating intricate machinery. So many steps in a set of activities occur automatically by habit driven by subconscious.

You need to read Charles Duhigg book 'The Power of Habit'[30] to fully understand the subject. Normally there is a cue or a trigger that sets automatic

176

unfolding of a set of actions. In the habit-loop after the action there is a reward or an accomplishment that makes it worthwhile.[30] This pattern is well recognized in circus, where an animal performs an act on a cue and is thereafter rewarded with some form of a treat. Same pattern is evident in the whales' jump and other acrobats performed by various animals at the SeaWorld.

We take for granted innumerable habits in day-to-day living. On waking up we go to kitchen, make tea or coffee and drink it. We take shower, change clothes and go to work. We sit in a car, drive few miles and reach our workplace. We don't concentrate on details of driving, acceleration, deceleration, taking a turn or stopping at the red-light as all these automatic actions are part of our learnt routine of habits.

However, certain pattern of behavior can be changed like on an off day or during vacation one can wake up late and get attuned to a more relaxed attitude. Some habits quickly build up in face of changing environment. If you are having vacation in a cruise liner you quickly temporarily acquire habits of overeating, taking extra meals or snacks or ice cream many times a day just because it is available. You look forward to multiple courses at the formal dinner and are still looking for a snack around midnight. As soon as you come back home, you quickly revert back to normal routine: habits of work, gym and controlled and balanced diet. These are the miracles of mind, the changing of the routines and habits in the changing environments.

Everyone has good and bad habits the fulcrum of your character is defined by tilts towards the side that predominates. Most of us are hardly aware of our habits. You need to do some introspection or ask a well-wisher or a friend to point out your bad habits. If you want to point out some of the bad habits in your friend, first make a list of his good habits and congratulate him for it before you gently remind him about his undesirable bad habits. It is appropriate to discuss good and bad habits amongst friends in a relaxed atmosphere and in privacy in a non-serious manner and begin the conversation by making fun of yourself by enumerating your own bad habits first.

Most annoying bad habits are picking nose and nail biting. The list of bad habits is long and depressing. The list includes: binge drinking, overspending, gambling, stealing, cheating, smoking and overeating junk food to name a few. In modern times these also include watching excessive television, overindulgence in Facebook or Twitter, texting while driving and being glued to the smartphone or the iPad even in a social gathering. Many of us have bad habit of overly criticizing others, procrastinating, being always late and tardy and unreliable, frequently complaining and interrupting others. Imposing and advising without being asked and always trying to dominate the conversation are not desirable traits. We can be uncompromising, short-tempered, lonely, selfish and depressed and worst of all addicted to drugs. We may habitually associate with losers creating a vicious cycle with a downward spiral in life. The list can go on and on.

Good habits are activities that make you happy, where goals are prioritized with positive will power and where you accept your failures as gates opening for better opportunities. When you do things with high self-assurance without seeking approval of others. Instead of being proud and defiant you are humble, helpful, considerate and gracious. You are benevolent and associate with kind and noble people.

Introspection is desirable from time to time to find one's bad habits and replace those with good ones. You need a positive willpower, a new focus and determination and repetitive reminders to do it. To quell a really bad habit one of the ways is to create 'post-it' reminders all around you. [30] If you are listening to somebody and you have an urge to interrupt because of your bad habit, repeat in your mind that 'I am not going to interrupt.' If you succeed reward yourself with a compliment for being successful in your accomplishment. To replace a bad habit one needs to change newer set of actions to a defined trigger with some sort of a reward.[30] You may fail in the beginning but repetitive attempts to change can be fruitful in a few weeks' time.

A transition by replacing bad habits by good habits can increase self-esteem. It can wipe out inner fears of uncertainties and bring peace and happiness of mind. Good habits glitter on the gates of happiness.

'Bad habits are our enemies because they hinder us for being the person we want to be.'

~ JOYCE MEYER

CHAPTER 45

'Yes...', 'Nooo', 'Maybe'- Learning the Art

*'A nice person is a 'yes' person, whereas a good person is a person
who accepts their responsibility in things and moves forward
and tries to constantly evolve and isn't afraid to say 'no' or challenge someone or be honest or truthful.'*

~ MIRANDA KERR

YOU ARE PULLED and pushed in different directions with various demands by your family. These include your children's activities, demands and expectations by their schools, your relatives, friends and neighbors and also at place of work and the community, where saying 'yes' is the only reasonable alternative to a disappointing 'no' to various roles you end up playing. One should learn the way to master the art and diplomacy of saying 'yes' 'no' or 'maybe'.

Neuroscientists believe that negative information like rejection creates a bigger surge of activity in the cerebral cortex than positive one. This makes it more difficult to forget negative hurtful memories that work as protective mechanism to remind us to avoid such circumstances in the future.

You play different roles at different stages in life; therefore, it is essential to prioritize these roles based on your commitments. You play a unique role as a student, as a spouse, as a father, as a son and lastly at place of work where an honest work should be your only priority. Proper care for your body including nourishment and exercise and however, some free time for personal or family entertainment are pertinent to keep a healthy body and a healthy mind. Important tasks for your day-to-day needs should be accomplished before you spare your time for something else. The jobs that give you satisfaction are worth pursuing. It is always important to find time for the community and for other compassionate deeds. It is crucial to inculcate these habits from the very young age to develop a kind and considerate demeanor for rest of your life.

We are surrounded by so many situations and requests in everyday life that we have to learn the art of this uncomfortable option as to how to say 'no' in life. Life is full of relationships and interactions that pulls you in different directions that saying 'yes' or 'no' or perhaps 'maybe' should be the norm in life, but it is not perceived that way. Typically the answer 'no' to anything is considered rude and impolite, whereas 'yes' is precisely the opposite. The polite answer 'maybe' lies somewhere in between yielding some personal choice.

An affirmative answer can unnecessarily increase stress in life. One usually feels guilty when you say 'no' to any request especially in a face-to-face encounter. But one has to prioritize and commit wisely and carefully.

Most people are good by nature. The character and trait of a person depends on his mind and intellect influenced by his upbringing, his education and various other factors. Human behavior can be summarized in two words as being 'nice or nasty'.[110] Considerate and helpful individuals are nice and they expect others to be holding the same values. In absence of these values in due course they invariably get angry and stressed. These nice individuals are afraid of offending others by saying uncomfortable word 'no'. In this process of trying to be too nice they lose their own health, wealth and happiness. You end up saying 'yes' when you really intend to say 'no'. Saying 'yes' all the time takes a toll on you and your personal relationships. 'They are too nice for their own good' and should learn the art of saying 'no'.[40]

Even saying 'no' to charities and worthwhile causes is prudent and logical for lack of resources or time. Even billionaires with big charitable trusts can't help each and every cause in the world. They help only a selected few and say 'no' to most other requests.

If someone feels close enough to ask you the favor to do something you typically feel obligated to entertain such request in affirmation and say 'yes' instead of saying 'no'. But by the same token by saying yes all the time you are fulfilling somebody else's wishes and not yours.

One is naturally disappointed when you say 'no' and it may create a friction. This 'no' word has lots of anxiety and lasting repercussions. Under certain circumstances especially at work place your superiors are not accustomed to hearing 'no' as the answer and expect you to work with a smile, no matter what the cost is.

There are of course circumstances where 'no' should be the logical answer and rather than saying 'no' you may keep quiet and work or do the work that is not yours in the first place or you work on things that you dislike or are uncomfortable doing it. This creates anxiety, anger and stress in your life. Best way to decline a request is to plan ahead and say 'no' in a gentle tone. If request comes totally unexpectedly reserve your answer: a 'yes or no' for a later date and time. Be consistent with your reply inspite of being asked repeatedly. This concept seems selfish on the surface but one should balance the time between what you enjoy doing or what you have to do. Getting stuck with work that you don't want will not only make you not happy but also increase your stress and misery. If you honestly can't comply any request learn the art to politely saying this 'no' word with various adjectives like:

"No, thank you...Sorry, not this time...I appreciate you asking me but sorry I can't help you due to prior commitments...No, I am sorry I can't help you...I will very much like to help but sorry I have other deadlines."

At times you have the option of meeting half way of the request or substitute their request with something else like: "Sorry, I am very busy I cannot spare all day but 'maybe' I will try to come for an hour or so if possible." Decision is yours.

"Sorry I can't help cooking due to other priorities but I can bring cookies...No, I am sorry I am not the right person for this project...." Give other options and let them pick and chose

You have to be genuinely polite and sorry for saying 'no' to avoid burning your bridges. However, you always should spare sometime for compassionate altruistic deeds of your liking in your time frame as it brings inner happiness and joy as it adds a 'purpose to your life'.

'A 'No' uttered from the deepest conviction is better than a 'Yes'
merely uttered to please, or worse, to avoid trouble.'

~ MAHATMA GANDHI

Part Five

The Spiritual Life

CHAPTER 46

Objectives in Life

'Spare sometime 'to reflect on as to what we seek in life...the search for a purpose (in life) is an elemental human quest - one we tend to put off...how an ordinary person can create an extraordinary change.'

~ NICHOLAS D. KRISTOF

PURSUIT OF HAPPINESS is goal of all human beings. However, the true goal and the purpose of our existence in life is defined in Vedic philosophy of Hinduism by 'purusartha'.[17,19,20,24,113] Word 'purusha' in Sanskrit means- man or an individual and 'artha' means- objectives of the human being. Purusartha stands for 'that which is sought by man; human purpose and the pursuit to the aim, or the end.' Purusha does not literally means a man in physical sense but the very soul of the individual self that cannot be defined by any gender. There are four human goals to lead a virtuous purposeful life in the world.

1. Ethical goals ('Dharma'): Right, lawful, moral and religious duties.
2. Material goals ('Artha'): Prosperity in acquiring wealth, materialistic possessions and other comforts in life.
3. Social goals ('Kama'): Pleasures to enjoy (including having children) in life for healthy existence.
4. Spiritual goals ('Moksha or Moksa'): Spiritual liberation or salvation and freedom from desires and sufferings. Moksha leads to salvation from cycle of birth and rebirth and unification with The Creator.

These are the blueprints, drafted and engraved to define purpose of life. So long as your material ('artha') and social ('kama') pursuits are based on ethical goals ('dharma') you can attain salvation ('moksha') even in your lifetime.[52] These objectives address the defining principals of living a disciplined harmonious life. Each component is like a wheel that is absolutely essential for a smooth ride, where life is a metaphor to a car or the carriage, traveling well balanced on all of its four wheels.

The True Ethical conduct of life - *Dharma*

Dharma in Sanskrit means 'purpose in life', what holds together and maintains cosmic order. It is the moral, ethical and virtuous practice that upholds, supports and maintains regulatory righteous order of the universe. It encompasses a large range of ideas such as duty, vocation and religion with correct, proper, ethical and righteous behavior. Education of mind and intellect with spiritual guidance leads to discovery of inner-self and helps fulfill the purpose in life by enriching one's life and life of fellow human beings. Many religions like Hinduism, Jainism, Buddhism and Sikhism preach living in compliance with dharma, which brings one closer to 'moksha' or 'nirvana'. Dharma also refers to teachings of Buddha (Buddhism) and Mahavira (Jainism).

'Let a man utter what is true; let him say what is pleasing. Let him say what is good for the other, even though it may offend him,' Manu IV, 138-9[24,71] 'There are many people who will say sweet things to please and flatter others; but rarely is a man who would say and hear the truth which is unpleasant to his ears but really conducive to his good.' (Vidhur Niti) It is our ethical duty not to mislead anyone.

Dharma not only incudes our duties to maintain, nourish and preserve our body and purify our mind and soul but also our duties (dharma) to our family, our neighbors, our community, other human beings, and our country and to the whole world. Knowingly neglecting our duty is betrayal of our dharma. One who is persistent in discharging his prescribed duties will not only attain immortality but also fulfillment of all his desires in the present life. (Manusmriti 2.5)[24,71]

The Material Prosperity - *Artha*

Artha means 'wealth' which is one of the vital pillars of worldly life. Everything requires money to acquire essentials (food, water, sanitation, education, house to live, health care etcetera) and comforts in life. Even possessions considered comforts or luxuries in the past have become necessities of life like a computer, a refrigerator or even a car. You need money to build roads and airports and to run any educational, religious and charitable institutions. Material possessions include minerals like gold and silver, factories, farmhouses, oil wells, research and development centers and all sources for generating energy. Even human work force are material wealth.

All kind of wealth is needed for sustenance of life. Without these resources life can be a living hell.

Accumulation of wealth and material possessions are acceptable, as much as you want, so long as you acquire these by lawful means and without deception, pretense, false premises, corruption, coercion or by overwhelming greed.[24] It is prudent to share some of your wealth and material possessions with the needy, the poor, the disabled and the elderly. These altruistic acts are essential gifts for the personal and overall happiness.

The satisfaction of worldly desires - *Kama*

Fulfillment of worldly desires and other legitimate pleasures of life are essential characteristics of Kama in life. In a sense the life is incomplete without these pleasures, so long as there is no overindulgence. One enjoys the pleasures in life through sense organs- eyes to admire the beauty, tongue to taste all kind of foods, ears to hear the melodies, nose to indulge all types of fragrances and skin to touch experiencing the ultimate pleasure of feelings and being physically intimate. Enjoyment of these sensual bodily and mental pleasures is the third objective of life- Kama.[113] The desire for sex is also Kama. 'This Kama (sex drive) is the motive force of the wheel of creation in this world and it inspires the desire for offspring.'[113] One should lead a disciplined life of control, contentment and moderation, as it is often difficult to be satisfied with Kama and it is easy to go astray.

The Salvation - *Moksha*

The final and the most sought after objective of life is Moksha, the liberation or 'Nirvana' in Buddhism. It is to understand The Self and to get freedom from all 'dhukhas' (sufferings) of life: disease, old age and death. Sufferings are inherent to life and thus unavoidable. To get rid of sufferings and 'physical unhappiness' from poverty, hunger and famine, preventable and incurable diseases is required. Getting rid of 'mental unhappiness' and thus of hatred, animosity, anger, jealousy and worldly attachments is as important. Lastly trying to prevent, forewarn and contain 'natural disasters' by helping in floods, earthquakes, devastating fires and taking part in preventing 'social ills' such as injustice, violence, lack of freedom and personal choices and acts of war are all part of liberation.[24,113] Freedom from sufferings by detachment and other means in the world is like bringing heaven on earth. In modern day idealism Moksha is not renunciation of life but the renunciation of evils.

Moksha is the spiritual means of The Self-realization and is to be one with the Creator God that frees one from the cycle of birth and death and brings enlightenment and infinite bliss. 'Nirvana' is enlightenment with liberation from all 'dhukhas' of the world.

IN THE END what counts is the quality and objectivity of life. Many visionaries died in their youthful years but left everlasting legacy behind for others to emulate and follow their footsteps. As Ralph Waldo Emerson correctly said, "It is not length of life but depth of life."

The objective in life is to play our part well on the world stage. We are like actors with varied personalities who play the scripted role on this world stage. Our personal character, society, culture and the community write this script. This role in a way becomes our duty. Everything is action and reaction, cause and effect and is predictable like the script. Predictable scripts in cosmos are that the wind blows, the water flows, the fire burns and the sun shines. Like an actor you have to play your part well in conformity with the dictates of life. The law of karma engraves the script. We still have a free choice and freedom to redefine ourselves and to craft our future for a happy ending. Happiness is achievable only when we diligently fulfill our objectives in life. Be the novice to change the paradigms of human quest and leave a legacy.

'You were put on this earth to achieve your greatest self, to live out your purpose, and to do it courageously'

~ STEVE MARABOLI

All Rivers run to the Ocean

*'God is one. He exists eternally, sages and the wise persons call
the same God by different names, but nevertheless He remains
the same One God.'*

~ RIG VEDA 1:64:46[2]

RELIGION IS THE fundamental grass root of human civilization. It gives direction and purpose to our existence. It gives us direction when our mind is led astray, gives us hope amidst pain and sufferings and energizes us to fight on when we are helpless. It motivates us as to how to love and be compassionate to other beings and most of all to be happy and contented and brings us closer to divinity.

Religion is an organized system of faith and worship, myths, beliefs and rituals, ceremonies, services and worship of God, The Divine supernatural Creator. Each religion has its own set of beliefs of creation, cause, nature and purpose of universe with moral codes. Major religions of the world are Christianity, Judaism, Islam, Hinduism, Buddhism, Jainism, Sikhism, Taoism and many others off shoots. Buddhism and Jainism are silent on God. About 15% of world population is non-religious, secular, atheists or agnostics.

Religion is not a prerequisite for us to thrive in the society but it gives us hope and uplifts our spirits to help our mind find a direction at distressing times. It brings discipline, order, integrity and morality to our relationships in the society. It brings peace and tranquility of mind by controlling our anxiety and desires and sows the seeds of real happiness.

Basically there are three aspects of any religion:

1. <u>Faith and belief in God</u>- God is The Divine power who is the ultimate controller of the world that He created. There is only one God that followers of the various religions call by different names.
2. <u>Prayers, religious rituals and ceremonies</u>: vary in different religions. Prayer, praise (Stuti) and devotion (Upasana) help make us understand God and discover our life's connection to Him. We are inspired to walk on the right and virtuous path. Type and the method of prayer vary but each is unique and sacred for practicing that particular religion. Each religious belief or ritual is engrained deep in his or her conscious and is virtuous and the Divine reality. Christmas for Christians is as much festive and divine as Hanukkah for the Jews, Ramadan for the Muslims, and Diwali for the Hindus or Gurpurb for the Sikhs. Various religious festivals bring in a sense of belonging and strengthen our beliefs.
3. <u>Spiritualism</u> by various ideals, ethics and morality is taught by all religions that have become central core for day-to-day living. Our belief in worship of God is as important to some as our determination to be honest and good. This brings discipline, control, coherence and peace of mind instead of chaos, agitation and unhappiness.

Spirituality and religion are intertwined and coexist. However, spirituality exists with or without religion. One discovers spirituality from within to find inner-voice of consciousness. Spirituality is unifying and inclusive and it resolves conflicts. It is the most important ideal tool that binds the modern pluralistic society. It is based on compassion, ethics and morality.

The basic doctrine of every religion of the world is to lead mankind to the Divine path. All religious teachings show us the virtuous path of truthfulness, righteousness, forgiveness, justice, contentment, compassion, tolerance and humility to bring peace and tranquility of mind to sustain happiness.

In true sense religion consists in realization of the Self.[115] It is spiritual relationship between the soul and the God. It is more than erecting places of worship. Religions of the world are not contradictory or antagonistic. They represent various faces of one eternal God. Central secret is that 'The Truth may be one, but there are various visions and adaptations of the same truth viewed from various standpoints. Once we understand this central crux there is no antagonism between various teachings. Instead truth lies on forbearance, understanding and harmony encompassing peace and intense love in absolute unity to become one voice of mankind. "The microcosm is but a miniature repetition of the macrocosm."' Said Swami Vivekananda.[115]

The practice of Buddhism can be summarized by a short phrase so eloquently elaborated by Dalai Lama[59] 'If you can't help others, at least don't harm them.'

Religion teaches us to have hope and patience with faith and mental equipoise. One needs to be calm and have endurance, as everything is impermanent. Nothing lasts forever: neither exalted pleasures nor dejected pain.[19]

The aim of the religion is to give hope to heal the wounded hearts. It helps spread peace and happiness and gospel of compassion, unconditioned love and nonjudgmental mercy.

No single religion has monopoly over doctrine of righteousness or ultimate goal of spirituality. All religions more or less teach the same message in different formats under different banners. Religion teaches: the truth, the righteousness, the love, peace, humility, graciousness and forgiveness. "Religion is to do right, it is to love, it is to serve, it is to think, it is to be humble" said Ralph Waldo. In a true philosophical sense all religions are one and the same depicted in different colors, all Gods are but one God called by different names. In essence we are all praying to the same God. Everyone has the birthright to pick his or her own religion, his or her own God. Love your God, get enlightened by his divinity but don't disrespect someone else's faith. "God has no religion" said Mahatma Gandhi.

Buddhism and Jainism are non-theistic religions that don't believe in the existence of God. Jains believe in independent 'I' called 'Atman' (soul) that is denied by Buddhists.[64]

One idea in all religions is to refrain from using term, 'little-I', this is the 'I' inferred from the selfish ego, referring to me, my achievements, my prides, my wealth, my name, my family and myself – all that is full of pride, greed and envy. Instead use the inclusive terms 'we, our and us'. Learn to use 'not little I but big I (Thou)', only the supreme God that created the world says, 'I' as 'I am He, the Creator, come to me, I will enlighten you.' We never get tired of using the egoistic words: 'I and me and mine' that have exhausted our spirits and robbed us from our happiness and peace of mind forever. 'Me and mine' and 'you and yours' are only illusion from our ignorance, we spend entire lifetime in these useless selfish thoughts...' (Ramayana, Aryanakand, verse 15). Only renunciation of our egoistic selfish acts and unending desires and our faith in religious tolerance can usher in everlasting happiness for everyone.

> *'Forgiveness, compassion, tolerance, brotherhood and feeling of oneness are the signs of a true religion.'*

> ~ SRI CHINMOY

CHAPTER 48

Consciousness - a way to Happiness

'The key to growth is the introduction of higher dimensions of consciousness into our awareness.'

~ LAO TZU

CONSCIOUSNESS IS THE cognitive awareness. This awareness pertains to both what is within the self as well as what is in the surrounding environment. It is to be aware of personal ideas, feelings, thoughts and conceptions Consciousness is essential to enjoy life and feel pain and pleasure and happiness. There is ever-shifting stream of thoughts that can swiftly change from moment to moment. It needs comprehension of brain as well as intact cognitive abilities. Life without consciousness is an empty echo devoid of any relevant meaning of true existence.

Consciousness has always remained a subject of varied definitions and interpretations by philosophers, psychologists, neuroscientists and theologians. 'Higher Consciousness' is the spiritual awareness with all its mystical divinity. It has been explained in detail in Upanishads as well in other religious teachings. There is a mind-body-intellect relationship of the consciousness with the outside world as well as an inner spiritual link to the soul.

There are three types of consciousness as defined by mystical psychiatrist Richard Maurice Bucke in 1905.[13]

1. Simple Consciousness that is awareness of the body and is possessed by many animals.

2. Self-Consciousness that is full awareness of the self, including mind and thoughts and is possessed by humans only.
3. Cosmic Consciousness is the spiritual awareness of life and order of the universe and is possessed only by humans who are enlightened.

There are other modern day definitions of consciousness that are not discussed in this text.

In the past many scientists viewed some aspects of consciousness with skepticism, but recently it has become a significant topic of research.

Cognitive consciousness: Physicians assess the degree and extent of consciousness by observing the patient's arousal and responsiveness by clinical examination. Cognitive consciousness is seen as a continuum of states ranging from full alertness and comprehension to a state of being totally unresponsive in coma.

There have been cases where persons in vegetative states, with supposedly unrecoverable brain damage due to massive head trauma, have shown positive meaningful activity in the brain (by fMRI) on verbally asking a pertinent question. At least some of these comatosed patients are not robots but have potential to enjoy some degree of inner happiness and pleasure on listening to music or on receiving hugs and reassurances from near and dear ones.

Self-awareness results from consciousness. However, it is not always fundamentally connected to consciousness as in a person listening to favorite music or enjoying other sensual pleasures, who can be so deeply absorbed in his own selective concentration of mind that he or she becomes temporarily oblivious to other surrounding activities like an absent-minded professor. There is a story of a Greek Philosopher who was so deeply engaged in solving a mathematical problem that a whole battalion of army with all that noise failed to draw his attention. He was completely unaware till a soldier wiped out the circle that the philosopher had drawn on the ground. What followed is anybody's guess!

Distractions by selective attention are common like talking or texting while driving and it results in significantly higher accident rates.

According to Sigmund Freud the mind comprises conscious and unconscious thoughts. This psychoanalytic theory is explained by using an iceberg metaphor. Conscious awareness is tip of the iceberg while the ice hidden below the surface of water, which is a lot bigger, is the unconscious feelings and thoughts.

Conscious mind represents everything that we are aware of, our thoughts, our speech, our daydreams, and all our plans and pleasures that guide our behavior. On the other hand, other acts which represent many day–to-day activities including a sequence of muscle contractions like holding a pen to write a letter, climbing the stairs, driving a car and similar other organized actions and thoughts are unconscious in nature. They influence our behavior without our awareness. Significant psychic manifestations can result from the hidden messages from the unconscious mind.

A strong positive mind helps us to keep our sanity and keeps us firm and saves us from slipping over the cliff.

Our conscious thoughts and actions unravel many routine issues, whereas, decisions about complex matters are tackled by the unconscious mind. Many of our thoughts are processed, analyzed and streamlined without our awareness. Thought progression in our mind refined by reasoning results in a better, more organized decision making.[27]

Human consciousness represents conditioning of mind and the brain to external sensory world of objects of desires. It is limited-consciousness as a product of limited-mind. 'We are product of contents of our consciousness: our thoughts, ideas, beliefs, desires and conceptions or misconceptions. That is what we are.'[55] Instead of outward sensory influences on individual consciousness we need an inward introspective transformation.

All of us share same happiness and pleasures and pains. This '*human consciousness*' inwardly is the same shared by every human being.[55] Global Consciousness Project has statistically correlated the coherent value of interconnected human consciousness. Random number generators (RNGs) based on quantum tunneling are normally unpredictable. However, at time of great events like 9/11, earthquakes and tsunamis it synchronizes the feeling of millions of people creating statistically significant peaks in RNG. It illustrates direct effects of collective consciousness reacting to global events like 9/11, tsunami and death of Princess Diana. Chance occurrence is one in a trillion odds.

'*Cosmic or Higher consciousness*' refers to awareness of the ever-existent Creator, The God and is also known as Super-consciousness or Objective consciousness. 'Mindfulness' is full awareness of the present-moment.

The concept of 'higher consciousness' rests on the belief that the average human being is only 'partially conscious' due to lack of a true spiritual knowledge in his untrained mind and restricted intellect. In that philosophic sense most humans are considered to be asleep as they are oblivious to the reality. One can attain the capacity to transcend ones' mind to a higher state of consciousness and achieve full human potential. The dark clouds of ignorance need to be removed to enrich mind and intellect.

The true consciousness is concealed by defilements ('doshas': lust, anger, greed, attachments and pride) covering our mind and intellect metaphorically like the clouds covering the sun or dust covering the mirror.

Metaphysically mind through 'higher consciousness' is spiritually linked to soul and The God. On the contrary atheists and agnostics believe that consciousness of mind is material and physical in realms of brain. There is nothing beyond physical body, there is no soul and death is finality.

In a secular context 'higher consciousness' has profound positive impact on mind and intellect and character and morals thus resulting in profound personal growth both for individual as well as overall welfare of the society at large. Conscious cognitive awareness of things that we like makes us happy while cosmic consciousness leads to the bliss ('ananda'), the best kind of happiness. We need cognitive awareness to really feel and enjoy happiness. Conditioned- consciousness is link to happiness through our mind, whereas, 'cosmic-consciousness is link to everlasting bliss through our soul.

'Like the waves in the oceans, the worlds arise, live and dissolve
in the Supreme self, the substance and cause of everything.'

~ *SHANKARA*

CHAPTER 49

Spirituality for Inner-happiness

'Spiritualty is meant to take us beyond our tribal identity into domain of awareness that is more universal.'

~ *Deepak Chopra*

Spiritualty gives us hope, energy and the direction that enlightens the path to long lasting happiness. For a longtime Western views searched for truth through the society, science and the nature, whereas, the East searched the mind, the body, the soul and The Self through spiritual teachings. West for a longtime neglected the search for the spirit and the soul. The answer lies in the fusion of two cultures as a paramount need of humanity pursuing with united efforts towards pure consciousness.[115]

Spirituality is the foundation, the pillar that supports our existence. There is immense power of spiritual world over material world as it awakens the conscious. It gives a purpose to life. Life would have remained aimless and selfish without any spiritual guidance. Spirituality wipes the dust of ignorance created by conditioned consciousness so that enlightened soul can shine through. It constantly reminds us whenever we run astray from righteous path. It is like a 'stop sign'. Whenever an evil thought or action crosses our mind, it makes us stop to reassess the situation. This inner-voice cautions us to use our power of discrimination learnt from previous experiences, knowledge and spiritual guidance. We may suppress this inner-voice. Once we suppress that inner-voice of reason and cross that threshold, it becomes easier and easier next time to go astray. Soon we are miles away from the righteous thoughts and able to justify our wrong actions. Even a thief can justify that he deserves what others have and even a murderer might think that his actions are justified like in case of honor-killings and murder for revenge.

About a decade ago, while visiting Big Island in Hawaii, I slipped one little piece of black lava rock in my bag. It was despite warning, 'Don't take Lava rocks, it may bring bad luck.' I couldn't sleep that night and had all sort of nightmares about impending bad luck. Although I don't believe in superstitions, next day we went back to the park to return the lava rock and I genuinely felt sorry for my action.

We are all good people doing wrong things at times. One needs to develop proclivity to follow spiritual and ethical path. Right thing is to periodically do introspection and try to be an honest, truthful and compassionate person. Everyone must change one's demeanor for the good. Merely feeling sorry does not mean anything unless we change our behavior for the better by repentance and transformation of mind.

One should not judge others. It is inconsiderate for anyone to judge other people's behavior as it generates unhappiness, anger, hostility and conflicts in relationships. Who am I to judge? Let God be the judge. However, some misdeeds or violent crimes are unpardonable. There are laws of the land to deal with the criminals. Some sort of rehabilitation and spiritual guidance, not necessarily prisons, can transform the mind gone astray to assimilate back in the society. The root cause of many crimes like poverty illiteracy and unemployment needs to be tackled.

One should try to go in the direction of 'a life of spirit' (sreya), the spiritual life rather than blindly pursue 'a life of senses' (preya), the materialistic life. The desires, the objects of our senses and the egocentric consciousness are all born out of our ignorance that binds us down to earth and keeps us away from spiritual path.[28] Purification of mind and body is needed by a clean balanced food, self-control, non-attachment, active practice of virtues and by altruistic compassion. Three 'D's of Hindi alphabet sums up virtuous path in this world.[105]

Daman (*continence*): self-control over organs of perception, greed and cravings.

Dan (*charity*)**:** donation of any kind- monitory, material objects, volunteering, educating others and our labor.

Daya (*Compassion*): mercy, kindness, forgiveness, empathy and benevolence. These three 'D' Sanskrit words are 'three Cs' in English: Continence, Charity and Compassion

A man ought to be ambitious of living a full life. Education, enjoyment of family life and accumulation of material possessions including wealth are norms so long there is honest earning and living. Moderation is the key. Excessive indulgence in any desire ultimately leads to unhappiness. Sublime happiness can be achieved by freeing ourselves from the bondage of materialistic attachments. Sincerity, purity, simplicity of mind and tenacity of a purpose can bring true celestial happiness. The path to enlightenment is to follow the 'Middle Way' and avoid being caught and entangled in any extreme.[15]

The spiritual path at first needs awareness of physical material knowledge and intellectual knowledge ('Baudhik-gyan') before one can imbibe the spiritual knowledge and 'Ataman-gyan' (knowledge of self). One attains true peace and lasting happiness after freeing oneself from destructive distractions (our 'doshas' or deficiencies) like worldly pleasures, anger, fear, lust, greed and ego. As described in Geeta true peace is attained by the stable mind when there is equanimity, where person is not perturbed by troubling dualities of life: pleasure and pain, success and failure, honor and dishonor. This tranquility of mind leads to true joy with lasting happiness.[19]

Worldly man likes to pursue the easily available materialistic path of sensory world, where these three levels of sensory perception, mental reception and intellectual assimilation create a sense of attachment with '1-ness' of ego.[19] Self portrayal through ego causes all the sorrows and miseries in the universe because power of discernment is eclipsed by delusion of ignorance (avidya). A spiritual spark is essential to illuminate and sustain higher consciousness to wean us away from egocentric selfishness.

One should have self-control over mind and senses by freeing oneself from desires and attachments without any craving for fruits of actions and to practice austerity, compassion and benevolence.

Religion is not a prerequisite to spirituality in the modern pluralistic era. Instead it is based on ethics, secularism, morality and idealism of one world. You don't have to believe in God or any religion to be a good and kind human being. Spirituality is inner awareness of discovering your inner-voice. 'A kinder, gentler atheism echoes a striking shift in religious culture' said David Skeel. As much as a third of Millennial children, born after 1980s, have no religious affiliation.

Complexities of the modern world with rising wave of crimes need a permanent solution not a quick, temporary Band-Aid. It seems people have lost values of moral compass with no sense of right or wrong. Spirituality acts as a guardrail, overlooking the path of our conscious lead by our inner-voice. Spirituality is the thread that holds all the pearls brilliantly in harmony like a garland of love and compassion. 'Forget what you give but never forget what you receive.' [110] Spirituality is essential in this modern selfish pluralistic world to reinforce everyone with an honest, moral, ethical and compassionate conduct to attain true happiness.

'To me religion is an agreement between a group of people about what God is. Spirituality is one-to-one relationship.'

~ STEVE EARLE

CHAPTER 50

Religion and Inner-Values

'Humans can manage without religion; they cannot manage without inner values.'

~ DALAI LAMA

ONE OF THE fundamental human goals is aspiration for happiness and aversion for pain and suffering. Apart from positive will, power of mind and intellect, spiritual and moral guidance from inner values of religion is obligatory in most human beings to reach this goal. In modern day globalization, universe is shrinking and a coherent tolerant ethical approach is essential to avoid conflicts and create a sense of universal togetherness. Religion teaches righteousness, forgiveness, compassion, love and humility. It is through these universal core values. It teaches us that every human being is the same. Understanding the concept of 'one world' ingrained in these inner values can make life of every human being happy and heavenly.

The basic doctrine of every religion of the world is the same, to lead mankind to the righteous path. In true sense religion consists in realization of self and God.[115] It is spiritual relationship between the man and the God. Through this we understand the true meaning of every religion and their inner values. It lights the spirit of kindness and compassion that ignites and fosters universal brotherhood where 'me and mine' is no different from 'you and yours'. It is where all of us, despite our religious and cultural differences, are one and the same. We can better understand God by shedding our egoistic attitude by practicing these inner values. It is more than erecting places of worship.

One can practice these inner values with or without any religious beliefs. Good values are not monopoly of any religion. Many modern age youngsters and scientists don't believe in God. They frequently ask as to 'who has seen the God?' It is very fundamental but hard question to answer. There are many things in the world that exist but we are unable to see. We can't see the air. Many things that normally we can't see need special organs of perception like smell, sound and feeling of touch. We need some kind of energy and a connection to it; like we need electricity for the electric bulb to glow and the source of electricity. In the same way we need mysterious energy of an 'inner-eye' to see the 'inner-self' and The God. Our prayers, devotion and meditation can light this path that is very long and difficult to achieve, it is razor sharp and narrow. It is more like feeling God and his close proximity with an actual illusion of seeing him- atamsparsh (ataman: soul, sparsh: touch).

There is interesting dichotomy of living in the modern society: secular outlook to reach one's community and the world, and at the same time be spiritual and holy to reach God. Secularism and spirituality, although seem to be contradictory but these can coexist creating harmony of mind for the personal benefit as well for benefit of everybody. Life is the flow of water in a river with two banks, secular and spiritual. Somehow we have to build the harmonious bridge of inner values to connect. Both aspects are important in modern times to live happily in peace and harmony. Frequently we fail to wipe the dust of prejudice from our mind and draw hasty unrealistic conclusions and wrong inferences.

Religion is: the truth, the righteousness, the love, peace, humility, graciousness and forgiveness. One should respect the values and beliefs of fellow human beings without contradicting his or her religion. 'Religion is to do right, it is to love, it is to serve, it is to think, it is to humble" said Ralph Waldo. Religion brings dynamic spirit of togetherness.[20] You can practice all of these virtues even without believing in God.

There is emergence of interfaith and multifaith groups in present pluralistic society in many countries. These groups include and respect both theistic and atheistic values without criticizing or being judgmental and without undermining any one. These groups explore the inner values and foster a harmonious platform for an open dialogue on a regular basis and especially at time of any crisis at local or national level.

There are people who have no faith but share the best practices of spirituality and its inner values - fostering togetherness in community, living ethically and morally with everyone irrespective of their beliefs.

Most conflicts in the world happen in the name of religion. Every religion harbors few fundamentalists who by wrong interpretations of their strong beliefs ignite the spark of hatred, revenge, divisiveness and violence.

Thomas Jefferson had skeptical religious worldview blending personal freedom and faith. He crafted and helped pass a statue of religious liberty in 1786, that was 'meant to comprehend, within the mantle of its protection, Jew and the Gentle, the Christian and Mahomedan, the Hindoo, and the infidel of every denomination.' This represents the earliest secular version of modern era.[73]

Recently Pope Francis said in an interview in 2013, "Church should be a home for all and not a 'small chapel' focused on doctrine, orthodoxy and a limited agenda of moral teachings. The dogmatic and moral teachings of the church are not all equivalent. The church's pastoral ministry cannot be obsessed with the transmission of a disjointed multitude of doctrines to be imposed insistently. We have to find a new balance, otherwise even the moral edifice of the church is likely to fall like a house of cards, losing all freshness and fragrance of the Gospel."

Dalai Lama has eloquently discussed secularism in his recent book 'Beyond Religion, ethics for a whole world.'[60] He recommends a sustainable universal approach comprising ethics, inner values and personal integrity. This approach transcends religious, cultural and racial differences and appeals to people at fundamental human level. It is essential to have Inner-values and moral ethics in sense of togetherness to lead a true happy life.

'Say nothing of my religion. It is known to God and myself alone...if it has been honest and dutiful to society, the religion which has regulated it cannot be a bad one.'

~ Thomas Jefferson[73]

CHAPTER 51

The Law of Karma

*'Your right is to work only, but never to its fruits. Let not the
fruit of action be your motive, nor let your attachment be in
inaction.'*

~ BHAGAVAD GITA 2:47

'KARAM-YOGA IS DEXTERITY in action.' Karma means deeds that you do and
not the fate. Good karma invariable lead to happiness. All actions propelled
by the mind physically, mentally in thoughts and words are karma. Karma is
the fire, the energy and the spirit that keeps life moving in the cosmic wheel-
of-action. Its relevance is in cause and effect and action and reaction and in
terms of reward or punishment. Karmas performed by man on the world
stage have long lasting repercussions that resonate in this life and beyond. It
all depends on your philosophy, unless you are such a simple-minded naïve
atheist who believes that you may escape the moral scrutiny in this life and
thereafter and will escape the consequences of your karma.

Karma concept explained in simple terms 'as you sow, so shall you reap'[110]
is a part of action and reaction theory, in other words the cause and effect phenomenon. The activities in 'Karam Yoga' are aimed at two paths: 1) Actions
with motive ('Sakam Karma': 'sa'- with, 'kama'-desire for fruit), it creates anxiety for success or failure and 2) Actions without motive or desireless actions
('Nishkama Karma'). Mind is at peace and is tranquil as there no anxiety (for
the fruits of your action).[113]

Law of Karma is interplay between desire (ischa), action (kriya) and effect (phal- fruit of action). There needs to be conformity in our thoughts, speech and action. The faculty of discrimination (viveka) and contemplation (vichara) by mind-intellect complex selects the appropriate choice to act.

'Karam Yoga' (Yoga of Action) is 'performance of any action' as the wheels of the world can't turn without karma, which is absolutely essential for motion of life. Individual has to perform actions for even simple act in life like eating, drinking, sleeping, walking, talking and other day-to-day activities. As Bhagwad Geeta (3:5) says: 'No person can exist without performing actions.' 'The attainment of success in action (occupation) is yoga.' ('Yoga karamasu kaushalam'- Bhagwad Geeta 20:50).[19,113,114]

When we are in distress, we do prayers and try to do some good charitable deeds like helping the poor and needy, hoping to get relief from distress (as reward for good deeds). At times it seems that our prayers are answered. Are these the result of our prayers and good deeds or are these a part of a pre-destined plan or fate? According to Vedic philosophy it is in the present life where we earn the fruits of our past deeds 'parabadha karma'. Pain and pleasure are part of our destiny that we earned by our karma in previous embodiments. To an extent our 'samskaras' (trait, temperament) are predetermined by our past 'karma' and the knowledge and degree of perfection of our soul. Our traits ('gunas') are exhibited in three categories:

'Tamasic' is typified as darkness being lazy, inert, ignorant and dull witted living a life of relative inactivity.

'Rajsic' temperament people are full of energy and are very ambitious and egocentric and are engaged in all forms of activities in life to seek power, wealth, name and fame.

'Satvic' people are sublime, compassionate, merciful, forgiving, selfless and altruistic.

These three traits are present in varying degree in everybody with one trait dominating over the others. Tamasic acts are destructive; rajsic acts binds him to the world, robbing him of spirituality, whereas, satvic acts set him on the path of freedom and liberation.[81] Past actions to a great extent determine one's dominant trait. The character of a person is not defined by isolated instances of some virtuous deed, when even a 'tamasic' person may help others to get recognition, but it is determined by his or her entire attitude in life. Usually our tendencies overlap under different circumstances at different times. No one is perfect all the time. On the other hand, some people may never improve and their life becomes a downward spiral of bad habits.

Helping and willingness to serve others is always a righteous act and is undoubtedly good karma. We want to donate for a good cause and want to be recognized and get applauded. These 'rajsic' acts are also good karma. However, when we give anonymously without desire for recognition and applause, that type of donation is a step higher. In that case it is simply to help without selfish desire-prompted motives.[21] 'Man's right is to perform actions, not to desire fruits, Whether or not he reaps the fruits is in the hands of The Creator' -Bhagwad Geeta 2:47.[19] Desireless actions free us from the feeling of happiness or sorrow associated with success or failure.[113]

Rhetorically speaking everyone has the 'free will' to consciously make the choice for his or her actions. Good karma is honest living and earning by honest means. Love, compassion, empathy and doing pious deeds for welfare of others are good karma. On the other hand, bad karmas originate from a self-centered mind full of hatred, jealousy, anger, lust and apathy.

There are laws in the society and in the community at large and in the country as a whole for the crimes committed and punishment thereof in this lifetime. However, spiritually speaking there is justice rendered by The Creator. He is just in every sense. Many erroneously believe that wheels of fortune tilts and turns to whichever side (a sum-total of all good or bad deeds) are heavier at the time of justice. However, there is reward or punishment for each and every good or bad deed.

'Law of destiny' only refers to his past and makes him a victim, whereas, 'Law of Karma' infuses the spirit of creative activities in the present moments focusing for the future.[20] What is destiny? We find many poor people afflicted with pain and sufferings despite being honest and hardworking people all their lives. On the other hand, the world is full of thugs and criminals who have all the riches and luxuries and are leading a comfortable life. Why this apparent disparity? Why a virtuous man is stricken in pain and suffering and the sinful man enjoying life full of luxuries? Is it all result of our fate? The only plausible explanation found in all the readings is that these are 'parabadha karma' a consequence of past deeds from our previous life, being realized in the present life. 'He is a product or an effect of his past actions or karma.'[21] Our present miserable sorrowful state may have resulted from pursuing negative values in the past. Presently we have opportunity to do a thorough introspection by finding and eliminating our harmful character flaws and transforming those with persistent deliberate efforts to improve our lives.

One is capable of improving ones' lot by picking up the right choices by replacing hatred with love and jealousy with praise. Destiny is governed by the deeds of the past while 'Law of Karma' gives him the choice, opportunity and the power to bring a change. 'You can change your future by transforming your present.'[21] We have the option of either improvement with self-realization or remain in the cosmic cycle of life and death. This is in essence of philosophy of karma in Hinduism.

Most religions have spiritual philosophy about karma. It is well elaborated in 'Gurbani' (Sikhism), Bible and other holy scriptures. 'Give them according to their deeds, and according to the wickedness of their endeavors: give them after the work of their hands; render to them their desert.' (Psalm 28:4)

Although fruits of 'good karma' are positive and pleasing, however, all karmas keeps one imprisoned in the cycle of death and rebirth.[81] According to Buddhism karma is neither a 'destiny' nor a result from cosmic retribution system. All things in life are impermanent due to physical conditions, feelings, perceptions and other unavoidable factors. These lead to restlessness and agitation of mind resulting in indecision, stress and suffering. Mind clouded by worldly cravings and desires becomes impervious to wisdom and results in egoistic inconsiderate karma with misconception of 'I and me and mine' in the forefront.[16] Wisdom and purity of mind are essential for good karma. 'When a man thinks, speaks and acts with a good intentioned mind happiness follows him like his shadow.'[15]

Self-effort against background of destiny modifies the past. Destiny is no longer determined solely by the past Karma. In-essence one becomes architect of ones' fate. The past reformed in the present is the future.'[19] You have to do good deeds in life to rectify the past and brighten the future. You have that power now to make that change. You need to curb your ego as it feeds on memories of the 'past', hopes and expectations of 'future'. Anxiety and agitation of mind (about fruits of action) ends up robing the 'peace and happiness of the present'. You have lots of choices; at least you can endeavor to leave a legacy of love, compassion and empathy.

ESSENCE OF KARAM YOGA

First duty of Karam Yogi is 'not to hate your-self'
Have faith in yourself, before you develop faith in others
Self-esteem strengthens power of mind and brings positivity
Be positive and keep company of good people
Follow your conscious
Don't copy others, follow your own ideals
'Don't fear as fear of fear robs happiness'[110]
Don't act with weak mind or fickle resolve
Develop mind to resolve, resist, restrain and renounce
Develop power to resist evil thoughts and actions
Develop character, integrity, wisdom and nobility
Works is worship- work passionately and avoid inactivity
Have 'Viveka' to discern between right and wrong
Don't injure anybody by your actions, thoughts and speech
Avoid extremes, as 'moderation' is the key to happiness
Be considerate, forgiving, kind and humble
Indulge and enjoy in activities with 'mindfulness'
Work incessantly without attachment
A man without ego can rule the world
Don't work for penance or fruits of your actions
Don't work for name, fame, applause or approbation
Don't have prejudice, be judgmental or have malice
Never work for retribution or vengeance
Work selflessly 'without ego'
Remove 'I, me and mine' from your vocabulary

Live with non-attachment and self-abnegation
Accumulate wealth by rightful means and share it with the needy
Be altruistic, truthful and righteous
Help others and be kind, merciful and forgiving
Don't expect 'gratitude' as it loses its purpose and spirit behind it
Develop relationships without conflicts, expectations and demands
Enjoy 'present moments' by forgetting past and worries of the future
Work for liberation of 'soul' from all bondages
Get guidance from spirituality, idealism, morality and ethics
You don't need to be a Sanyasi to live a spiritually divine life
In Sanyasa, don't renounce the world, only renounce all evils
'Don't give up the world, live in the world by karam yoga'[115]

CHAPTER 52

The Power of Prayers

'It is much easier for me to see a praying murderer, a praying prostitute, than a vain person praying. Nothing is so at odds with as vanity.'

~ DIETRICH BONHOEFFER 1928

PRAYER IS A set order of words or thoughts addressed to the object of worship, The Creator The God as a solemn request for help or expression of thanks. It is the devotional path that takes us to God and helps us feel His Presence. In the difficult discerning moments when man feels helpless, weak and desperate, he surrenders himself to the Almighty and asks for his help and guidance to sail the ocean of pain and sufferings and to seek joy and happiness.

Type, mode, wording and frequency of prayer vary in different religions. These are sacred to ones' faith. Prayer in the morning and in the evening is acceptable norm in many religions and cultures. 'Salaat' (Islamic prayer) is performed five times a day.

Prayer has a crucial importance in the life of a believer. It is a practice of faith that inspires hope. It brings humility as pride is stripped and mind becomes peaceful and tranquil. Praying inspires to cultivate noble thoughts and helps eradicate the evil ones from our mind. James 4:8 says, "Draw near to God and He will draw near to you." In Chapter 11 Gospel of Luke Lord Jesus was praying with his disciples. One of his disciples asked. "Lord, teach us how to pray?" And so Jesus taught them, The Lord's Prayer is most commonly performed prayer by all denominations of Christian faith.

For Jews prayer (Tefilah in Hebrew) is continual integral part of everyday life. Jewish Prayer to seek wisdom is:
'So teach us to remember our days
That we may get us a heart of wisdom.'

The purpose of Buddhist prayer is a practice of meditation and inner reconditioning to awaken our inherent inner capacities of strength, compassion and wisdom to replace the negatives with the virtuous karma.

Prayer is a central part of Sikh devotional life with beautiful hymns (Hukamnama), meditations (Naam Simran), devotional readings (Paath) and five daily prayers (Nitnem Banis).

Hindu, Sikh, Jain's and Buddhist prayers are done in the morning and evening or at any other time to bring us closer to divinity.

Prayers strengthen our faith and give us hope, dispel our fears and show the righteous path when we are lost in miseries, indecisions and other encounters in life. By praying at the trying times we seek His love, protection, guidance and comfort.

The power of prayers coming from depths of one's heart gives solace and peace to the agitated mind and controls our arrogance, false-pride and anxiety.

Collective prayers done at the time of calamities and other national or international disasters, tragedies and wars tranquil the minds and bring in hope and advance the processes of healing. Simultaneous and multimodal prayers by different interfaith and multifaith groups bring a new purpose to the cause and broaden our vision. Local MultiFaith Council of Northwest Ohio draws together diverse faiths, in mutual respect, friendship, cooperation and service. Our group regularly meets to discuss varied current or controversial issues for better understanding of everyone's perspective. Council fosters peace, love and compassion.

A sincere prayer is recited to have the strength and guidance at the time of undertaking a difficult task in life and death situations to invoke the courage and hope. As a trauma surgeon I frequently faced many life and death situations, when a patients' life was slipping away every second. At these crucial times when virtually patient is dying under the knife (in and out of surgery), I have frequently prayed silently to God to save the patient and to seek healing power in my hands. Many times I have asked God, "Please God save this dying person in lieu of all the good karma I have ever done in my life." I am sure other persons also ask for guidance from the higher one in these difficult times. My wife routinely prayed to God while scrubbing for any difficult surgery or a delivery, or during a procedure. Many times I had taken critical trauma patient to surgery without any identity of patient except knowing their sex and approximate age. At other times when patient was dying from massive injuries, I merely had seconds to talk to the available family member to say, "I am running to surgery to try to save his life. Please pray for him as I am doing the same." The power of prayers, collective one by the family and the others who want to save the dying patient brings hope and lessens the agitation and anger. How much prayers help and change the outcome only the sufferers can estimate as I have seen some miracles in my life? Even if I have the privilege to save one person in my lifetime, I feel honored and thank God for His helping hands.

Prayers can reduce stress and agitation of mind resulting in peace and happiness. Comforting words of empathy work like soothing balm to the agitated mind. These words are far better than saying 'sorry' as people like your support and not to be pitied upon.

The positive outlook of your mind, your faith and prayers and a good support system give you hope and courage and is conducive for better outcome by helping the immune system. A recent publication from Harvard in 2013 by Aizer and colleagues[1] reported that married cancer patients fared better than patients who are single. They were found to have less advanced cancers because of earlier diagnosis. They are more likely to get definitive treatments and have a better prognosis and a reduced incidence of dying from certain cancers by 20%: varying from 12% in liver to 33% in head and neck cancers due to a close family support.

Stress reduction strategies like meditation; yoga, prayers and relaxation exercises enhance the immune system. People who pray regularly live longer.

Optimistic patients, who take cancer or other deadly diseases head on also live a little longer than their counterparts. Look for the sunshine in dark gloomy times in your life. Instead of fear and worries, look for the rays of hope under the dark clouds. Other techniques to augment healing and reduce stress before chemotherapy or surgery is massage, meditation and yoga, 'say "Om" before surgery' as reported by Dr. Oz.[85] A group of patients were asked to listen to special audiotapes before heart surgery. A calm voice speaking over gentle music urged patients to close their eyes and remember the place where they were very happy and comfortable.[85] This technique was very helpful by significantly reducing their stress level.

According to Vedas:[2,24] 'One prays not only for one's spiritual, mental and physical welfare but also for that of others…that includes entire mankind' said Sudhir Anand.[2]

However, never pray for impossible things like 'let money grow on trees or sunrise in the west.'

Never prey to bring harm to others.

Prayers from a deceitful heart are seldom sincere and are never answered.

Prayers are not a substitute for action. Pray for help only after your best efforts. 'God help those who help themselves.'[110]

Pray for yourself. Others should not pray for you unless you are sick, physically or mentally incapacitated.

Pray for others welfare.

One of the prayers in Upanishads: 'Asto ma sad gamya, Tamso ma jyotir gamaya; Mrityorama amritam gamaya.' symbolizes man's endeavor to tread the righteous path. It translates:

'O God1 Lead us from untruth to truth,
Lead us from darkness to light.
Lead us from death to immortality.'

Prayers seek faith and shower us with a gleam of hope, inner-peace and happiness.

'In the happy moments, praise God
In the difficult moments, seek God
In the quiet moments, trust God
In every moment, thank God'

~ ROBERT ALBERT WOOD

Buddhist Prayer for Happiness:

'May all living beings have happiness
and the causes of happiness
May all living beings be free from misery?
and the causes of misery
May all living beings be never be separated
from happiness and devoid of misery
May all living beings be in equanimity?
free from prejudicial attachments and aversions'

Jewish Prayer

'Let love and justice flow like a mighty stream
Let peace fill the earth as waters fill the sea
And let us say: Amen'

Muslim Prayer

'Our Lord! Give us good in this world and good in the Hereafter, and defend us from the torment of fire with Thy kindness, O Benevolent of the benevolent.'

CHAPTER 53

Body, Mind and The Soul

'Water washes off impurities of body, truth exalts mind, knowledge and strict devotion to duty elevate the soul and possession of ideas refine the intellect.'

~ MANU[24,71]

THERE IS AN intimate relationship between body, mind and soul, the three pillars of human existence. Man has tried to understand this complex question since the dawn of civilization. Religions have tried to shed light on these Devine relationships with some success. However, it has been often confused by varied mystical explanations accompanying rituals and biased explanations, myths and superstitions. Spiritual understanding with theological, scientific and psychological discussions has failed to completely demystify the mysteries of body, mind and the soul and without this trio happiness has no relevance or existence.

Here are some Vedic concepts:

The universe is composed of 'inanimate' (lifeless material objects: Prakriti) and 'animate' (live; Jiva) forms.[2] Material objects like a stone or an object made of iron are composed of atoms and have no consciousness. Animate subjects like human beings and animals are conscious and have cognitive faculty of mind. The human consciousness is called the soul (ataman: Jeevatman), which has only finite knowledge, strength and power of action. The formless soul when manifesting in living body is the consciousness that can act, create and feel. It has desires, envy, pain and pleasure and can think and acquire knowledge and wisdom. In essence it has free will to act.

Material objects are inert and without any cognition of mind with neither any feeling nor any capability of action. According to Hinduism, the universe is made up of matter (Prakriti) consisting of five 'tattva' (substances), which are earth, water, fire, air and ether (space) that by their attributes (properties) impart sense of smell, taste, light, touch (air touching the skin) and sound (through the space) respectively. Five organs of perception of the human body comprehend these attributes.

Body changes, mind evolves and intellect grows with passage of time. Ego is the real perceiver of sense objects through mind. However, all objects are finite and ever changing in a state of flux. Body mind and intellect are also dynamically changing and adapting and are cohesively held together by the soul ('ataman') like the thread that hold the beads in a necklace.[19]

The ultimate entity governing everything is omnipotent, omniscient, eternal Creator (God), called 'Parmatman' (The Supreme Soul).

Vedic literature illustrates qualifying traits of matter, soul and God by three Sanskrit words *Sat-Chit-Anand* (Sachidanand): 'sat' implies -to be, to stay, to remain, to eternally exist, 'chit' means -to be aware, to be conscious, to have experience: and 'ananda' connotes- to be happy, to be full of joy, and to be free from sorrow.[2,113]

Prakriti (matter) is existent 'sat' as it always existed. One can change its form but it cannot be destroyed. It has neither consciousness nor any bliss ('ananda').

Soul ('Jeev-ataman') is 'sat-chit': 'sat' as it is existent (exist all the time without any beginning or an end). It cannot be destroyed. It is 'cit' as it gives awareness and consciousness to the body. It has the capability to know, to understand and to experience pleasure and pain. However, it is devoid of bliss.

God is *Sat-Chit-Anand* as He is ever existent, always fully aware of everything (pure consciousness) and full of eternal and everlasting bliss ('ananda')

There is trinity of spiritual inter-relationship between material objects, soul and the God. This is called 'Traitvad' (three eternals).[2] However, in monism, the non-dualistic Vedantic view everything in universe is one Brahma, one God.

Our quest to understand our physical body is never ending. Scientifically there is significant understanding of anatomy of complex human machinery. Its physiologic functioning is becoming clearer. How to completely diagnose and repair its malfunctions have taken quantum leaps? We have been able to prolong human life but quality of life with aging is another whole issue. In spite of all these advances the fact that humans are mortals and it is neither possible, nor desirable to think otherwise. When we die what is left is a dead body. Instead of physiological existence of body, pertinent issue is the relevance of life as a human being in relation to larger than life issues.

The mysteries of mind have been the subject of study since times immemorial. Vedas and Upanishads have described in detail the analysis of interrelationship of body, mind and soul. Mind is functional only in a live body. Mind ('manas') is intimately connected to and is the controller of physical body with cognitive powers through five organs of perception ('Jnanendriyas') and reactive powers through five organs of action ('Karamendriyas'). While the body deals with objects, mind deals with thoughts with emotions and the intellect ('Budhi') deals with thoughts, ideas and decisions.[21]

There are four faculties at work in a human being in any given situation:

1. *Physical* is the most gross and rudimentary. These are basic neurologic reflexes like when one withdraws ones' hand on accidently touching a hot object.
2. *Mental* is dealing with emotional level. It is like expressing anger or love at someone verbally, physically or with body language.
3. *Intellectual* when using its determinatory logical powers to make the response balanced and well thought out. It is like staying calm and composed in adversity because anger will be counterproductive. It is an art to control angry outbursts and other emotions effectively. Intellect gives power to discern right from wrong.
4. *Spiritual* is the subtlest of all. It is the ultimate, when you try to dissociate yourself from attachments like pleasure and pain, anger and hatred to become equipoised, kind, considerate, forgiving and compassionate.

Right thinking with a logical mind and the intellect reduces conflicts. Moral, ethical and spiritual values bring in better understanding in human relationships refining our thoughts and actions. Personal introspection to assess one's correlation with the universe is ultimate self-knowledge. Once you understand the basic rule of life that 'you are no different from others as all beings are the same', you attain self-perfection. Most of us are too ignorant or too busy or are incapable of taking this path of humility. This path leads to Self-realization and enlightenment. Person who understands Self, has no ego, has no 'I and me' and enjoys immense happiness. Through self-realization he comes closer to and merges with The Supreme Soul.

Thoughts are fuel for human existence. Thoughts begin in the mind, take shape, get nourished and reside in subtle body (mind and intellect). The various stages of thoughts are in: the Mind (Manas), Intellect (Buddhi) and finally Ego (Ahamkara). Mind (Manas) develops doubt, indecision and restlessness at first impact of stimuli through cognitive awareness. After experience of this first impact, there is analysis, decision and determination by the intellect (Buddhi) and the person becomes calm as disturbance disappears. Ego results when 'doubt and decision' reside in the same person. This awareness gives rise to concept of limited- 'I', 'me', 'mine', 'I-ness' 'I decide', 'I want' and 'I am the boss.' Conditioned consciousness (cita or chitta) makes us aware that these thoughts belong to us conditioned in our mind. When this conditioning is eliminated chitta merges with pure consciousness resulting in eternal bliss: 'Sat-chit-ananda' with absolute existence- true knowledge- and eternal bliss.[21]

Man perceives the outer world through his sensory organs conditioned to his own interpretation. Ignorant person colors his world with his own egoistic perceptions, whereas, a man of steady wisdom sees life from within- inwards, from inner-voice and values based on spiritual and moralistic standpoint in an equipoised tranquil mind.

Ignorance is metaphorical to darkness that needs light of knowledge. There is hardly any trace of light in a cave or in a house with a small window, this dim flicker of light merges with sunlight outside when the walls are blown away. Similarly, when the walls of mind, intellect and ego around us are torn apart, our ignorance disappears; darkness is replaced as it merges with light of unconditional 'Pure Consciousness'. In Hindu philosophy there are three paths to attain pure bliss:

1. Yoga of Devotion (Bhakti Yoga) is the spiritual path of utter devotion, love and faith in God. It is the easiest path for the common man to totally surrender to God. It does not involve extensive yogic practices. With humility devotee takes refuge in God and becomes fearless and at peace under his protection. At the end of this path he abandons all desires and eliminates ego.

   'Engage your mind always in thinking of Me, become my devotee, offer obeisance to Me and worship Me, surely you will come to Me.' -Bhagwad Gita 9:34

2. Yoga of Knowledge ('Jana Yoga' is also called 'Gyana Yoga'). It is a discipline of attaining wisdom with an in-depth study of knowledge of ourselves and our spiritual relationship with the Creator. It needs a thorough understanding and introspection with steadfast determination, concentration and needs meditation to attain this goal of self-realization. 'There is nothing superior to knowledge. Without knowledge man is like animal.'[18] -Bhagwad Geeta 4:38.

   'By means of science, man attains freedom from ailments, by means of spiritual knowledge he gains salvation.' -Yajurveda 40:11.

3. Yoga of Action' ('Karma Yoga') is the 'dealing with the law of Karma; 'as you sow, so shall you reap'. Virtuous deeds bring happiness, whereas, sinful acts bring pain and suffering. Selfish acts bind the soul. By purifying one's heart one can provide self-less service to humanity without any ego.

'Without being attached to the fruits of activities, one should act as a matter of duty, for by working without attachment one attains Supreme.'-Bhagwad Gita 3:19

We can break the 'wall of mind' through the path of devotion ('Bhakti Yoga'), break the 'wall of intellect' with path of knowledge ('Jana Yoga') and break the 'wall of ego' by path of action ('Karma Yoga'). What remains after breaking these walls is 'Pure Objectless Awareness',[21] that brings 'ananda', as there remain no doubts, no desires and no misapprehensions. This is blissful spiritual insight into Atman.

During deep sleep the soul gets self-illuminated as it transcends the physical world. In deep dreamless sleep, there is no desire or dream, intelligent soul knows nothing, and there is nothingness within or without, a state of pure bliss.[86] On the other hand, dreaming soul creates its own world of pleasures and desires and is full of ignorance and illusions.

Spirituality purifies the soul. When all the senses are stilled and the mind is calm and at rest and the intellect does not waver; man attains freedom, as he is no longer a slave to his passions.

'Self is the rider, and the body the chariot, the intellect is charioteer, and the mind is the reins. The senses are the horses; the roads they travel are the mazes of desire. The self is the enjoyer when united with the body, the senses and the mind.'[91]

'The senses obey the mind in a wise man, mind is commanded by intellect, intellect by ego and the ego is under control of self. The self is the Supreme Being'[81] the omnipresent immortal creator Himself in Vedantic non-dualism belief. However, in dualism, it is believed that when one knows self, he is closer to the Supreme and not the Supreme himself.

Spiritual, moral and ethical duties of dharma enlighten our individual soul as it transcends our mind in the realms of pure consciousness. In the final stages of enlightenment one is completely detached from bondage of life and gets liberated from cycle of rebirth, and in this salvation, he merges and gets assimilated with the Supreme. One has to discard 'apparent-self' that is full of desires and egos and know the 'Real-Self'. The immortal is the one whose heart's desires are dead, knots to ignorance are untied and he understands the highest truths.

'We who are so lucky as to be born into the light—who see it every day and never think about it, we're blessed. We could have been born shadow souls who live and die in crimson darkness, never even knowing that somewhere there is something better.'

~ L. J. SMITH

221

CHAPTER 54

The Soul

'To your enemy – forgiveness, To your opponent --
tolerance.
To a friend -- your heart.
To a customer -- service.
To all men -- charity.
To every child -- a good example,
To yourself – respect, To mind—knowledge, To
Intellect—wisdom, To ego—selflessness and To
soul—liberation'

~ *UNKNOWN*

THE SOUL IS the supreme controller of life as it is the ultimate center of all thoughts and knowledge, desires and feelings and actions and deeds and awareness. Only human soul has the choice of a free will and is responsible for its actions.[2,24] Soul is eternal (existent: sat), has limited awareness (chit, cit) but unlike God it doesn't have bliss (ananda). God is *sat-chit-ananda* (Sachidanand): eternal with supreme awareness and unending bliss.[2,24,72,86] On the other hand 'Prakriti', the material cause of the universe comprising all non-living objects and physical bodies of all living things without soul are by itself inert physical matter in subatomic state.[2] It is limited with existence (sat) and without other attributes.

Soul controls ego, intellect and the mind. Mind directs the senses in various pursuits of life. The mind-intellect complex is the discriminator for assessing a suitable response for a desire, a thought or an event. One should always entertain pure thoughts for the good of the self and of others and harbor only righteous desires and refrain from sinful acts and vice. -Yajur Veda[24] Soul is the inner-voice always directing to the righteous path. Somehow we don't always listen to that inner-voice. It is that inner-voice which in the end preserves the character, honesty and integrity of a person by engaging his mind in the direction of noble thoughts and deeds.

The character of a man depends upon the power and control over his thoughts. After listening to inner-voice which is modified by past experiences and knowledge, wisdom (mind-intellect complex) takes over in providing a suitable response in terms of karma. Happiness, cheerfulness and fearlessness spring up in the mind from within when a good action is performed, whereas, when the action is evil in nature a sense of shame, fear and distrust follows. He who follows the inner-voice of the inner-self and acts accordingly, enjoys the bliss of 'moksha' (salvation) with incandescent enlightenment.[24]

Upanishads as the essence of Vedas are full of poetical depiction of the philosophy of mind and the soul. In 'Brahadaranyak' and 'Chhandogya Upanishads'[90,95] there are famous soul-searching dialogues to explore the nature of reality between King Janaka and Maharishi Yajnavalkya who was the disciple and prodigy of Uddalaka. Vedehi Janaka was not only a well-revered king but also a philosopher and a sage who used to engage in deep spiritual and philosophical discussions.

The dialogues go as such: "What is the source of light in the world?" Innocently King Janaka asked Yajnavalkya.

"The Sun"

"What is the source of light when the sun is set?"

"The Moon"

"What happens after the sunset when there is no moon?"

"There is the light of fire to guide us. When there is no fire the sound of speech leads us to the source. Person moves in the direction of the voice."

"What illuminate the path, when sun and moon have set, and there is no fire to burn, no candles to light and speech has ended?"

Yajnavalkya said, "The self. It is this light of the 'Self' that guide man to sit, to walk, and to work and to return home."

When king asked about 'Self'?

Yajnavalkya replied, "The Self is the Pursha-the inner person lodged in the heart; so potent that it illuminates with true knowledge and the truth. The inner person dwells in two states: one in this world and the second in the other. When born, he is embodied and joined with the evils of the world. When he dies, he leaves his body and abandons all evils. In that state the inner person sees both the evils of this world and joys of the other."

Soul is That Inner-person that endures pains and sufferings, joys and sorrows, and gets perfected in cycles of life and death according to Hindu philosophy.

There is famous philosophic discussion in Chhandogya Upanishads'[86,90] about soul (Atman) and its relationship with God (Parmatman). Sage Uddalaka asked and taught his son Shvetaketu a few philosophical questions to probe his intelligence after he returned from 12-year of study in 'Gurukul' (school). Uddalaka discussed in detail, the origin of things like 'Primal-Being' and 'Existent' ('sat') that cannot come from non-existent ('asat'). He also taught him about cosmic elements: 'heat-light, water and food' that are essential for existence. These three basic elements (three element doctrine) in their finest form maintain vital functions in man.[95] Even in today's age of scientific advancements we totally agree with importance of these three elements in order to nourish and sustain life.

Uddalaka gave example of rivers and oceans, as all waters coming from different rivers become imperceptible in the vast ocean. "Tell me more?" as Shvetaketu asked again.

Uddalaka gave analogy of honey. "Bees collect sweet juices from many flowers, fruits and trees. In honey all the collected juices assimilate and sources of various juices become imperceptible. Just as you merge with the Existent, The Being, your individual identity becomes imperceptible; you assimilate and become part of it."

Essential component of every living being is one and the same invisible Self or 'Ataman' (soul). At every step of teaching to his son, Uddalaka repeatedly said, "tat tvam asi" (That is you), to drive the point home to Shvetaketu.

These words have become cardinal philosophy of 'Vedanta' in Hinduism. 'This monistic (non-dualistic) view is different from the dualistic concept where human soul is perceived to be separate and not the same as God. At Salvation it merges with but remain distinct from Parmatman- Supreme soul 'atat tvum asi' - 'thou art not that' (O Soul! You are not God).'[24]

Just as a bird tied by a string is agitated and restless flying from one direction to another and finds no resting place until it is untied from the string, same way in human beings there is no peace of mind as mind is always wandering in different directions till it alights from all its attachments. [19-21] Similarly, the soul is in the bondage and it needs to be freed from all attachments of the world to attain deliverance.

The purity and conviction of one's own soul is essential. 'What is good for you is good for the others.' What is painful to you is painful to others. It should be the guiding principal of life.

The final goal, beyond birth and death cycle is salvation, when all good karmas have worked out, the soul is pure and perfected, there is nothing left to draw it back to 'birth and rebirth' cycle. There are no attachments and it is in perfect harmony and assimilates with Him. That is the final emancipation of the soul. It is like the river running into the ocean, not lost within its vastness, but truly conscious and aware of its oneness with divine infinite.

Katha Upanishad[79] says, 'Beyond the senses there are objects, beyond the objects, there is mind, beyond the mind there is intellect, the Great Self is beyond the intellect...beyond the great is The Person (Pursha, God). Beyond the Person, there is nothing-this is the goal, the highest road.' That self is hidden in all beings and does not shine forth.'[79]

The body is mortal, but the self (soul) is unborn, has no body and is 'immortal'. The soul suffers pleasure and pain in the incarnate body, but bodiless self is untouched by these.[86]

Existence of soul or self is denied in Buddhism.[64] According to Buddha 'the belief in eternal soul is a misconception of human consciousness.' 'Anatta' – no-soul doctrine of Buddha dictates that both the eternal soul theory: 'I have a soul' and the material theory: 'I have no soul' are obstacles to 'nirvana'. They both result from 'I am' misconceptions that cause difficulties in life.

Buddha did not find any eternal soul. 'When one sets no value on the body, or on sensation, or on perception, or on mental construction or on consciousness, he becomes free from the passions and he is liberated...rebirth is destroyed.'[15]

On the other hand, Jainism believes that souls exist in plants, worms, ants and wasps. Jains believe that immortal soul is individual and independent from other souls.

Soul and the spirit are important in Christianity. However, the Bible does not give a formal definition of the concept of soul resulting in different interpretations. There is dualistic concept of soul where a God-given soul is distinct from an inferior earth-bound body. Only human's 'rational soul' is immortal and capable of union with God.

Judaism believes in the concept of soul. Earthly existence of the man is meant for another and better existence for another and better world. Abraham is told by God, "Depart from this vain world: leave the body and go to thy Lord among the good." (Testament of Abraham) They believe in future world of resurrection rather than immortality. Kabbalah has three types of 'correlating' conduits in the soul:[49] There are The Pathways of Wisdom (*chochmah*), The Gateways of Understanding (*binah*) and The Bridges of Knowledge (*da'at*).

In Islamic view, soul is made of 'nor' (pure light) that belongs to Allah only, the pure light cannot harass people out of its body. Every soul has only one chance to enter the world and pass its defined time. Once time is over the soul is taken back.[50]

Soul is the inner-voice within us, the voice of virtue, but at the end we make our own choices with our free will. Soul is the key, which by spirituality and worship and prayers and good deeds can open the gates of heaven with everlasting happiness.

'When there is nowhere else to turn, turn inward. Enter into the sacred silence of your soul and ask for healing, guidance and personal peace. '

~ MICHAIEL BOVENES

CHAPTER 55

Meditation for Happiness

'Meditation is dissolution of thoughts in Eternal awareness or
Pure consciousness without objectification, knowing without
thinking, merging finitude in infinity.'

~ VOLTAIRE

MEDITATION, SPIRITUALTY AND true happiness are interlinked as they transcend the mind in the realms of contentment, self-control, peace and tranquility. The word 'Yoga' is derived from Sanskrit root: 'yuj' (to yoke) meaning to yoke or to create bondage between individual consciousness or the 'soul' with the universal consciousness or 'the spirit'. It is a physical, mental and spiritual practice of yogic discipline that originated at the dawn of civilization in Vedas in ancient India. Yoga is undertaken to attain peace and tranquility of mind and to endeavor a spiritual union with the divine Creator. Various forms of yoga are described in Vedas, Upanishads and in Bhagwad Geeta. 'Jana yoga' (yoga of knowledge), 'Bhakti yoga' (yoga of prayer), 'Karma yoga' (yoga of action) are just to name a few. West is familiar with only 'The Yoga of Meditation' and 'The Yoga Sutras of Patanjali', which includes 'Hatha Yoga' that defines yoga as 'the stilling of the changing states of the mind'. Yoga is a spiritual and an ascetic discipline, a part of which, including breath control (Pranayama), meditation, and the adoption of specific bodily postures (Hatha Yoga), are widely practiced for health and relaxation.

227

These yogic exercises discipline your mind and control your body. There is a widespread use of this discipline in the West with various names like 'Bikram Yoga', 'Lotus Yoga' and 'Aqua yoga' etcetera.

Various yogic practices originated in India and were later undertaken by Jainism and Buddhism. Gautama Buddha, the founder of Buddhism was born as Siddhartha to a Hindu king in India and subsequently got enlightenment (Nirvana). Buddhism has grassroots in Hinduism. Later on after brutal War of Taksila, Hindu King 'Ashoka the Great' converted to Buddhism and spread it to many Fareast countries including China and Japan. In The United States Swami Vivekananda undertook the first wave of introduction of Yoga to the west in 1893 when he attended 'Parliament of Religions' conference in Chicago.[115]

Yoga of Meditation is the practice of self-introspection where one trains one's mind in intense focus of concentration into sublime consciousness by a single pointed attention. It is a training to use the mind beyond its limits. It is a process of contemplation or reflection where one transcends into a heightened level of awareness. It promotes relaxation, builds life's force of internal energy and enlightens the mind. Meditation also transpires one to develop and accept new habits and get rid of the old and the unwanted ones.

Discipline and purity of mind are prerequisite of initiation into meditation. Unless you learn the know-how and ability to control and discipline your mind, you will have a long and tedious road ahead for meditating successfully. In the true traditions the first step is to start with strict practice of 'Yama' (rules of behavior or moral disciplines,) and 'Niyamas' (rules of self-discipline or physical disciplines) in daily life (chapter 8, Page 29) to purify the mind. How true it is to be able to meditate with a pure mind in the modern day life is subject to individual interpretation? However, only a wise and noble person will have the time, ability and aptitude to pursue this lifelong ardent art of meditation.

A learned and dedicated guru (teacher) is paramount to teach the art of meditation. Various books, courses, groups and seminars are available. Persistence and repetitive practice is essential for success.

Meditation should be done in a relaxed atmosphere in a dimly lit quiet place. One should first eliminate lethargy ('avarna') and distraction ('vikshepa') as dullness makes you sleep that is so common in meditation and distraction keeps your mind preoccupied and wandering with innumerable other disturbances.[19] Distractions like background sounds from a television or buzzing of a smartphone nearby need to be avoided. In early morning alpha state when brain is relaxed seems to be more appropriate time, however, meditation can be done any time that conveniently fits into day-to-day routine. One should wear loose clothes and have an empty stomach. In the beginning it is imperative to have the same routine every day, which will subconsciously prepare ones' mind for the meditation.

A correct posture (asana) to feel at ease is conducive to physical relaxation and inner peace. You can sit crossed legged on a floor like a yogi or sit in a comfortable chair in a quiet place and should try to sit straight without bending the spine.

Some routine hand posture, meditation 'mudra' like thumb and the index finger touching each other or the middle finger touching the thumb or holding a rosary or 'rudhra' beads also is preparatory. Keeping the index finger tip under thumb signify holding down your ego (index finger).

For beginners a picture or an object could be placed in front of the eyes to help focus. You can also focus with your eyes closed bringing intensity of concentration on the middle of forehead: 'Trataka' (aka third-eye meditation) and imagining some sacred object or a deity or the formless creator in your mind. Once seated in correct posture slowly start chanting some 'mantra' or simply saying a sacred word like 'Om' repeatedly (a few times).

Just doing these prerequisites by habit will prepare your mind for meditation. When one gets attuned to the practice of meditation and becomes an expert he or she will be able to do meditation anywhere, anytime. However, one needs to get conditioned to the routine first.

Slow and a deep breathing in and then out ('Pranayama)' helps in concentration. One should try to feel and hear the flow of air in and out of the nostrils as well as feel and hear the flow of air in and out from the lungs. The aim is to focus your mind in so much intense concentration ('Dharana') that you withdraw yourself inwards and detach from all sensory impulses. If some-how some thoughts crop up in your mind, it is good that you have noticed this distraction. Get rid of these unwanted thoughts by concentrating on deep breathing inhaling and exhaling to focus on meditation. You follow your thoughts as they come and disappear with deep breathing to get detachment from thoughts.[102] With eyes closed you concentrate on the sounds and learn to dissociate yourself and say 'I am not that sound.'

Meditation ('Dhayana') needs to be intense and uninterrupted 'single pointed focus' after excluding all other movements of thoughts and feelings. Only when your mind is merged in absolute stillness and is unable to perceive any external stimuli you may be able to connect with your Inner-Self. At first it seems like a distant soft echo, an imperceptible trace of an undertone sound, a gentle whisper coming from the outer world. With more practice and concentrated focus slowly the sound will become clearer and more audible as your mind transcends to your Inner-Self creating so high a volume of the amplified sound and incandescent light that drowns you in universal awareness of your Inner-Self.[110]

In last state there is a complete absorption ('Samadhi') of mind in Self-Realization. This state of 'pure consciousness' can be attained only when the mind is completely detached from 'conditioned consciousness'. When in deep sleep we enter into a state of non-awareness (unconsciousness) but when we are in 'samadhi' we enter a state of 'pure consciousness' with total awareness of Self. 'Dhayana, Dharana and Samadhi' are progressive stages of medita-tion. Golden triad of Buddha's teaching is: Good Conduct, 'Samadhi' and Wisdom. As you enter 'samadhi' one transcends and the wisdom awakens.[102]

'Meditation is not about feeling a certain way. It is about feeling the way you feel' said John Kabat-Zinn. Meditation is an art to regain immense inner pleasure by relinquishing the confines of your physical conscious and by tran-scending your mind into the reality of cosmic sub-consciousness.

'Prayer is you speaking to God. Meditation is allowing the spirit to speak to you.'

~ DEEPAK CHOPRA

CHAPTER 56

Mindfulness – A transformation for True Happiness

'Sometimes you need to disconnect and enjoy your own company.'

~ UNKNOWN

MINDFULNESS IS AN art of meditation by continuous clear awareness of the present moment. The yoga of meditation has been described extensively and practiced since Vedic times.[19] Gautama Buddha's upbringing consciously or subconsciously was influenced by that philosophy till he rediscovered himself to attain nirvana (enlightenment). Buddhists pursued this art and later it spread from India to Far East. Mindfulness practiced by Buddhists for thousands of years has found its way into mainstream modern day living with worldwide acceptance since 1970's when Jack Cornfield and Jon Kabat-Zinn brought the practice of mindfulness to the West. However, it is practiced in a secular way without much spiritual overtones and is becoming increasingly popular.

Mindfulness is a state of active tranquil moment-to-moment awareness of one's body as well as the feelings and thoughts including the mind and our surrounding environment without labeling it good or bad by being non-judgmental. The present moment is the only one that counts, it being a historical connect between elapsed moments of yesterdays and what is still to come in the unknown future. Mindfully enjoy by being aware of the present moment, here and now and with full concentration of whatever you are doing like eating and walking by enjoying each bite and each step respectively. You become oblivious to surroundings, as your mind and body are aware and focused at the same place at the same time.

To attain true 'nirvana' one does not need to run away from the present but should enjoy 'by stopping and touching deeply the present moments.'[41] Mindfulness is an attempt to completely submerge in the present and to enjoy every fabric of these precious moments. It is a unique art of day-to-day living to the full extent in the existing moment with total awareness.[91]

Mind is mostly imprisoned and preoccupied with day-to-day worries and insurmountable desires. It needs to be freed from these distractions by completely getting absorbed in the moments of today by mindfulness and to get rid of intrusive self-created sufferings.[102]

Since development of Mindfulness Based Stress Reduction (MBSR)[88] program by molecular biologist from MIT, Jon Kabat-Zinn (1979) there has been an extensive use of mindfulness practice across the globe. Mindfulness has moved into the mainstream classrooms and industrial and support programs. It calms the kids, make them kinder, and sharpen their brains with higher graduation rates.

There is resurgence of the old avenue of mindfulness for health and happiness. It has immense benefits in various fields of our everyday life. It reduces anxiety and helps to combat depression, substance abuse and other mental states in day-to-day life. It reduces chronic pain and helps insomnia. It lowers cortisol level and helps increase immune response. It reduces inflammatory cytokines that in turn create a friendly environment for aging. It also decreases risk of cardiovascular disease (high blood pressure and heart disease). Mindful meditation reduces cellular damage from highly reactive oxygen atoms known as free radicals. It may slow biologic aging by stabilizing telomeres. Mindfulness is good for cardiovascular health and may be helpful in maintaining ideal weight. It reinvigorates the mind and body with new energy to work more passionately without distractions. It fosters relationships and increases self-esteem and inner peace as well as tranquility and happiness.

Buddhist monks highly trained in meditation are found to have brain with more functional connectivity and a higher state of consciousness indicated by more gamma-wave activity on electroencephalography (EEG). On long term follow-up 'Meditators are found to slow age-related decline in grey matter in the brain.' With consistent attentiveness during repeated meditation exercises one can strengthen attentiveness like increasing muscle mass by physical exercise according to Kabat-Zinn.[88] Neuroplasticity is the ability of the brain to adapt and rewire and it can be achieved with brain exercises of mindfulness.

Slow deep breathing increases oxygen supply to the brain. It relaxes the mind, reduces stress and decreases the heart rate due to parasympathetic vagus-nerve activity, which is triggered on exhaling. This meditation technique of slow deep breathing using abdominal muscles (diaphragmatic breathing) reduces stress, anger and panic attacks. It is helpful when one is trying to focus or concentrate.

Mindful Meditation is typically done in basic erect sitting posture on the cushioned floor or a chair and in a quiet place. However, it can be done anywhere and anytime, even while standing and at place of work. One needs to avoid common distractions of daily life and suppress the urge to keep in touch with others especially due to ready availability of digital media. Everything else can wait while you pursue total focus on mindful moments. Practice concentration of mind with a focus on 'breathing in and out' as you feel the movement and sound of air moving in and out through the nostrils and also focus on air moving in and out of your lungs. Acknowledge your distracting thoughts and bring the attention back to breathing. Learn to ignore all distractions. Start mindful practice around 5 to 10 minutes each day and gradually increase it till you become proficient in it.

'Mindful breathing meditation' has been recommended to calm mind.[41] It calms personal emotional storms like intense unsurpassable anger and hate. You assume a sitting or standing position and you breath deep in and out using abdominal muscles. You should not fight anger but instead bring the anger to the surface of the naval by repeated deep breaths. Concentrate on mindful breathing and be aware of rise and fall of abdomen. The storm of anger will pass away within 10 to 15 minutes and you will become calm.

'Mindful walking' is wonderful ways to walk aimlessly without any destination, enjoying the moments by stopping at every step you take. You 'breathe in and out' mindfully, feeling the movement and sound of air, feeling the vibration of sound of the steps and feeling the fragrance of the earthly air. Breathe in and breathe out and walk one step at a time to watch color and beauty of the flowers and the leaves. Be aware as you enjoy each step of the present moments as it is like walking in the paradise touching happiness in pure mindfulness of nirvana.[41]

'Mindful music therapy' is mindful listening with complete awareness to every rhythm and note, enjoying every pitch and convolution of voice. It can be classical music, slow tempo music, soothing new age music or relaxing instrumental music. Mindful music therapy has been used to boost spirits and immune system in terminal cancer patients.

'Mindful Eating' and other modes of mindfulness can be practiced simply while doing housework like cleaning, cooking and painting. Whatever you are doing admire and enjoy each minor step of activity with full concentration.

In essence mindfulness is total awareness of the present moment. Fill yourself with the sight, sound and the smell of everything around you. Every aspect of nature is marvelous as nothing is good or bad. Enjoy doing everything in life with mindfulness to alley all your fears. It is like the world is at a standstill and frozen in the present moment in the microcosm for each of us to enjoy its wonderful existence. Enjoy these moments of immense beauty and intense happiness in the present, as these dynamic ever-changing moments will be gone in the very near future. Enjoy the present moment without being judgmental and be constantly aware of what you thinking and feeling. Mindfulness makes life happier by reducing stress at all levels. For mindfulness all you need is *(1) quietness* (without any disturbances- internal or external) while sitting, standing or walking, *(2) mindful focus on breathing* in and out, *(3) full absorption in present moments* (whatever you are doing*).* When your mind wanders away- just *refocus on breathing and (4) be non-judgmental.*

> *'Peace is present right here and now, in ourselves and in everything we do and see. Every breath… and every step we take can be filled with peace, joy and serenity... We need only to be awake, alive in the present moment.'*
>
> *- THICH NHAT HAHN*

234

Part Six

The Ultimate Goal

CHAPTER 57

Idealism, Secularism and Happiness

Imagine there's no countries
And it isn't hard to do
Nothing to kill or die for
And no religion too
Imagine all the people
Living life in peace...'

— *John Lennon, 1971*

HAPPINESS IS A byproduct in pursuit of excellence. It is closely intertwined with ideas, ideals, ethics and morality. Positive psychology of mind cultivates positive ideas to foster happiness. High ideals and ethics resolve conflicts to bring harmony in relationships and generate empathy and compassion in a kind and considerate mind. A positive atmosphere promoting individual well-being is as important as well-being of all around us. We are happy if everyone else is happy. 'Happiness begets happiness.'[110]

Idealism is the philosophy that defines the central role of refined ideas. It is a spiritual interpretation based on personal experiences of life. The experiences may differ in the different states of mind of the same individual. Same event or an experience can likewise create a different impression in minds of different individuals. It is not independent of mind as it is experienced through it. 'In naïve idealism perceived reality can be different from true realism.'[110]

Spiritualism germinates and nourishes ethical ideals, which ends up making the world a better place to live. The ideals not only reinforce nobility of mind but also fertilize human conscious. A proclivity for following moral, ethical and spiritual ideals in this pluralistic society is necessary for progress. It makes us strive for absolute truth, goodness and perfection. True love under these ideal conditions can easily envision trust, compassion, humility and happiness. Idealism at large lies in the ability to seek for equality, tolerance and acceptance in the face of diverse personal, religious and cultural divides. In true ideal world every one is a part of one big happy family. True idealism is often impossible and unattainable beyond the concepts of the world, as it exists today. High ideals of dreams, hopes and vision of one-world is the key to universal happiness.

Individual point of view based on personal goals is self-centered, whereas, societal point of view centers on ideals that are inclusive and suited for everyone and that varies in different communities and cultures. Worldview on the other hand lies in more elaborate and comprehensive wider vision, a melting pot for harmonious integration rather than confrontational attitudes.

According to Dalai Lama[60] there are two pillars of secular ethics in the concept of inclusive approach in this pluralistic society: a), Shared humanity with shared aspiration for happiness with avoidance of suffering and, b), interdependence for day-to-day existence. When we inculcate these two basics of ethical ideals in our mind it will bring forth an abundance of generosity, love and compassion to the forefront of our mental attitude. The ideas constantly evolve in this dynamic world but both idealism and realism view the truth as absolute, permanently enduring and immutable. Feeling good about doing the right thing is reaffirmation that one is on the right track and in possession of the high ideals. Cultivating gratitude and idealism in our daily lives inspire others to be a part of the quest to make the world a happier place to live.

Ideas and ideals reflect the inner refinement of conscious with evolution of mind from ordinary luminance to brilliant incandescence. Eleanor Roosevelt reflected that 'Great minds discuss ideas; average minds discuss events; small minds discuss people.' 'Words without action are hypocritical.'[110]

Secularism is a forum where society does not adhere to religious biases or beliefs. 'It should not be seen as absence or lack of faith but rather a positive moral creed' according to Phil Zukerman in his book 'Living a Secular Life'. Secular morality is based on ideals of individualism to become considerate and empathetic towards others, 'not harming others and helping those in need'. It is a 'drive to purity, self-transcendence, and sanctification' says David L Brooks. A belief in secularism can tear down walls of hatred that exist in the world today. We can practice religious diversity as well as secular ideals to make world a happy place to live.

Intellectual courage nourishes and preserves ethics, ideals and morality. Idealism and secularism philosophy can be applied in multifarious directions: like in world peace, in spreading education, in fighting hunger and in eradicating poverty and discrimination on the bases of ones' color, cast and the creed.

An idealist seeks answers to the true meaning and the purpose of life in the continuous search of happiness. If every one of us tries even a little to make a difference in the world it will be altogether a happier place to live. It is when minds and ideals are cohesively bound together like bricks and mortar that can result in true happiness. Idealism is deeply rooted in honesty, integrity, perseverance and compassion.

'One should always aspire to entertain pure thoughts for the good of the self as well for the good of others around him by trying to have only righteous desires and thus try to renounce sin and vice. One should aspire for purity of mind and shun wickedness and thus have the courage to perform acts of great public good.' Yajur Veda[24]

Rather than pure idealism a pragmatic approach is necessary to achieve happiness in the world. Instead of mere ideas and theories one has to find reasonable and logical way of doing things or of thinking about problems and issues that is based on dealing with specific situations. One should try to be inclusive and not be oblivious to legitimate concerns of others. Idealism and secularism dwell in morality with personal transcendence full of selfless deeds of love and compassion.

'Let it never be said by future generations that indifference, cynicism or selfishness made us fail to live up to the ideals of humanism...' said Nelson Mandela on accepting Nobel Peace Prize in 1993

Some simple ideals of the wise to practice are:

All human-beings are equal irrespective of cast, color and creed
Don't be judgmental
Listen to others' point of view
Don't be argumentative
Respect every ones' rights
Be inclusive not divisive
Don't hate: anyone, any religion or ideology
Always try to be kind, compassionate and forgiving
High ideals uplifts everyone
Freedom of press is as important as personal freedom
Everyone has freedom of choice including choice to disagree[110]

'The darkest places in hell are reserved for those who maintain their neutrality in times of moral crisis.'

- Dante Alighieri

CHAPTER 5 8

Compassion - a link to Happiness

'There is no exercise better for the heart than reaching down and lifting people up.'

~ JOHN HOLMES

COMPASSION IS AN emotion that you feel on seeing pain and sufferings of others and motivates you to help them get out of their plight. It is sympathetic awareness of their distress that inculcate a desire to alleviate their sufferings. There is so much inequality, discrimination, injustice and prejudice in all walks of life that simple empathy and feel only emotional about their sufferings does little unless you are motivated to help. Selfless kind altruistic behavior kindles the feeling of compassion that transcends your mind where you not only want to help but also have a genuine desire to 'share in their sufferings'. Compassion without acting on this impulse to help is an empty jargon and is an exercise in futility. It is the desire to help someone who is hungry or sick or in pain or in trouble.

Compassion brings more happiness to giver than recipient.

Acts of compassion lead to bonding and a positive sense of accomplishment helping general well-being, cardio-vascular and immune systems. There is lowering of the heart rate and a decreased agitation of mind. It lights up 'brain reward system' through impulses and neurochemicals that bring pleasure and happiness. Compassionate people whose happiness comes from 'doing good to others' have favorable gene profile with less inflammation and better antibody and antiviral activity that is conducive for health.[35,117]

You must try to inculcate considerate compassion in your deeds. Motivation to help others open the gates of opportunity and widens the horizon, as you are no more blind-eyed to sufferings around you. It is frequently difficult to measure the extent of sufferings even with an open empathetic mind. Often the scene can be dramatically gloomy where every corner is dark and neglected. There are weak and the poor helpless hungry children, forgotten and ignored orphans and poor widows, poverty stricken unemployed illiterate people and heart rendering plight of suppressed and deprived individuals. Slaves of child labor and sex-trade victims for prostitution are other examples that can awaken our conscious if we have one and have the time to listen to it. If not this what else can awaken us from the slumber of selfish neglect.

A sense of connectedness with under-privileged creates a spiritual and compassionate bond of solidarity where our own happiness or suffering is no different than theirs. Compassion is a rich powerful word; it is more than pity, kindness or benevolence. It is transformation of behavior to share in someone's grief and to suffer in his or her pains by participation and collaboration. Degree and the extent of help have more to do with intensity of desire that comes from within and depends on lot of other factors including time and other resources. One can device in strategies by networking and partnerships to collaboratively help by compassionate acts without needlessly duplicating the efforts. Once this sense of compassion is aroused in an individual don't compel them to do more. Try to be a part of compassionate world by individual and collective acts to make a world of shared sufferings, a happy place to live. Happiness that you germinate in others and harvest yourself as the giver is beyond any definable limits.

Working on POWs during Indo-Pakistan conflict in 1965 as a young aspiring surgeon in-training I quickly learnt the true and practical meaning of compassion to alleviate their pain, to be considerate treating their injuries and listen to their conflicts of mind with compassionate reassurance. I did not know anything about Geneva rules of treatment of POWs but I followed rules of humanity engraved deep in my conscious. I treated injured POWs and our own soldiers with same degree of love and compassion. I felt so proud and happy treating them all with utmost gentle care. The compassionate bond between a patient and a physician are based on no religion or geographical boundaries.

Empathy makes you feel the experiences and sufferings of others. In *compassion* you are directed to positive feelings with kind warm thoughts towards others, whereas, empathy can generate unpleasant negative cumbersome feelings, 'bad decision-making, burnout and withdrawal.'(Paul Bloom, Professor of Psychology at Yale –WSJ December 3-4, 2016) Empathy undoubtedly is a virtue that can backfire with negativism as it makes us unreasonable and biased in conflicting issues. Either side of issue can generate empathy.

'Insula and cingulate cortex' of brain are activated in empathy from painful experiences. Compassion, on the other hand, activates 'ventral striatum' that deals with reward and motivation. (Paul Bloom)

'Compassionate world is possible when every human being treats others as they wish to be treated- with dignity, equality and respect.' Toledo is actively pursuing to become a compassionate city. Bob Moyers of Liberty Center, Ohio is known as Mr. Happy. He always talks about compassion, forgiveness, happiness, unconditional love and Jesus Christ.

It is imperative to instill the spirit of empathy and compassion in children at an early age before they adapt to present day self-centered egoistic culture of 'me-me generation' that is full of narcissism and indifference. Low-empathy teens develop aggressive behavior, flawed understandings and conflicts in relationships. As a parent you must engage young children in empathetic deeds by involving them in kind acts of giving, helping and serving the needy and immersing and nurturing their mind in sprit of compassion.

Abnegation is an act of sacrificing personal interests by helping others. Compassion overshadows selfishness, vanity and pride. Compassion brings humility, love and kind-heartedness to the forefront.

The Compassionate deeds will not only bring happiness to others but also to the giver as well. Compassion is contagious whereas apathy is demoralizing.

Compassion reclaims purpose in life. Treat everyone with fairness, equality, humility, mercy, grace and compassion and without any vanity and ego.

Every religion teaches love and compassion but love and compassion have no religion, these are echoes from the inner-self.

'Love and compassion are necessities, not luxuries. Without them, humanity cannot survive.'

~ DALAI LAMA

CHAPTER 59

Live a Purposeful life

*'Your life won't be perfect, but it can be purposeful. Live for
something bigger than yourself and leave a mark on the world.'*

~ *JAR OF QUOTES.COM*

LIFE IS FULL of timeless moments that bring credence to our existence. A purposeful life entails far more than pursuit of happiness. It goes way beyond our sensual existence as it is based on the true idealistic goals of life. Rather than staying confined to our cozy nest we need to crack this shell of our comfort zone and discover the outer-world and adjust to the changing circumstances. We need to balance our life and remain focused in our endevours instead of running aimlessly in different directions.

Imagine you are in the middle of the battlefield of life and you are surrounded by all other entities. You in the middle is the one who counts the most. You have to know yourself and pursue the life and the dreams you see fit. You have to know yourself inside out with full awareness. You have to know everything around you to comprehend, progress and achieve. Remember you are the lead character; you have to play the drama of life with other actors on the world stage in natural environment suffused with man-made architecture and technology. You have to understand and interact with the world around you to lead your life and define a purpose for your existence.

The circle of life is:

Me in the middle – central focus of life

Around Me – 'outwardly' as the world and the people around me
Within Me – 'inwardly' as consciousness, inner-voice, The Creator

We have to know all the three elements to purposefully thrive in life. Being a human is the most precious gift. We have the will, the choices and the opportunities and the freedom to pursue life in our endeavours. Me matters the most but we have to know and build relationships with others and lead the life that is best for us.

The central focus of life is me that creates the basic question - Who is me? First step to find the purpose of life is to *discover yourself*, as to who you are and what are your strengths and weaknesses? Everyone is so different with diverse personalities, dreams and expectations. There is no simple answer for your aspirations: you may want to become an artist, a policeman, a doctor, a computer scientist, an entrepreneur or an astronaut. You may want to explore different galaxies; the sky is the limit.

Full awareness of your thoughts, feelings and emotions is the key for progression. You need full personal awareness in all dimensions of life. It gives the opportunity to make necessary changes to live in the present moment. *Emotional intelligence* builds relationships and is helpful in personal as well as professional growth.

You need to have *trust and confidence* in your abilities and to *motivate* yourself to maximize your potentials. Best is to dwell in your strengths and work insistently to achieve. This will help you to cross the threshold of your confines. You can always do better with a positive enforcement of your psyche. Real growth is beyond your imaginary boundaries of success. You can lose track of time in your prolific periods when the work is of your liking, as it will invigorate your abilities to passionately confront all the challenges. Remember there is no limit for success and progression. You should remain *positive and optimistic* without any fear and set your own *values and goals*. Keep focused by working to the best of your abilities. Work done with good intentions does not need any explanation.

The world and the people around me need attention. Try to understand by carefully *listening* to them to know as to who they are, what they need and what are their feelings and expectations? Are they important and what is their relationship to me? Do I have any duties or obligations to them? We need to build relationships by solving conflicts. Many times all they need is the listening ear. 'If you can't help anybody at least don't hurt them.'[110] Be *gracious* and *forgiving* and *appreciative* to people around us. Remember to treat others the way you want to be treated. Mindfully enjoy life and the gifts of the nature in the present moment. Try to be a *good neighbor* in your community and be a good citizen of the world.

Self-introspection to reflect on your conscious, your inner-voice is essential to lead the right path. Listen to your inner-voice to discover the outer-world in order to become a forgiving, kind and considerate and loving and compassionate human being. Try to understand others and be empathetic and helpful and somehow find solution to their problems if you can and you have the time and resources to do that. Dedicate to a cause. You can passionately pursue a purpose that may seem simple and straightforward like helping in a soup kitchen. What you need is patience and commitment for the cause.

Remember you are the central figure surrounded by the others: your neighbors, your community and the society, the universe and their needs. Inwards within you is consciousness, your inner-voice, The Creator Himself, The God if you are a believer, or the unknown entity or simple a question mark?

In essence you live the life the way you deem fit. You define purpose of your existence. A happy comfortable family life and a good paying job is everyone's dream. But at the end of the day think if you have done any worthwhile thing for someone else, a simple act of kindness without expecting any reward or appreciation.

Compassion, honesty, forgiveness, service and sacrifice sanctify the true meaning of purposeful life. Leading a meaningful life with love and compassion brings in immense happiness. Everyday I witness young and the old volunteers in the hospitals trying to help the sick patients to bring a flicker of smile amidst their pains. People who help others achieve their dreams or give them their shoulders to lean on and cry are the true angels and their helping hands are The Hands of God. They serve the purpose of our existence, as they are our true gardeners of life.

> *'Put your hours to be productive, your weeks to be educational,*
> *your life to be experience of growth, to change and to grow.'*

> ~ IYANLA VANZANT

CHAPTER 60

Salvation – The Final Destination

'The work of salvation, in its full sense, is about the whole human beings, not merely souls; about the present, not simply the future; and about what God does through us, not merely what God does in and for us.'

~ N T WRIGHT

PURPOSE IN LIFE is to live fully, enjoy the moments of everyday life and to make it complete and worth living. But somewhere in our journey we need a spiritual connect in order to understand The Creator and seek the 'real purpose' in life. Sooner it happens in life better it is. Salvation is the liberation from all those attachments that robs the peace of mind and causes all types of confusion manifesting as pain and pleasure, happiness and sorrow and success and the failure. The road to salvation is difficult, long and tedious and not easily achieved. First you need to clean your body and then purify your mind and the soul. You have to seek the truth for the mind, purity for the intellect and perfection for your soul by discarding all sins. Enlightened liberated souls attain super-consciousness and everlasting bliss.

The union of soul to the body is called its birth, whereas, dissolution of this union is called the death. True salvation or emancipation is liberation from this cycle as the soul is perfected and is without any fears, doubts, sorrows and attachments. Salvation is liberation from the cycle of births and rebirths- it is called 'Moksha' (Moksa) in Sanskrit by the Hindus and 'Nirvana' by the Buddhists. Other synonyms for salvation are kaivalya, mukti, union with God and enlightenment.

At death the body dies, whereas, cremation or burial is mergence of 'ashes to ashes and dust to dust' while the immortal soul is reborn in another body. Rebirth depends on karma in the past life and the state of perfection and attributes of the soul. Desirable rebirths occur according to ones wishes, desires and karma in the past life. If you spent all your life chasing money and were virtuous, you may be born in riches, but not so if You have been sinful and were chasing the wealth by crimes and deceits. If you were after knowledge you may end up being a noble person, a scientist or an inventor. According to Hindu philosophy, being born in a poor or a rich family is no accident but you are reaping the fruits of the past karma. Some persons are highly intelligent while others are not. Even children born in same families have different aptitudes, IQs (Intelligence Quotient) and different outcome in life becoming successful or utter failures. If you believe in justice of God you can never accept the notion that such differences are brought by acts of God. These are not His thoughtless acts.[113] He is neither partial nor unjust. We are all children of God and He is fare and loves us all the same. In the present life we are only reaping the fruits of our past karmas. This manifests as states of happiness or sufferings in the current life. We all have ups and downs with pleasure and pain in life as fruits of good and bad karmas in the past life.

There is justice and orderliness in His creation as principals of rebirth and laws of karma (action and reaction) are inseparable.[113] We have to be virtuous, altruistic, considerate and compassionate in selfless deeds (Sakam karma) to make the difference.

It is only after complete detachment and disassociation from earthly objects, desires and ego that a person finally transcends to selfless awakening of mindless reality. He is liberated and attains moksha as he merges with 'Parmatman' (Supreme-soul). This Self-Realization is the Cosmic Union that cannot be described in words. It needs to be experienced. This is the journey from darkness to light when ignorance created by ego dissolves on gaining true-insight experiencing Eternal Bliss full of contentment, joy and love.[3,123]

You achieve moksha when you conquer your mind with egoless detachment to attain pure, motionless tranquil state with inner transcendental awakening: mindlessness, thoughtlessness and actionlessness. This is attainment of Divine Consciousness, a dispassionate state in which all earthly bonds of the soul are dissolved and the soul is free to be with God in a state of immense bliss.[3]

In Buddhism the main focus is to allay sufferings of life because according to Buddha focusing primarily to attain 'nirvana' will lead to more attachments and more sufferings. Chanting or copying of 'sutras', prayers, altruism and other virtuous karma will increase your merits for a desirable birth and bring you closer to enlightenment that will end rebirths, thus attaining 'Nirvana' to become free from all sufferings and existence.[15,62]

Buddhism teaches a *Noble Eightfold Path* for Nirvana:

-Right Understanding of 'four noble truths': The existence of suffering, the cause and the end of suffering, end of the pain
-Right Resolve: Renounce bodily pleasures, Do no harm to anyone and be kind to everyone
-Right Speech: No gossip, lie or slander
-Right Karma: Do not kill, steal or engage in unlawful sexual act
-Right Occupation: work at a job that does not harm anyone
-Right Effort: to eliminate evil, develop good conduct in a clean mind
-Right Mindful Contemplation: to be aware of your deeds, words and thoughts to free yourself from desires
-Right Meditation: to concentrate and focus in your unwavering calm mind

In Nirvana one transcends to a state of blissful nothingness. Buddhism is silent on God and does not believe in the existence of soul. The noble path of Nirvana in Buddhism is no different from the principals of rightful ethical living in Hinduism practicing both moral ('yamas') and physical ('niyamas') disciplines in life (Chapter 8, Page 29), the essence of 'Gurbani" in Sikhism or 'The Ten Commandments.'

Anger, greed, hatred, pride, ego and attachments are our inadequacies ('doshas'), which act as our eternal enemies that derail our mind and hinder our quest for happiness. True salvation lies in winning over these obstacles. Salvation is not renunciation of all possessions and living an acetic life but in true sense lies in renunciation of evil desires, selfishness, apathy, jealousy, hatred and other negative destructive traits. Vivekananda asked the individual who is trying to achieve moksha to come out of his narrow-minded vision and combine the ideal of service to humanity with the ideal of renunciation and cease to think of his individual salvation.[115]

One doesn't have to be religious to achieve moksha. Spiritual path helps one to follow the ethics of life, by being truthful compassionate and considerate, by karma-yoga in passionately and selflessly performing good deeds and by austerity and by altruism. You can even reach the ultimate goal by simply leading a moralistic life. This will make your existence worth living in this life and beyond. You can attain salvation (moksha) in your lifetime if your material ('artha') and social ('kama') pursuits are based on ethical and moral ('dharma') values.[52]

There are pragmatic ways to practice idealism in this utopian society where for your salvation you don't have to relinquish all comforts and live an ascetic life in seclusion. The attachments of mind and the brain to outward sensory objects need to be deflected inwards to the inner-voice to transform conditioned-consciousness to pure-consciousness leaving no room for egoistic self-centered desires as conditioned mind will be replaced by a selfless, kind, considerate and empathetic mind.

True meaning of many rituals in Hinduism need to be redefined and reinterpreted[19] by a meaningful modern day approach:

'Yajna' instead of ritual of prayers, offerings and chanting mantras around agni (fire), 'Yajna' gets defined by self-dedicated work in any activity.'

'Tapas' instead of religious austerity that ranges from simple self-denial to rigorous yogic acetic ordeals, 'Tapa' gets defined by self-denial and self-control of ego.'

'Sannyasi' instead of being a religious ascetic who has renounced the world, 'Sannyasi' is portrayed as the one dedicated to self-perfection by renunciation of all evils, desires, anger and fear.

'Moksha' in pragmatic sense means- liberation from all undue attachments and evils of the world to enjoy bliss of heavens in this very embodied soul. It is nurtured by morality and ethical idealism and can even flourish equally in secular as well as spiritual attitudes of love, tolerance and compassion.

'The salvation of mankind lies only in making everything the concern of all.'

~ ALEKSANDR SOLZHENITSYN

CHAPTER 61

Heaven on Earth - Reality or a Myth?

'The mind is a universe and can make a heaven of hell, a hell of heaven.'

~ JOHN MILTON

MIND AS THE instrument of thoughts has the key to happiness with the capacity and the power to make our life a living heaven or hell. A considerate and caring positive mind triumphs in love, laughter, contentment and compassion. It brings in happiness to make the life worth living. On the other hand, a person that dwells in negativity sees only the adversities in life and is full of hatred, jealousy, anger, restlessness and misery. He is not only living in hell but he has same real hell in store for him in future.

The long journey of life begins with the birth of an innocent child that quickly learns cooing, smiling and giggling. Learning process in children is influenced by various sources, from his parents, his siblings, teachers and others imbibing both good and the bad traits. Imperfections and impurities of mind can be engrained by various bad influences that transform mind to become flawed in character and convictions. Presently an egocentric mind of millennial is in the forefront; 'The Me Me Me Generation' blowing 'me me and mine' jargons. 'That is mind of a self-centered narcissistic personality where the wisdom is clouded by ego and vanity.' (Time Magazine, August 2013)

According to religious teachings there is a heaven and a hell. I don't dispute their teachings and beliefs and conception of reality as they see. Heaven is supposed to be full of all the luxuries and comforts and all that we can ever dream of, whereas, the hell is place full of all miseries. Is heaven or hell a reality or an Illusion? For argument sake where is heaven? Is it situated beyond the distant skies, beyond outer space and beyond all galaxies? Is there seventh heaven? Has any living being ever seen it? Does it really exist and where does it exist? Concept of heavenly design and pleasures and amenities it offers varies in different cultures and religions. Is there one or more than one heaven? If it is one, who's God is present there? Is everyone's God one and the same? If God is omnipresent, being present everywhere, is he present in hell as well? He is, He has to be - being omnipresent. Is heaven a physical place or merely a conceptual luxuriously pristine myth? Do heaven and hell really exist? Was this concept created for humans to make them follow the virtuous path and avoid being sinful? It seems there are more questions than authentic and verifiable reasonable answers. The big realistic question is 'are heaven and hell right here on this living earth?'

'For an intelligent man, this promise of heaven is nothing more than a charming hallucination. Such a vague goal cannot be sufficiently encouraging to coax out of an intelligent man all his enthusiasm and sincerity.'[19] 'Paradise is not a place, it's a state of mind', is a realistic interpretation of Frank Sonnenberg.

'Every intelligent person who has enthusiasm and courage to muster life and lives virtuous life like an angel upon earth ruling over circumstances and smiling at adversities, leads a heavenly life.[19] Our ideals need to be spiritual or even secular and not necessarily religious.

We live in a materialistic society full of temptations, seduced by desires and myriad of luxuries. Unending cravings for acquisition of more wealth and materialistic possessions breeds more greed, creates anxiety and fear-jeopardizing happiness.

Anyone, rich or poor, young or old person can make his life miserable of his own making. One doesn't need to wait till after death, one's life can be a living hell or heaven while still living on this earth.

We can try to make appropriate changes in our life to make it more pleasant and live a heavenly life. We can lead our life by careful introspection and change our modus operandi to channel our desires and our actions and thoughts in the right direction by transforming ourselves and eliminating bad habits and erroneous beliefs. There is crisis of consciousness.[55] Our individual consciousness results from conditioning of our mind and brain respectively - *outwards* from desires of the sensory objects that seduce us to indulge. Instead we need to look *inwards* to transform. Everyone's pleasures and pains and sufferings are the same and this 'human consciousness' inwardly is the same shared by every human being.[55] We need to bring a change to sublimate human behavior by transformation.

We must realize that:

1. *All beings are the same.* What is good for you is good for others as well.
2. Practice *moderation* and follow the *Middle Way* without overindulgence and by avoiding extremes of earthly desires as well as extreme practice of ascetic discipline and in the process ending up torturing one's body and mind.[15] Behaviors of extreme nature can make the life miserable and happiness impossible. There is no middle path between good and evil or right or wrong.
3. Follow your *inner-voice* to be *righteous* and *truthful* in our thoughts and deeds. *Desires* lead to short-lived happiness. We live a disorderly life in this chaotic world by being a slave to our desires. Sensory perception of a beautiful *object* creates a *thought* to admire it: like admiring the sunset, a garden, Eiffel tower or Taj Mahal. The thought of owning it does not cross your mind. 'A *thought to have* that object creates *desire* (ischa).' We can surrender to that thought and indulge in it or we can suppress it or try to control it, creating a conflict.[55] Suppressed-desires cause *conflicts* leading to loneliness, anger, fear and misery. Good desires are to excel and to get better in life such as desire for knowledge and self-reflection and desire to help others with love and compassion.
4. '*Desire for Wealth*' and other materialistic things are not contrary to any religious or moral practice so long as these are earned by honest means. Wealth is essential for both personal needs as well as need for the family and the society. Wealth does not proportionately increase

happiness; on the contrary it can enhance more greed, more desires, selfishness and restlessness. Curbing ego and vanity and sharing some of one's wealth with less fortunate and the needy brings true happiness. True legacy of a person lies in as to what he has done for the society at large.

5. '*Karma*' is the not fate, it is creator of fate in this life and beyond. According to the law of Karma good or bad deeds are rewarded accordingly. Selfless pious deeds rendered with a compassionate heart are of the highest merit. These are to work with passion and do it to the best of your abilities?

6. '*Spirituality*' (Sadhana) is ego-transcending practice for self-enrichment and self-realization. There is liberation from bondage with dispassion. Spiritual and religious guidance is essential for inner peace and values. It also includes caring for the needy and the poor by empathy, compassion and philanthropy.

7. '*Discernment*' (Viveka) is the positive learning process by objective distinction between right and wrong in our thoughts words and deeds. By abnegation 'Viveka' prepares our mind for contemplation and keeps it away from preoccupation with worldly attachments.[20]

8. '*Detachment*' (Vairagya) is a negative process of dispassion by detaching oneself from all urges and agitations of mind. In olden days in 'Vairagya' people used to leave all worldly ways and live the life of an ascetic in the forests for contemplation and meditation. This interpretation of vairagya modified in modern context. 'it is neither the only way nor is the right way.' One can live a better and fuller life and doesn't have to live necessarily in dreadful conditions. In older age obligatory duties to family and the society need to be partly shared. One can minimize ones' responsibilities by gradual process of detachment if possible under the given circumstances. Relinquishing these duties altogether is pure escapism and defeats the purpose of life. You should gradually withdraw yourself and find time for introspection. You don't have to be an ascetic to enjoy blissful happiness in life.

9. *Rectify your shortcomings:* One can live a heavenly life on earth by avoiding notorious '*doshas*' (deficiencies, inadequacies) of mind by controlling organs of perception and action. By rectifying our inadequacies (doshas) like desires, anger, greed, attachments and ego and vanity (kama, krodha, lobha, moha and ahamkara) we can transform ourselves to be considerate, forgiving and compassionate. Everyone should constantly strive to remove these inadequacies in life to make this world a happier place to live.

10. *Anger and greed* like a vicious disease are the most powerful enemies of man. By abandoning desire one becomes happy, by relinquishing greed one becomes prosperous, by renouncing anger one finds peace and by dispelling jealousy and hatred one finds love and tolerance.

11. *Curb your Ego:* Egoistic '*I-consciousness*' is the root cause of miseries in the world. We are erroneously proud of 'me and mine', our name and fame. 'One who can curb ego discovers oneself' and gets true enlightenment and liberation ('moksha') in this world and beyond. One should keep away from the ego wall of display. 'The ego needs to go' and it is the hardest and last thing to let go.

12. *The Art of Listening* fosters understanding and resolves conflicts. 'Life is a process of relationships. Instead of being vocal or argumentative try to listen to your wife, husband, children and neighbors, also the wind and birds.'[55] Listen, watch, observe and appreciate the pristine beauty in everything with mindfulness.

13. *Seek real knowledge: Ignorant mind* is eclipsed with superstitions and fantasies that result in flaws and conflicts of mind. Ignorance (Avidya) is lack of true knowledge (Satya-Vidya). We can replace ignorance of mind with true knowledge by contemplation, discernment[81] and self-reflection.

14. *Don't chase the elusive happiness* as it is just like pursuing one's own shadow. Pleasures are insatiable. These passionate flames within can only be quenched by self-control.

Basically you can make your life heavenly if everyone is trying to lead a meaningful life, works passionately and earns honestly, and if everyone is truthful, compassionate, considerate, and empathetic and have control over ever-increasing desires. However, there are all kind of people and most of us are egoistic and selfish and are reluctant to any change. A small percentage of us are even deceitful and engage in many types of unlawful criminal activities. It is only in the absence or rehabilitation of such people that the world can be transformed to a living heaven.

Only positive thoughts and actions can bring in the best within us. On the other hand, negativism has toxic mix of envy, resentment and hatred.

In essence, 'good people go to heaven and bad people go to hell.' Good or bad resides within us. Good people are the angels that create heaven. 'Heaven is a choice you must make, not a place you must find. (Wayne Dyer)

Is quest for heaven in afterlife real or a myth? According to Stephen Hawking, 'There is no heaven, it is a fairy story.'

Life will be worth living and heavenly if a person has his mind and intellect under control and in harmony and is no longer a slave to his desires. This liberated self-illuminated soul attains moksha and lives in a state of everlasting bliss. The '*liberated soul*' can exist with or without earthly body. Mukt-jiwa (liberated living-human), the enlightened soul is leading a blissful life while still living in the human body. Such a man gets rid of ignorance, breaks all the shekels of worldly attachments and gets liberated from cycle of birth and rebirths to attain everlasting bliss. We spend all life in fear and anxiety of events after-death. No one asks the pertinent question as to what happens before-death? Only living a life of love and compassion is bound to bring happiness in this life and beyond.

Like most of us, I am religious and believe in prayers and existence of God. The creator rewards everyone fruits of one's karma. All of us endeavor to get liberated and attain moksha and go to heaven. There are religious beliefs and prophecies that I don't want to dwell in. I believe in pluralistic society and respect everyone's right to choose his or her religion or no religion. I love and respect them all.

Let us assume you behave in a righteous and compassionate manner and lead a pious life and regularly pray to God. Well that is great. You not only destine yourself for heavens above in afterlife but also may end up living happy heavenly life on the earth as well. Heaven and hell exist on this very earth.

On the other hand, one can be non-believer in God, not believing in hell or heaven but as long as he conducts his life ethically, compassionately, morally and righteously, he can make his life happy and contribute immensely to make the world a heavenly place for others as well.

'I don't know whether to believe in hell or heaven exist after you die. But I do know that both places exist on earth and you don't have to die to experience them.'

~ UNKNOWN

Part Seven

The Synopsis of Happiness

CHAPTER 62

ABC of Happiness

A

- Ability to appreciate others point of view
- Ability to understand yourself and know your strengths and weaknesses
- Ability to use your strengths and rectify your weaknesses
- Associate with right kind of people who are considerate, kind, hardworking, truthful and honest
- Agree to disagree with grace and humility
- Avoid greed, jealousy, hatred and vengeance
- Avoid 'avidya' (ignorance of mind) by knowledge
- Avoid company of people with bad habits who are sinful, addicts and alcoholics
- Avoid apathy, the sign of egoistic selfishness
- Avoid ego as it binds you with selfishness, false-pride, hatred and narrow vision
- Avoid greed and unnecessary desires
- Avoid superstations and enjoy myths for legendry values
- Avoid preconceived ideas as these are often erroneous
- Attachments lead to love, envy, hatred and short-term happiness
- Attachments cause expectations and conflicts
- Abnegation is the key to conquer mind
- Altruistic considerate and kind helpful people are blessed with happiness

- Awakening by transcendental transformation
- Angels are ordinary people who are quick to help anyone in distress
- 'Ananda' (eternal bliss) can be attained by meditation, mindfulness, contemplation and Self-realization

B

- Be Positive in attitude, Positive in willpower,
- Be kind and considerate for everybody's welfare
- Be knowledgeable of your work and profession as knowledge is key to happiness
- Be truthful, kind and humble
- Be helpful to others
- Be an angel of happiness by acts of compassion, kindness, forgiveness and unconditional love
- Behaviors of extreme nature can make the life miserable and happiness impossible
- Benevolent individuals are happier and have better gene profile
- Benevolence increases antibody and antiviral activity and decreases inflammation
- Bondage is source of limited transient happiness and many conflicts and miseries
- Before labeling someone 'unreasonable' try to understand his or her perspective
- Breaking the shell of Ego opens the reservoir of happiness
- Believe in yourself to be happy

C

- Character
- Calmness
- Contentment

- Compassion
- Control (Continence)
- Charity
- Commitment, trust and integrity
- Civil and Courteous
- Curb overindulgence in desires
- Curb your ego, stay away from "I, me and mine'
- Curb yore anger and greed
- 'Communication skills' improve happiness
- Conquered mind is 'Pure Mind' in tranquil quietude
- Conditioned consciousness attuned *outwards* to sensory world causes pleasure and all the pains and sufferings
- Consciousness that you have is shared by all in *World-Consciousness*
- Compassion is the moral fabric of human existence

D

- Dispel darkness of your mind by knowledge
- Discernment: to distinguish between right and wrong, truth and lies, follow the righteous path -inner-voice
- Do good '*Karma*', selfless deeds are of the best kind
- Death, disease, dukha (sufferings) and decay like old-age are part of life
- *Daya* (kindness), *daman* (self-control) and *daan* (charity) are virtues that bring happiness
- *Dharma* is your moral duty to your family, your community and your nation
- Don't be a slave to your desires
- Discard bad habits
- Death wipes away all attachments
- Death of Ego ceases all troubles
- 'Die while living' to be reborn spiritually as Ego dies with the death

E

- Ego is self-destructive as it only brings false happiness.
- Ego's death ceases all troubles
- Egoless attitude of detachment brings real happiness
- Excess of everything is bad, don't overindulge
- Eat balanced nutritious food
- Exercise makes mind and body healthier and happier
- Empathize and be compassionate
- Eternal happiness results from liberation of mind

F

- Faith in-self generates high self-esteem & happiness
- Fear comes from a weak pessimistic mind, conquer it
- Fear causes anxiety, anger and unhappiness, curb it
- Fear and anger brings stress and unhappiness
- Failures are guide to success
- Follow your conscious and inner voice
- Follow your goals with passion and commitment
- Follow the right path to secure real happiness
- Free yourself from conflicts and duality of comparisons
- Freedom from all desires, attachments and unreasonable beliefs ushers happiness
- Freedom of mind and body
- Forgive and forget
- Forgive others to be forgiven

G

- Good Karma
- Goodness of heart
- Good company
- Good thoughts and actions

- Graciousness, gratitude and gratefulness
- Genteel and humble
- Good habits enhance happiness
- Grateful heart is filled with humility, compassion and happines

H

- Happiness is the goal in life
- Happiness is elusive and impermanent
- Happiness lies in simple pleasures
- Happiness grows in a positive mind
- Happiness comes from contentment, continence and compassion
- Happiness due to wealth and material possessions is transitory
- Happiness achieved by gratification of desires is short-lived and breeds addiction
- Happiness can never be bought
- Happiness from attachments (bondage) is transitory
- Happiness is marred by preconceived convictions
- Happiness is eroded by expectations and demands
- Happiness comes when you discard anger, jealousy, hatred and greed
- Happiness comes on helping others
- Happiness comes with harmony of mind, body and soul
- Happiness of others increases your happiness
- Happiness thrives and flourishes in the present moments
- Happiness radiates when you forgive and forget
- Happiness grows with acts of compassion
- Happiness flourishes by acts of giving and sharing
- Happiness begets happiness
- Happiness is everlasting bliss on self-realization
- Happiness and sufferings are two sides of the same coin, can't discard one without the other
- Happiness is the fountain of love and compassion
- Happiness is not possessing it but enjoying it[110]
- Happiness is within you discover it

Bibliography

1. Aizer, AA, Chen, MH, McCarthy EP et.al. Marital Status and survival in Patients with Cancer, Journal of Clinical Oncology-on line, JCO Nov1, 3852-3853, Nov1, 2013, On line September 23, 2013

2. Anand, Sudhir: Who is God, Does God have Shape or Form. Ask Publications, Los Angeles, 2009

3. Anand, Sudhir: The Essence of Hindu Religion with Introduction of Vedas and Yoga. Ask Publications, Los Angeles, 2000

4. American Society of Addictive Medicine (ASAM): www.asam.org/DefinitionofAddiction-longversion (accessed in 2013)

5. Atheism a la mode: http://www.newhumanist.org.uk/1421

6. Barlow DH: Abnormal Psychology: An Integrated Approach (5th edition), Thompson Wadsworth, 248-249, 2005

7. Bao, Y, Han, J and Hu, F et. al.: Association of Nut Consumption with Total and Cause –Specific Mortality. The New England Journal of Medicine, 369:2001-2011, 2013

8. Bernstein, Elizabeth: We Actually Get Nicer with Age, Personality Traits Improve on Their Own, and It's Possible to Speed Change Along, Elizabeth.Bernstein@WSJ.com, Wall Street Journal, April 22, 2014

9. Bhadula, Ragini: A piece of my mind: The Good Physician. Journal of American Medical Association (JAMA) 310 (9): 909, 2013

10. Blouin, AM, Siegel, Jerome et. al.: Human hypocretin and melanin-concentrating hormone levels are linked to emotion and social interaction, Article 1547, Nature Communication 4, March 2013

11. Boomerblog: www.boomerblog.sdsu.edu/2011/06/third-age-the-golden-years-of-adult...

12. Brenhouse, Hillary: North Korea: One of the Happiest Place on Earth? Time, June 1, 2011

13. Bucke, Richard Maurice: Cosmic Consciousness: A Study in the Evolution of the Human Mind. Innes & Sons. pp. 1–2, 1905

14. Buddha, Gautama: www.budsas.org/ebud/whatbudbeliev/297.htm

15. Buddha: The Teachings of Buddha. Bukkyo Dendo Kyokai, Kosaido Printing, Tokyo 2001

16. Burnod, Y et.al: Parieto-frontal coding of reaching: an integrated framework. Review article. Exp. Brain Res (1999) 129:325–346

17. Chatterji, JC: The Wisdom of Vedas. Quest Books, The Theosophical Publishing House, Versa Press, Wheaton IL, 1992

18. Chen, C., Burton, M., et al.: Population Migration and the variation of Dopamine D4 Receptor (DRD4) Allele Frequencies Around The Globe and Human Behavior, 20:309-324, 1999

19. Chinmayananda, Swami: The Holy Geeta, Central Chinmaya Mission Trust, Mumbai 1996

20. Chinmayananda, Swami: Kindle Life, Central Chinmaya Mission Trust, Priya Graphics, Mumbai 2002

21. Chinmayananda, Swami: Self-Unfoldment, Central Chinmaya Mission Trust, Mumbai, 2007

22. Chalub, M, Telles, LE: Alcohol, Drugs and Crime, Rev. Bras. Psiquiatr. 28(supple. 2), S69-73, 2006

23. Chopra, Deepak: The Seven spiritual laws of success: A practical guide to fulfillment of your dreams. New World Library, 1994

24. Dayanand, Saraswati: Light of Truth, English Translation of Satyarth Prakash, Maharishi Dayanand Nirvanh Shatabdi Publication, 1984

25. Descartes Rene: www.lep.utm.edu/descarte/

26. Diamond, SA: Anger Disorder. What it is and What we can do about it?, Psychology Today, April 3, 2009, http://www.psychologytoday.com/experts/stephen-diamond-phd

27. Dijksterhuis Ap, Nordgren, Loran F.: A theory of unconscious thoughts, Association for Psychological Science, Volume 1-Number2, 2006

28. Diwakar, RR: Upanishads in Story and Dialogue, Bhartiya Vidya Bhavan, Bombay, 1988

29. Dubovsky, SL, Davies R and Dubovsky AN, : Mood Disorders, Chapter 10: 439:542, Textbook of Clinical Psychiatry by Hales, RE and Yudofsky, SC, 4th edition, American Psychiatric Publishing, Inc., Washington, 2005

30. Duhigg, Charles, : The Power of Habit, Why we do and What we do in life.', Random House, New York, 2012

31. Ellis, BJ and Boyce WT: Biological Sensitivity to Context, Journal of Association of Psychological Science, 70 (3): 183-187, 2008

32. Easterlin, Richard A et. al.: The Happiness-Income paradox revisited. Proceedings of National Academy of Science, Volume 107, no. 52, 22463-22468, 2010

33. Ferriss, Timothy.: The 4-Hour Workweek, Escape 9 to 5, Live Anywhere and Join The New Rich, Crown Publishers, New York, 2007

34. Fredrickson, Barbara L.: The emerging science of Positive psychology is coming to understand why it's good to feel good. American Scientist, 91:330-335, 2003 www.americanscientist.org/template/issue TOC/issue/394

35. Fredrickson, B L et al. (Steven W Cole): Functional genomic perspective on human well-being. Proceedings of National Academy of Sciences. http://www.pnas.org/content/early/2013/07/25/1305419110.abstrac

36. Funch, Flemming: Positive and negative emotions, Transformational Paths, Facilitator Training Manual by Flemming Funch.

37. Gibran, Kahlil: The Prophet, Alfred A Knopp, Inc. 1923

38. Gilbert, Daniel: Stumbling on Happiness. Page 220-221, Alford A Knopf, New York, 2006

39. Gross National Happiness Index Articles: www.grossnatinalhappiness.com/articles/

40. Grzyb, Jo-Ellen and Chandler, Robin: The Nice Factor, The Art of Saying No, Fusion Press, Satin Publication, London 2008, First published by Simon and Schuster in 1997 in Great Britain

41. Hanh, Thich Nhat, How to be Happy and Free Under the Banyan Tree, United Buddhist Church, Yash Printographics, Noida, India

42. Hameroff, Stuart and Penrose, Roger, The Orch OR Model of Consciousness (The conscious pilot-dendritic synchrony moves through the brain to mediate consciousness. Journal of Biological Physics, Volume 36, Number 1, January, 2010, www.quantumconsciousness.org/penrose

43. Happiness Index: A Short Guide to National Happiness Index.www.grossnationalhappiness.com/wp-contents/uploads/2012/04/short-gnh

44. Harrison, T M, Weintraub, M, Rogalski, E.: Superior memory and higher cortical volumes in usually successful cognitive aging. Journal of International Neuropsychological Society, DOI: 10.1017/S1355617712000847, 2012

45. Hawking, Stephen: www.hawking.org.uk

46. Helliwell, J, Layard, R. and Sachs, J.: www.earth.columbia.edu/sitefiles/file/sach.

47. Helliwell, J, Layard, R and Sachs, J.: World Happiness Report 2013, UNO 2013

48. Help-guide: www.Helpguide.org/toolkit/developing_em

49. Inner dimension: www.inner.org/audio/aid/5765/bridging.htm

50. Islamic View: www.islam44.net

51. Jyotirmayananda, Swami,: The Art of Positive Thinking, Yoga Research Foundation, Miami, 1988

52. Jyotirmayananda, Swami: Mysticism of the Mahabharata, Yoga Research Foundation, Miami, 1993

53. Kegel, CA, Bus AG and van IJzendoorn, MH: Differential Susceptibility in Early Literacy Instruction Through Computer Games: The Role of the Dopamine D4 Receptor Gene (DRD4), Mind, Brain, and Education: 5 (2): 71–78, 2011

54. Khan, Razib: Gene Expression, How the "fierce people" come to be. Discover, Friday Fluff, May 6th, 2011

55. Krishnamurty, J: Mind without Measure. Krishnamurty Foundation, Chennai, India, Second Edition 2005

56. Kluger, Jeffrey: The Pursuit of Happiness, Times, 182: 24-32, Time Inc., New York, July 8-15, 2013

57. Kurzwell, Ray: How to create a Mind, Viking Press, 2012

58. Kupperman, Joel J.: Classic Asian Philosophy, A Guide to the Essential Texts, Oxford University Press, 2001

59. Lama, Dalai: Ethics for The New Millennium, Riverhead Books, Penguin Putnam Inc., 1999

60. Lama, Dalai: Beyond Religion, Ethics for a whole world, Harper Collins Publisher, India 2012

61. Lama, Dalai and Cutler C. Howard: The Art of Happiness at Work. Riverhead Books, Penguin Group Inc. New York, 2003

62. Lama, Dalai: Live in a Better Way, Reflections on Truth, Love and Happiness. Edited by Renuka Singh, Viking Penguin, New York, 2001

63. Lama, Dalai: Destructive Emotions. How Can We overcome Them? A Scientific Dialogue narrated by Daniel Coleman, Bantam Book, Random House, New York 2003

64. Lama, Dalai: A Profound Mind, Cultivating Wisdom in Everyday Life. Edited by Nicholas Vreeland, Harmony Books, Random House, New York, 2011

65. Lama. Dalai: How to See Yourself as You Really Are. Translated by Jeffery Hopkins, Atria Books New York, 2006

66. Lazarus, Richard S, Folkman, S: Transactional theory and research on emotions and coping. European Journal of Personality: 1(3): 141-169, 1966

67. Lazarus, Richard S: Progress on cognitive-motivational-relational theory of emotions. American Psychologist: 46(8): 819-834, 1991

68. Lees SJ, Booth FW: Sedentary death syndrome, Can J Applied Physiology, 29 (4): 447-60, 2004

69. Leonhardt, David: Maybe Money Does buy Happiness after all, The New York Times, Business, April 6, 2008

70. Lyubomirsky, Sonja: The How of Happiness, A New Approach to Getting the Life You Want, Penguin Books, 2008

71. Manu-Smriti: Edited by JH Dave, Bhartiya Vidya Bhavan, Bombay, 1975

72. Mahadeva A Sastri: Amritbindu and Kaivalya Upanishad, Thomas and Co at Minerva Press, Madras, 1898

73. Meacham, Jon: Thomas Jefferson, The Art Of Power, Page 197, Random House 2012

74. McCullough, David: Morning on Horseback, The story of an Extraordinary Family, A Vanished Way of Life, and The Unique Child Who Became Theodore Roosevelt. Simon and Shuster, page 31, 1981

75. Miller, R., Wankerl, M. et al.: The serotonin transporter gene-linked polymorphic region (5HTTLPR) and cortisol stress reactivity: a meta-analysis. Molecular Psychiatry, (4 September) doi: 10.1038/mp.2012.124

76. The Mind-Body Connection, NIH Medicine Plus, 3:1 (page 4), Winter Issue 2008

77. Montross, L., Depp, C., Daly, J. et.al, Correlates of Self-Related Successful aging among Community-Dwelling Older Adults. American Journal of Geriatric Psychiatry: 14(1): 43-51, 2006

78. Mostofsky, E, Mittleman, M et al.: Outbursts of anger as a trigger of acute cardiovascular events: a systematic review and meta-analysis. doi:10.1093/euheartj/ehu033, European Heart Journal, published on line March 3, 2014

79. Muller, F Max: The Upanishads, The Sacred Books of the East Part 2, Dover Publication, 1962

80. National Cancer Institute at the National Institute of Health: www.cancer.gov/cancertopics/factsheets/diet

81. Nikhilananda, Swami: Aatambodh- Self-Knowledge of Sri Sankaracharya. The President, Ramakrishna Math, Madras, 1947

82. O'Brien, Barbara: About.com.Buddhism, Karma: www.buddhism.about.com/od/abudhistglosseryg/karmadef.htm

83. Oswald, A., Blanchflower, D.: Is Well-Being U-Shaped over the life cycle?, Social Science and Medicine, 66(6): 733-49, 2008

84. Outlaw, Frank: in book by Ziglar, Zig: Better Than Good, Creating a Life You Can't Wait to Live, Page 54, Jaico Publishing House, 2009

85. Oz, Mehmet: Mind and body, Say "Om" before Surgery, Special Issue Time, How your mind can Heal your Body, Volume 161, No. 3, January 20, 2003

86. Parrinder, Geoffrey: Upanishads, Gita and Bible, A Comparative study of Hindu and Christian Scriptures. Association Press, 1963

87. Piccard, Bertrand: in book by Ziglar, Zig: Better Than Good, Creating a Life You Can't Wait to Live, Page 62-63, Jaico Publishing House, 2009

88. Pickert, Kate: The Art of Being Mindful. The Mindful Revolution. Time Magazine, 40-46, February 3, 2014, New York

89. Positively Present; www.positivelypresent.com/2010/03/3-sh

90. Prabhavananda, Swami and Manchester, Fredrick: The Upanishads, The Breath of Eternal, Vedanta Society, Mentor Book, New American Library, New York, 1948

91. Psychology today: www.psychologytoday.com/basics/mindfulness

92. Robinson, Sara,: 'Bring Back The 40- Hours Work Week': www. salon.com/2012/03/14/bring_back_the_40_hour_work_week

93. Rudolf, Robert: Work Shorter, Be Happier? Longitudinal Evidence from the Korean Five-Day Working Policy. Journal Happiness Studies, August, 2013

94. Sadock, BJ and Sadock, VA: Kaplan and Saddock's Synopsis of Psychiatry, Behavior Science/Clinical Psychiatry: Substance-Related Disorders, 12:385, 10th edition, Lippincott, Williams and Wilkins, 2007

95. Scharfstein, Ben-Ami: A comparative History of World Philosophy, From The Upanishads to Kant, State University of New York Press, 1998

96. Scott, CL, Hilty, DM and Brook, M: Impulse-Control Disorders, Chapter 15: 781-802, Textbook of Clinical Psychiatry by Hales, RE and Yudofsky, SC, 4th edition, American Psychiatric Publishing, Inc., Washington, 2005

97. Seligman, EP and Royzman, Ed: Happiness- Three Traditional Theories, July 2003: www.authenticha, www.pursuit-of-happiness.org

98. Ship, Amy N, MD: The Most Primary of care- Talking about Driving and Distraction. New England Journal of Medicine: 362:2145-2147, 2010

99. Siegel, Dan: Science of the Mindful Brain, www.kripalu.org/article/480

100. Siegel, Jerome et. al.: Is this peptide a key to happiness. Online edition Journal of Nature Communications, March 5, 2013

101. Simon, Naomi M: Clinical Crossroads, Treating Complicated Grief, Journal of American Medical Association: 310(4): 416-423, 2013

102. Sirshree: The Five Supreme Secrets of Life, Unveiling the Ways to Attain Wealth, Love and God. Wisdom Tree, 2008

103. Sitholey, P, Agrawal V, Vrat, S: Indian Mental Concepts on children and adolescents, Indian Journal of Psychiatry, 55:6, 277-282, 2013

104. Spolsky, RM: Mind and Matter: The Monkey Business of Pure Altruism. The Wall Street Journal, Review section, September 28-29, 2013

105. Swami, Mahatma Anand: In the Dark Woods: Publisher: Vijaykumar Govindram Hasanand, Delhi, India. 1998

106. Steve Taylor, Out of Darkness, From Turmoil to Transformation, Hay House publication, 2011

107. Treatment solutions: www.treatmentsolutions.com/worldwide/ (2013)

108. Transformational Processing Institute www.worldtrans.org/TP/TP2/ TP2A-35HTML\

109. Trinkaus, E.: Late Pleistocene adult mortality patterns and modern human establishment. Proceedings National Academy Science USA 108(4); 1267-1271, 2011

110. Unknown

111. Vaupel, James W.: www.demogr.mpg/de/en/institute

112. Vayikra, Rabbah 1:6; see Talmud Nedarim 41a. Inner dimension: www.inner.org/audio/aid/5765/bridging.htm

113. Vedalankar, Pandit Nardev: Essential Teachings of Hinduism, Book Three, Veda Niketan, Arya Pratinidhi Sabha, South Africa, 1991

114. Vivekananda, Swami: Karam-Yoga, The Yoga of Action, 18th Impression, Advaita Ashrama, Nabajiban Press, Calcutta, 1991

115. Vivekananda, Swami: What Religion Is in Words of Swami Vivekananda? Edited by Swami Vidyatamananda, Advaita Ashrama, Nabajiban Press, Calcutta, 1991

116. Westen, Drew: The Scientific Status of Unconscious Processes: Is Freud Really Dead. Journal of American Psychoanalytic Association, 47(4), 1061-1106, 1999

117. Wheeler, Mark (news about Steven W, Cole): Be Happy Your genes may thank you for this: But different types of Happiness have different affects, UCLA study shows. www.newsroom/ucla/edu/portal/ucla/don-t-worry-be-happy/247644.aspx

118. Wikipedia: https://www.wikipedia.org/

119. Wills, Gary: Inventing America: Jefferson's Declaration of Independence. Doubleday, 1978

120. WHO, World Happiness Report 2015: www.theglobeandmail.com/news/national/article24073928.ece/BINARY/World+Happiness+Report.pdf

121. WHO, The World Health Report 2001- Mental Health: New Understanding, New Hope, cited 2008-10-19

122. WHO Report, Depression: A Global Crisis, World Mental Health Day, October 10, 2012, Federation of Mental Health www.who.int/mental_health/management/...

123. Yati, Balakrishna: From Darkness to Light: Life's Journey. Edited by Kewal K Mahajan and Rahul Mahajan. L.B.S. Charitable Trust, Dalhousie, India 2003

124. Ziglar, Zig: Better Than Good, Creating a Life You Can't Wait to Live, Jaico Publishing House, 2009

Author researched about 200 articles and books in various formats to write this book. Most of quotes are referenced in bibliography or in the text. Some quotes with unknown authors are written between quote-unquote. Every effort was made to acknowledge original authors. Any inadvertent omission will be remedied in future printing.

Acknowledgements

- Thanks to my teachers and parents who kindled the light of knowledge.
- A debt of gratitude to my wife Rajni, who is not only professionally successful obstetrician and gynecologist and an academically accomplished teacher but also a loving wife, mother and grandmother. She was born in the basement of a home in a small city in Burma-British India during bombardment by Japanese planes in 2nd World war. She was evacuated as 36-hour old infant with her parents as political refugee in one of the last planes that left for freedom before Japanese occupation of Burma.

Dr. Rajni Sharma is also well versed in Sanskrit and is follower of Swami Dayanand Saraswati. Rajni and the author read about 200 books, spiritual and scientific articles in journals, magazines and newspapers to help write this book. She made the author understand the real meaning of spiritualism and morality in relation to day-to-day karma; as 'honest passionate work in any field and helping those in need' is as or even more important than prayers in temples and Churches. Both are practicing Hindus and the founding members of The Hindu Temple of Toledo.

She has spent hundreds of hours with the author researching, critiquing with valuable suggestions from the concept to the final version of this book. She edited the book. As a perfectionist she has been an inspiration for the author to write and rewrite these words to their satisfaction. The work would have been incomplete without her expertise.

- To our son Dr. Sameer Sharma for constant encouragement to pursue this project and to our multitalented younger son Maneesh for literary critique.

- To our friend and great community resource Supriya Joshi for designing the book cover and web page with her graphics.
- To Sumit Mukherjee and his talented son Adit for help in setting up and support for web and Facebook page.
- Thank you Arya Pratinidhi Sabha of America for igniting spiritual awakening and especially its trustee Shri Girish C Khosla, Arya Pathik, editor of monthly magazine Navrang.
- Special thanks to Pandit Anant Dixit of The Hindu Temple of Toledo for instilling spirit of divinity and spiritualism.

Authors Biography

Om P. Sharma, MD, was born and raised in India. After receiving his medical degree, Dr. Sharma earned his board certification in surgery and practiced at a prestigious medical institute in Northern India before moving to the United States in the early 1970s.

As a trauma surgeon, Dr. Sharma faced many life-and-death situations, as well as the moral, ethical, and ideological challenges, learning to pursue physicians' duty not only to heal the injured bodies but also their weakened minds with empathy and compassion.

Dr. Sharma has published over forty articles in peer-reviewed journals and delivered scientific lectures in many countries around the world. He was Trauma Director and Clinical Professor of Surgery; President and Chairman of Board of Surgical Society and The Hindu Temple of Toledo. After retiring, he decided to turn his mind to the human quest for happiness.

Dr. Sharma lives in Toledo, Ohio, with his wife Rajni. They have two sons and five grandchildren.

'Comprehensive reference book... True Happiness is a serious affair'

'It is one of the <u>finest and most extensive investigations on happiness</u> and the human condition ... a very comprehensive review of the philosophical, psychological and spiritual foundations of personal happiness. ...a focus on personal meaningfulness as well as wide ranging sociological-cultural aspects of humans living with more mutual support... in the global society of mankind. The book is made more effective by the use of famous person quotes at the start of each chapter, the use of stories and metaphors ...openly shared personal references and life experiences...focused on the less theoretical and more practical aspects of designing one's own path toward happiness. It includes not only new behaviors and experiences to implement but also a detailed presentation of the blocks to achieving happiness that is frequently encountered in the course of life... a <u>virtual road map</u> for persons who are serious about improving the quality of their lives.... "Synopsis of Happiness" A B C's of Happiness. It is an alphabetized compendium of the most essential elements to consider in the development of one's personal quest for happiness. ... <u>must read for those interested in improving the lives of those they love as well as themselves.</u>

~ Jacob Elliot, MA, Ph.D. Clinical Psychology

Member American Psychological Association, International Society for Neurotherapy and Research, Certified Global Neurotherapist Initiative Instructor
Past Associate Editor for the Journal of Neurotherapy

'...a rare collection of principles of happy life...Reader is tempted to read faster with the urge to grasp without delay what lies ahead in the following pages. ...the author has done in-depth and extensive research in writing this book.
He has really done genuine service to the society at large.'

~ *Krishna Nanda, CPA*

'Dr. Sharma has shared with readers his multi-dimensional view of happiness, in pursuit of which each of us is living. The book is a very enlightening account of Dr. Sharma's philosophical views, reflecting his rich cultural and social background, and encompassing different aspects of happiness.'

~ *Mohan C. Pandey*

Senior Indian Diplomat, Former Ambassador to Iraq
Senior Director and Head, International Department ASSOCHAM, India

Made in the USA
Monee, IL
28 April 2023

32533756R00167